Crosscutting Social Circles

Crosscutting Social Circles

TESTING A MACROSTRUCTURAL
THEORY OF INTERGROUP RELATIONS

Peter M. Blau &
Joseph E. Schwartz

WITH A NEW INTRODUCTION BY PETER M. BLAU

TRANSACTION PUBLISHERS
New Brunswick (U.S.A.) and London (U.K.)

New material this edition copyright © 1997 by Transaction Publishers, New Brunswick, New Jersey 08903. Originally published in 1984 by Academic Press, Inc.

Library of Congress Catalog Number: 96-38937
ISBN: 1-56000-903-9
Printed in the United States of America

Library of Congress Cataloging-in-Publication Data

Blau, Peter Michael.
    Crosscutting social circles : testing a macrostructural theory of intergroup relations / Peter M. Blau and Joseph E. Schwartz ; with a new introduction by Peter M. Blau.
        p. cm.
    Originally published: Orlando : Academic Press, 1984.
    Includes bibliographical references and index.
    ISBN 1-56000-903-9 (alk. paper)
    1. Social groups. 2. Intergroup relations. 3. Intermarriage. 4. Social structure. 5. Cities and towns. 6. Cities and towns—United States. I. Schwartz, Joseph E. II. Title.
HM131.B587 1996
305—dc20   96-38937
                                                                CIP

For Reva

Contents

Introduction to the Transaction Edition

I am the sole author of this new introduction to *Crosscutting Social Circles,* which was the expressed preference of the book's co-author, Joseph Schwartz. The book presents our joint project of extensive tests of a macrostructural theory I had developed (Blau, 1977). My writing this introduction alone makes it possible to start by expressing my debts to Joe for the important contributions he has made to designing and performing the tests and their presentation. Although I have some knowledge of statistics, it is not sufficient for me to have been able to decide on the appropriate procedures and apply them to the various tests without his help.

I want to take the opportunity provided by the republication of the tests of my macrostructural theory to offer some reflections on two developments in my so-ciological thinking and my conception of social theory. The first pertains to my interest in social structure, structural sociology, and macrostructural sociology. The second refers to my changing conception of social theory: from grand theo-ries—broad systems of meaningful interpretations and conjectures; via theories derived from and close to research results (what Merton [1968: 39–72] called "theories of the middle range"); and then, in contrast, to strictly deductive theo-ries; ultimately to explanatory theories formulated in abstract terms grounded in research as well as tested in it by their logical empirical implications.

Social Structure

The early political interest of mine in Marx's theoretical analysis of class differ-ences undoubtedly affected my conviction of the profound influence of social condition on people's lives. My subsequent reading and admiring of Durkheim's structural analysis of the *division of labor* gave me a clue for conceptualizing these influences of social conditions as the external constraints of social structure on people. Later I published a paper on the analysis of such influences, which have come to be known as contextual effects but which I considered to be "Structural Effects" (1960).

The essential idea underlying the concept of structural effects is that people's relations and conduct are affected by their social environment. But what is the social environment? Clearly one's social environment is composed of people. To study influences of the social environment on all members of a collectivity one must discover how every member is affected by the characteristics and actions of all members except one's own. In laboratory studies, this can be done experimentally by assigning experimental subjects to groups in which varying proportions of other members differ from him in respect to the presumed causal attribute or attitude. But one cannot usually experiment with work groups or other small groups outside a laboratory, and experiments are out of the question for large populations, which are the primary concern of macrosociology. Consequently, statistical procedures must be used to substitute for experimental controls in most cases. To ascertain the influence of a group's or population's social environment on its members, one must separate for every one how all the others' characteristics, excluding one's own, affect oneself. This can be done statistically by comparing every person's attitude Y in groups with different proportion of members with trait X while holding constant everyone's own trait X. A structural effect is indicated if individuals, whether or not they are an X, are more likely to exhibit Y in groups with many than in groups with few X's. The cross-tabulation procedure I used for this study was primitive, but more advanced valid procedures are now available to analyze structural or contextual effects.

The research on which this paper was based was designed to study how group pressures in a public welfare agency influenced whether caseworkers were more concerned with helping poor people or with enforcing eligibility procedures. Although my interest in structural effects did not diminish, I became more interested in the influences of objective structural conditions than those of cultural values reflected in opinion climates and surveys. I also was becoming less interested in studies of small groups than in macrosociological studies of entire communities or societies. Both of these changes may still have been the influences of Marx's macrosociological analyses of the effects of material, economic conditions on people's lives. Yet I did not want to confine sociological analysis to economic factors, inspired by Durkheim's study of the division of labor, the prototype of social structure in my opinion, which provided an important clue for characterizing it, as I only later realized.

Social structures have emergent properties which are independent of the properties of individuals. They are independent in the sense that no individual can have equivalent properties and that they do not reflect properties that individuals have. (They are not independent, of course, in the sense that they could be derived or observed if there were no people or no information on people.) These attributes characterize an entire population but none of the individuals in the population have or could have one. What they primarily refer to are the differences among the members of a population in various respects. As I put it at the beginning of the book where the theory here tested was first presented, "To speak of social structure is to speak of social differentiation among people, for social structure...is rooted in the social distinctions people make in their role relations" (Blau, 1977). Empirically, social structure refers to the distribution of a population among social positions in any dimension, as the division of labor perfectly illustrates.

Are all differences among the members of a population structural attributes? Many but not all: only those that affect social life, the social distinctions the members themselves make in their social associations, particularly whether in-group associates are distinguished from others. (Underlying the degree of these distinctions is the strength of in-group affiliation or salience, which some attribute to cultural influences, but I find the distinctions' visible effect on social life sufficient without such attribution.) This criterion provides an empirical measure for whether unusual differences—say, being left- or right-handed, or having had one's appendix removed or not—are significant structural conditions that affect social life. Measures of central tendencies, like means or medians, are not proper operational indicators of structural characteristics because they are equivalent to individual attributes, whereas measures of dispersion, like standard deviations or covariances, are, for they are unlike any individual attribute including that used to derive them.

There are two kinds of distinctly social characteristics populations have, both properties that an isolated individual cannot have: the differences among members in various respects, and the relations between them of various kinds. Location in any dimension of social differences is referred to as a social position in that dimension, such as a person's religion, occupation, education, or income, but also differences that are not conventionally called social positions but affect social life, such as age and sex, and even voting for a certain party. Social relations can be casual acquaintances, colleagues, friends, lovers, spouses.

A generic distinction in social relation of any kind is that between in-group relations of members in the same positions and intergroup relations of persons in different positions. In dyadic relations, like spouses, which are analyzed in our research, or mutual friends, the rates of in-group and of intergroup relations are complementary, for the two must sum to one (100 in percentages). Hence, the intermarriage data reported in this book can be translated into in-group marriages by subtracting the rate from one (or doing so for a correlation or regression coefficient, but for this case the sign must also be reversed).

The structural approach has been adopted in microsociological as well as macrosociological studies (Wellman, 1988). Both forms of structuralism are concerned with the causal relation between differences in social positions and patterns of social relations among those in different positions, but they assume opposite directions of influence between the two. Network analysis is the study of the social structures of small groups; macrostructural is that of the structure of large populations. The central terms of network analysis are the net's links bestrewn group members and its nodes where the members are located. The latter correspond to macrosociology's social positions in various dimensions and the former to its rates of social relations, though neither of these terms corresponds fully to that used in network analysis. One reason for the difference is the sheer magnitude of the size difference, but there are others in conceptualization, and particularly in the assumption about causal direction. An important meta-assumption shared, however, is that the most fundamental influences are strictly structural, albeit using different conceptions of structure.

Social structure in network analysis refers to the network of links, in contrast to our use of the term *social structure* for the various differences in a population, its members' differences in social positions or group affiliations. Both approaches consider social structure to govern the other aspect of social life, but what network analysts mean by this is that the network structure affects the roles of those located in various nodes, whereas for students of macrostructures it means that the multiple differentiation in social positions influences the rates of social associations linking persons in different positions.

The network assumption of causal direction may be satisfactory for experimental studies of small groups, because the experimental designs usually impose the network on the group, and also because their only concern about persons in the nodes is their decisions and outcomes in the experimental task as influenced by their network location. There seem to be good reasons for making the opposite causal assumption in macrosociology. The social relations in a population, though they may modify some differences among people, rarely affect changes in their most salient positions, which are primarily influenced by major differences in a population. The differences in major positions of the most salient dimensions, like religion, race, national origin, or social class, are either ascribed or strongly influenced by family background and therefore cannot change or are greatly resistant to change but exert strong influences on social relations, as indicated by the particularly strong prevalence of in-group and proximate relations in these respects.

The assumption made in macrostructural analysis, therefore, is that a population's structural differentiation influences intergroup as well as in-group relations (but in opposite ways) in all major dimensions at any given time. Whereas people's relations and conduct may have feedback effects, these do not occur instantaneously but over the long run. Illustrations of such long-run consequences are those of differences in fertility rates among ethnic groups, and among persons with different religious affiliations, which effect changes in the population that slowly alter its structure, its distributions along these lines. Even the actions or interactions of persons in very powerful positions have immediate effects on population distributions, which are our defining attributes of social structures. (Genocide is fortunately one of the rare cases when actions have direct effects on restructuring ethnic and other population distributions. War may also have short-run effects.)

In short, a population's structure normally changes only as the result of actions of past generations, not those of its current members. This is the reason for my disagreement with the view that the analysis of structural effects on people must be complemented, as Giddens (1986 [1984]) assumes, or implemented, as Coleman (1990) does, by the study of the effects of the choices and acts of individual agents on the existing structure. For the actions of individuals hardly ever have short-run effects on the current structure of the population defined, as here, by the population's distributions in multiple dimensions. To be sure, historical trends that change a population and restructure its members' distributions in multiple dimensions are not independent of human conduct. Of course not. What else could have created them? They are not, however, the product of the deliberate actions of the population's present members but the emergent unintended result of actions and interactions of many persons in past generations. For instance, whereas differential rates of fertility, migration, and suicide are consequences of acts of individuals that alter the future population distributions, the human acts effecting these changes in population structure were surely not motivated by doing so. Whereas historical change results probably in good part from past human actions, this cannot be studied cross-sectionally, only historically.

Social Theory

I turn now to the changes in my conception of theory during my career, postponing further discussion of macrostructrural concepts until later, as these have been affected by developments in my view of theorizing. In the small midwestern college where I, a recent immigrant from Europe, first heard the term *sociology* and then majored in it, I was fascinated by grand theory. Marx's and Freud's impressed me most, and two other theoretical analyses I greatly admired were George Herbert Mead's *Mind, Self, Society* (1934) and Fromm's *Escape from Freedom* (1941). In conformity with what was customary among theorists I was disdainful of mere empirical research. A number of recent publications attempted to integrate Marx and Freud, including Fromm's book. Stimulated by them but wanting to be original, I chose for my bachelor's thesis to try to relate the theories of Freud and Mead, two great theorists, but also two grand, even grandiose, theories.

When I went to graduate school at Columbia University after the Second World War, I became interested in research and its relation to theory under the influence of Lazarsfeld and, particularly, Merton. This led to my revising my ideas about social theory to a preference for theories closely related to empirical studies—

what Merton was later to call "theories of the middle range." Accordingly, I carried out two empirical case studies of work groups in government agencies in the framework of Weber's theory of bureaucracy for my dissertation, which was later published in revised form (1973 [1955]). Although my conception of theory has further changed, I have never entirely forgotten, and returned with renewed emphasis to, my conviction that research is essential for theory.

The research on work groups in government agencies aroused my interest in the then burgeoning field of small groups, which led to my teaching, jointly with two colleagues at the University of Chicago, one of the early courses on small groups, and which stimulated my first theoretical book. It is, in contrast to the macrotheory tested here, a mostly microtheoretical analysis of exchange processes occurring in interpersonal relations (Blau, 1986 [1964]), though with some extension to macrosociological processes. The linkage between empirical research in this case involved the theoretical analysis of ideas that originated in the empirical analysis of my observation of the social interaction among government officials. This is not the only function of empirical research for theory, but it is one contribution it makes to their development.

I was visiting Pitt Professor in American History and Institution at Cambridge University in 1966/67. Faculty at Cambridge are also members of colleges, and I was invited by King's College to become a fellow. My office at King's was part of a suite of three rooms—two studies and a large anteroom—which I shared with Richard Braithwaite. I knew he was a well-known philosopher of science, but I had not read anything by him, not even his famous book *Scientific Explanation* (1953). We became quite friendly. I enjoyed his company and conversation, and I made up for not having known his academic work not only by reading some of it but also by becoming a great admirer of his contribution to theorizing and a convert to his approach.

Braithwaite is a strong advocate of deductive theorizing. His reason for this approach, as the book's title implies and he specifies at its outset, is that he considers the objective of science to be to explain the results of empirical research, and theory is what does explain them, but only deductive theory does so rigorously. He clarified this by answering the question how one explains any empirical proposition, the results of empirical observations and analysis about the relations between two or more variables. His answer is that one explains an empirical proposition by a more general proposition from which the empirical one can be logically deduced.

How does one explain the general theoretical proposition in turn? The same way—which is not really the same but merely using the same procedure on a higher level of abstraction—that is, by finding a still more general principle as explicans that logically implies the explicandum, the less general theorem. Although Braithwaite's claim that all there is to explanation is deducing a proposition from a broader generalization has been criticized by other philosophers who consider explaining also to require providing meaningful interpretations, Braithwaite's is a pure form of deductive theorizing. It is not the only form, however, nor is the idea that scientific theories should be deductive systems Braithwaite's most original and greatest contribution. We shall return to what is presently.

Before leaving for Cambridge I had started, and after my return I continued, a large program of quantitative research on the internal structure of formal organizations of several types—government agencies, department stores, hospitals, academic institutions, factories. Our research revealed interesting regularities in the first two types of public audiences studied, and these results were replicated in quite different kinds of organizations. For all types, the empirical findings showed similar relationships of an organization's size, the differentiation of its internal structure along various lines—its structural complexity—and the relative size of its administrative as well as managerial component.

Influenced by my recent interest in deductive theorizing, I tried to explain these findings by formulating a deductive theory, which was later published (Blau, 1970). I sent a copy to Braithwaite to show him how greatly he had influenced my conception of theory. He wrote back a polite letter but said that he was not the first to formulate a deductive model of theorizing and added that I had just too many research findings in my paper for his model of theorizing. What he implied was that I had not realized what his most original contribution was. He was right, but I have since.

Principles of logic have been known since ancient times, but the nomothetic or deductive model of scientific theorizing was first used, I believe, in theories by nineteenth-century economists, notably Jevons. More explicit formulations, however, were developed only in this century now coming to a close. An important pioneer, in my view, was Wittgenstein, whose *Tractatus logico-philosophicus* (1963 [1921]) specified the generic logical principles of scientific theorizing. This work was inspired by Russel's famous formulation of mathematics as a rigorous system of symbolic logic (Whitehead and Russel (1957 [1910–13]). The *Tractatus,* in turn, greatly influenced the logical positivism of the Vienna circle, whose best-known member was Carnap. Wittgenstein himself, however, was critical of their neo-positivistic use of his ideas.

The Vienna circle stressed that a scientific theory must consist of a system of logically related propositions and that the theory's meaning rests not on some philosophical interpretations but purely on the verification of the empirical implications logically implied by the theory. Thus, logical positivists tried to link theories to empirical evidence as well as logical deduction, but their claim that logical implications of theories can verify them poses a serious dilemma. The statement that the truth of more general propositions can be based on the accuracy of less general ones deduced from them is a logical fallacy—affirming the consequent. Since logic demands that only less general statements can be deduced from more general ones, how can particular empirical results validate more general theories? They cannot, which is the dilemma. Popper (1959 [1934]) found a way out of this dilemma. (Some logical positivists had tried to do so by using as the criterion of a theory's import not its *verification* but only its *verifiability*. Popper would also deny that theories are verifiable, though his implicit assumption that those not yet falsified are valid is in effect hardly different from the verifiability assumption.)

Yet Popper did make an important contribution to the philosophy of science (notwithstanding my critical parenthetical remark). For it makes a difference whether we accept a theory repeatedly tested and never negated as probably true but subject to further tests and to being superseded by another, or whether we consider it to be true and are fully expecting it to be verified. The contribution Popper made was that he suggested a method of scientific theorizing that not only conforms to rigorous logic but in addition makes theories empirically testable without violating logic. His great insight was to discover a principle for testing theories implicit in the logic of the hypothetical syllogism.

A hypothetical syllogism—if A, then B—logically precludes accepting A (the general statement) on the basis of evidence for B (its logical implication), but it requires the rejection of A (the general antecedent) on the basis of negative evidence for B (the deduced consequence). Hence, empirical tests can falsify theories from which the predictions tested are deduced but they cannot verify them. The method of testing theories by evidence that their empirical implications are not falsified is Popper's falsificationism. It implies that scientific theories are never absolutely true but always subject to be superseded.

In my enthusiasm over deductive theorizing, I went overboard. Not that I started to neglect the importance of research for scientific theory, just as Popper did not, but I also followed him in considering the only role of research to be to test theories once formulated and to have no role in formulating them. The last I no longer consider to be accurate, nor do I still think that it is what Braithwaite implied by his comment that my organizational theory stays too close to empirical results. I concede that Braithwaite may have a point, though I am not sure whether this was his intent, but I have come to disagree firmly with Popper's assumption that research has no role in developing scientific theories, as will be explained presently. I arrived at this criticism of Popper, however, only after completing work on the macrostructural theory under consideration.

This theory was developed the year I spent at the Netherlands Institute for Advanced Studies (NIAS) in Wassenaar, when I was strongly identified with Popper's as well as Braithwaite's conception of strict deductionism. Accordingly, I did not bring a set of data and preliminary analysis, having decided not to start with empirical results but to first formulate a macrostructural theory and conduct research to test it afterwards. This resolve did not make it true, of course, that the theory I worked on was not affected by research at all.

Of course, my roughly thirty years of research experience, as well as my background, influenced my sociological thinking. The long-term interest of mine in social structure has been noted. My interest in inequality and class differences dates back even further to my adolescence when I started reading Marx, and it was revived later in a large study on stratification and mobility conducted in collaboration with Duncan (Blau and Duncan, 1967). Finally, the new theory was undoubtedly influenced by the organizational research I conducted for many years and the theory based on it about the formal structure of organizations. In short, it was not unrelated to my research experience that my marcosociological theory turned out to be a structural one and concerned with inequality. To be sure, there is a difference between starting a theory to explain a set of research findings and trying to build it without such a specific foundation. Both are legitimate ways to develop social theories, but some research knowledge is essential, in my opinion.

Abstract Forms of Theorizing

My conception of theorizing has continued to evolve while I developed this theory, during the time Schwartz and I worked together on the research in this book, and even in the dozen years since. I finally realized what Braithwaite's major contribution was while I was working in Holland. His major criticism of my theory of organizational differentiation was not that it was derived from empirical research but that the theoretical concepts were too close to the empirical variables. Some of the theoretical concepts, like differentiation and complexity, are somewhat removed from empirical measures and encompass several, but others, such as administrative or managerial component, simply reflect empirical indicators. Braithwaite's greatest insight was that the defining criterion of a theory that explains empirical results is that, at least, some of its major terms must not be empirical variables but *abstractions* from them that encompass more than what the variables represent. In Braithwaite's own words (1953: 76):

> A theory which is hoped may be expanded in the future to explain more generalizations than it was originally designed to explain must allow more freedom to its theoretical terms than would be given them were they to be logical constructions out of observable entities. A scientific theory which, like all good scientific theories, is capable of growth must be more than an alternative way of describing the generalizations upon which it is based, which is all it would be if its theoretical terms were limited by being explicitly designed.

My basic conception of social structure has been discussed above, and I had already formulated it before coming to NIAS. To summarize: Social structures are characterized by emergent properties, which are not equivalent to any of the individuals composing them. The most distinctive structural property is the differentiation of individuals in various dimensions. Another social factor is relations among individuals, and the most distinctly structural kinds of social relations are intergroup relations, because these refer to the relations between persons classified by their different position and thus connect different groups or classes. Whereas microstructural studies analyze the influence of network structures on the roles of individuals in various positions, macrostructural research analyzes the effects of structural differentiation among positions in various dimensions on rates of intergroup relations.

The members of a large population, particularly in modern societies, differ in virtually innumerable ways. One cannot develop a theory in terms of these many differences, which would violate Braithwaite's criterion that theoretical terms be abstract as well as the principle of simplicity or parsimony. To solve this problem I tried to conceptualize generic aspects of social differences that apply to all particular differences among many elements in an aggregate and also are independent of the distinction between any two elements. I only later realized that my distinction is an application of Simmel's brilliant insight of distinguishing social forms from their contents.

I may have been influenced unawares by Simmel. For I always considered this distinction, which he made in the first chapter of his major book (1908), a profound theoretical contribution, though I only later realized its full significance for social theorizing. What Simmel gave to sociology with this distinction are ways for formulating abstract theoretical terms out of the welter of social reality. Competition is an abstraction that does not exist without an empirical content, such as rivalry among lovers, athletic contests, political elections, or economic competition. What is conflict—a fist fight, an argument, a war, a disagreement? It is the abstract social form reflected in all of them, with which we can construct theories that are testable by their manifestations in empirical contents.

Parameters are what I have called the three major theoretical terms of the theory—three social forms into which one can classify any of the many dimensions of differences among people. Since these are discussed in detail later, I merely describe them briefly now. Heterogeneity refers to differences in a population in terms of nominal categories, such as race, religion, national origin, or occupation. Inequality refers to differences in a rank order or continuum, such as education or income. Intersection, which is the most important dimension, and which is explicitly derived from Simmel's concept of crosscutting social circles, refers to the independence of one dimension of social differences from others (or of several dimensions from one another). A question that arises is how these abstractions from the concrete differences in contents can vary. The answer is that they differ in degree: how great a population's heterogeneities or its inequalities in various respects are, or how *weakly* differences in one dimension are related to those in others—how close to orthogonal they are.

The core of the theory are the effects of these three forms of differentiation on the rates of intergroup relations in a population. The intergroup relations examined in the tests are the proportion of all recent young brides in a metropolis whose grooms differ from them in the dimension under consideration. The three major theorems stipulate the effects of degree of heterogeneity, inequality, or intersection on rates of intergroup relations. To test the theorems, measures are used that refer to empirical representations of the three forms of differentiation and of rates of intermarriage. All measures are defined in terms of chance expectations.

Degree of heterogeneity is the chance expectation or probability that any two persons differ in a specific nominal attribute, be it ethnic background, mother tongue, birthplace, or any other categorical attribute. Degree of inequality is the expected—which is the same as the probable (and also as the average)— difference between any two persons in a given rank order, such as socioeconomic status, earnings, or another continuous variable. Degree of intersection is the chance or probability that any two persons alike in one characteristic are unlike in others, for example, people of the same religion who differ in socioeconomic background, birth region, and the other characteristic in the data set.

The social structure of a population encompasses its members' differentiation in all dimensions. It has been conceptualized as the multidimensional space of social positions among which a population is distributed. The degree of differentiation—in heterogeneity, in inequality, and in one dimension's intersection with others—is not the same in various dimensions, and it also differs for the same dimension among populations. Once it is easier to envisage three dimensions in a spatial image than a large number, it is, paradoxically, easier to visualize the three abstract than the many empirical dimensions as a social space.

Intergroup relations are simply indicated by the rate or percent of all relations of a given kind—in the tests all marriages of women under twenty-five—that involve two persons who differ in a certain respect, for example, who belong to different ethnic groups, or who were not born in the same region. The theory, as the measure of the dependent variable indicates, predicts only the probability of intermarriages, since rates are probabilities, and does not predict whether a particular couple is or is not intermarried, which implies that it is not a deterministic but a probabilistic theory. This is a weaker form of theory, which cannot explain or predict that a cause has a specific effect, as a determinist theory can, but only that differences in the causal impact determine differences in the chances or probabilities that those subject to the impact are affected.

It is inevitable, however, that genuinely sociological theories that seek to explain effects of structural conditions are probabilistic and cannot determine which individuals in a population will be affected. For the conditions in a population's social structure, as here defined, are the same for all its members, which implies that differences in these conditions—in the degree of structural differentiation and the strength of its influence—are necessarily the same for all. Since structural differences are the same for all members of a population they cannot determine which members are actually affected, only the differences in the chances any one is affected, which is reflected in the rate or percent of those who are. Structural effects do not conflict with the assumption of free will, because they only exert constraints on our decisions and permit free choice within these limits, though often only at the sacrifice of other options in order to take advantages of one.

Initially I considered the definition of social structure—as multiple dimensions of social positions among which a population is distributed—to indicate also a structure of life chances. In other words, I believed that the same concept also reveals the opportunities provided and the constraints implied by the limits that the asocial structure imposes. On second thought I realized that this is misleading, however, because the definition fails to make a sufficient distinction between positions and people occupying it. This can be illustrated with two different hypothetical cases of limits to opportunities. If more single women than men are college graduates, some of the women who do want to marry are constrained by the fewer male college graduates to sacrifice their educational ingroup preferences and marry men who have not graduated from college. If colleges admit fewer students than apply to them, some of the persons who had chosen to go to college are constrained to find a career that does not require a college education.

How do the two cases differ? The first constraint was exerted by the insufficient number of *persons* in positions on the educational ladder to satisfy choices of a certain relation. But the second was not exerted by too few persons who chose a college education but by too many, which has the consequence that there are too few available *positions* in colleges for the large number of applicants who want to go to college.

The distinction is confounded by the practice in studies of social mobility to define opportunities for structural mobility up (or down) by the difference in a matrix between the distributions of respondents and those of their fathers. If more sons than fathers are in professional occupations it is taken as an indication of good opportunities for upward mobility. Although it is true that this indicates that today's labor force had good opportunities for moving up into the professions, it does not indicate existing or future opportunities. Only further expansion of the demand for professional services would create a need (implicit vacancies) for professionals and opportunities to become one.

Concluding Comments

The tests presented in this book are simple correlations, not multiple regressions. I want to mention briefly later tests of this theory that increase confidence in the results of the tests here presented. The reason Schwartz and I decided to use simple correlation procedures is that we wanted to know whether the theory is robust enough for its predictions to prevail over other possibly disturbing influences. In particular, we wanted to protect our tests against the misuse of the phrase *ceteris paribus*. Theories in the social sciences always implicitly assume their predictions to be protected by this phrase of "other things being equal." But a literal interpretation of this phrase makes it impossible to falsify a theory because any negative result can be excused by saying that some other influences interfered. This is especially bad for a deductive theory which cannot be tested unless falsifying it is a possibility.

What we ignored, however, is that a simple correlation may appear to confirm a prediction though it is actually a spurious result of parallel influences of some other structural conditions on both variables, the presumed independent and the dependent one. For this reason, I later also performed tests of the theorems regressing every intermarriage variable on its predictor and, as controls, all other structural variables on which we had data that exerted an influence on it (1994: 53-89). All but one of these seventeen empirical tests confirmed the predictions, and so did, as will be seen, nearly all of the tests here presented. The regression tests that confirm that the correlations are not spurious increases confidence in the more robust tests of the theory in this book.

In conclusion, I outline my final conception of social theorizing. It continues to be largely based on Popper's and particularly Braithwaite's model of theorizing, with some more emphasis on the significance of research for theory. I agree with their central argument that scientific theories are ideally formulated in logical terms as deductive systems of interrelated propositions that imply empirically testable predictions. I prefer Braithwaite's additional criterion for a satisfactory theory to Popper's, that its propositions be formulated in abstract terms rather than that they state universal laws. Popper's favorite illustration of a "strictly universal statement"—"all ravens are black"—indicates my reason. Though it clearly refers to all black ravens, the statement is so concrete that it is virtually identical with the empirical statement "all ravens ever observed are black." Moreover, I doubt that this universal statement could be falsified, because if a bird with all attributes of ravens except for the feathers were found, then claims of falsification could be refuted by stating that blackness, as other distinct attributes of ravens, define the species.

On the other hand, unless some, and perhaps ideally all, theoretical terms are abstract, theories cannot logically imply truly new predictions in quite different substantive matters. For abstraction implies generality, and its degree implies generality's scope. This suggests that advances in theory that explain some theorems by discovering a new one from which they can be deduced, which requires that the new proposition is more abstract and thus more general, produce a theory of wider scope and thereby make it, in Popper's terms, simpler, better, and easier to falsify.

As much as I admire Popper's insights about testing theories by failing to falsify their implications in research, I am critical of two of his arguments. The first, as just noted, is that the criterion of theorems is that they are universal statements. The second is his dismissal of the role of research for developing theory as of no concern to a philosopher's logical analysis (1950 [1934]: 31–33). Even if one agrees with Popper's criticism of inductive logic, practicing scientists hoping to contribute to scientific discovery cannot ignore the significance of research for doing so. There is truth in the Baconian conception that the distinctiveness of science rests on its grounding in empirical observations, which distinguishes it from mere logical reasoning and mathematics as well as metaphysical speculations and superstitions. I learned already in graduate school of the important role of research in constructing, as well as testing, theory, but I tended to neglect it in my early enthusiasm for deductive theorizing.

To give a few illustrations of this role: To formulate a theoretical explanation in abstract terms, these terms must be abstracted from empirical data. For theory to explain empirical reality, research must raise and specify the questions that need to be answered. Research also often produces unexpected insights that point in new directions and stimulate theoretical hypotheses—the serendipity pattern, as Merton (1968: 157–52) refers to it. The reconceptualization of empirical findings often provides the clues for abstract theoretical generalizations that explain them, particularly by revealing the common element implicit in several variables that were found to have the same influence. A great help for such reconceptualizing may well be Simmel's clue to discover the abstract social form from the observations of concrete empirical contents.

Peter M. Blau
September 1996

References

Blau, Peter M. 1960. "Structural Effects." *American Sociological Review* 25: 545–56.
———. 1970. "A Formal Theory of Differentiation in Organizations." *American Sociological Review:* 201–18.
———. 1973 (1955). *The Dynamics of Bureaucracy.* Chicago: University of Chicago Press.
———. 1977. *Inequality and Heterogeneity.* New York: Free Press.
———. 1986 (1964). *Exchange and Power in Social Life.* New York: Wiley.
———. 1994. *Structural Contexts of Opportunities.* Chicago: University of Chicago Press.
Blau, Peter M., and Otis Dudley Duncan. 1967. *The American Occupational Structure.* New York: Wiley.
Braithwaite, Richard B. 1953. *Scientific Explanation.* Cambridge: University Press.
Coleman, James. 1990. *Foundations of Social Theory.* Cambridge: Harvard University Press.
Durkheim, Emile. 1984 (1893). *The Division of Labor in Society.* New York: Macmillan.
Fromm, Erich. 1941. *Escape from Freedom.* New York: Farrar & Rinehart.

Giddens, Anthony. 1986 (1984). *The Constitution of Society*. Berkeley: University of California Press.

Mead, George Herbert. 1934. *Mind, Self, Society*. Chicago: University of Chicago Press.

Merton, Robert K. 1968 (1949). *Social Theory and Social Structure*. New York: Free Press.

Popper, Karl R. 1950 (1934). *The Logic of Scientific Discovery*. New York: Basic Books.

Simmel, Georg. 1908. *Soziologie*. Leipzig: Duncker & Humblot.

Wellman, Barry. 1988. "Structural Analysis." Pp. 19–61 in B. Wellman and S. D. Berkowitz, eds., *Social Structures*. Cambridge: Cambridge University Press.

White, Harrison C. 1970. *Chains of Opportunity*. Cambridge: Harvard University Press.

Whitehead, Alfred N., and Bertrand Russel. 1957 (1910–13). *Principia mathematica*. Cambridge: University Press.

Wittgenstein, Ludwig. 1863 (1921). *Tractatus logico-philosophicus*. New York: Humanities Press.

Preface

The objectives of this book are to present a macrosociological theory and to test it in research on the 125 largest metropolitan areas in the United States. Attention centers on the influences social structure exerts on intergroup relations. By *social structure* we refer to the distribution of persons among social positions that influence their role relations, for example, a community's racial composition, division of labor, ethnic heterogeneity, income inequality, or the extent to which educational differences are related to income differences. The theory is tested by deriving its implications for the effects of such structural conditions on intermarriage, as an important form of intergroup relations. Of course, we would expect the population distribution of a small neighborhood to affect the casual associations among neighbors. But it would be much more sociologically interesting if the population distribution of a metropolis with millions of inhabitants also affects the consequential decisions involved in mate selection, as the theory implies.

Our endeavor in this monograph rests on three convictions. The first is that sociological explanations, like those in other sciences, require formulating axiomatic theories from which the phenomena to be explained can be logically deduced. The second conviction underlying our approach is that theories that have been a priori developed must be tested by deducing from them new empirical predictions and confronting these with relevant research findings. Our third conviction is that the most distinctively sociological theories are those that explain patterns of social relations in a community in terms of the structure of positions among which the population is distributed, not in terms of psychological preferences or cultural orientations. These three assumptions are controversial and by no means accepted by all sociologists. The counter view is that sociological theories are fundamentally different from those in the natural sciences because they deal with human behavior which must be meaningfully interpreted and not merely logically explained, as Weber's concept *Verstehen* emphasizes. Similarly, not everybody accepts the deductive approach to theorizing. A number of social scientists—and natural scientists, too—think that the nature of the data with which they work requires an inductive approach and stress that theories have to be built from the ground up, starting with empirical findings and deriving theoretical generalizations of increasing scope by accumulating more and more related findings. Finally, many sociologists—perhaps most—seek to explain social life not in terms of structural conditions but in terms of the cultural orientations and psychological motives affecting human behavior.

Of course, there can be no doubt that people's behavior, including their interaction with others, is affected by their preferences and motives, which in turn are influenced by the culture in which people were socialized. However, social relations depend not only on cultural and sociopsychological factors governing individual dispositions and preferences but also on the social environment, that is, the population composition of the community and society. Whatever people's preferences, living in a black ghetto limits opportunities to associate with rich whites and exerts much constraint to associate mostly with poor blacks. The population structure of a community determines the opportunities for finding certain associates and hence constrains the prevalent social relations that occur. We consider the study of these external influences of the structure of social positions on social relations the most distinctive task of sociology. The effects of the opportunity structure of a community are often paradoxical and counterintuitive. For instance, many empirical studies have found that group differences discourage marriage, and our data confirm this result. One might extrapolate from these findings on individuals to the conclusion that intergroup marriage is rarer in communities composed of many diverse groups than in more homogeneous places. But the theory implies, on the contrary, that community heterogeneity encourages intermarriage, and the empirical data confirm this theoretical prediction.

The theory was initially developed in an earlier publication (Blau, 1977). To illustrate its wide applicability, the attempt there was to derive a large number of theorems and corollaries from a limited number of primitive terms and assumptions. The analysis here is confined to considerably fewer basic assumptions and theorems, only those that constitute the core of the theory, and the focus is testing the implications for intermarriage of most of these major theorems—all on which data were available. (Of course, no theorem has been excluded after testing it yielded negative results.) That the theorems being tested were formulated and published in advance serves as evidence that the theory was not tailored to fit the data. However, the empirical findings do require a few revisions of the original theory.

After analyzing the significance for social life of various forms of population distributions in a single dimension, we raise the question of how combinations of population distributions in several dimensions influence intergroup relations. When several kinds of social differences among people are closely related—

foreign-born tend to have worse jobs and lower incomes than natives—their effects reinforce one another, they consolidate differences in social positions and group boundaries, and they inhibit intergroup relations. On the other hand, when several dimensions of social differences are very weakly related, their influences mitigate or even counteract each other, and such intersecting social differences promote intergroup relations.

Weakly related group differences correspond to Simmel's concept of *crosscutting social circles*. In a pioneering analysis, Simmel dissects multiple group memberships, crosscutting social circles, and the resulting webs of group affiliation. He calls attention to the significance of these phenomena for modern society and civilization. Simmel was not particularly interested in the degree to which various kinds of social differences are related and the implications of such variation. In contrast, how variations in the degree of intersection of several social differences affect social life generally and intermarriage particularly constitutes the central culminating part of the theory advanced here, which is the reason that Simmel's concept has been chosen as the book's title. In large part, the theory systematizes Simmel's insights and makes them suitable for empirical testing.

We gratefully acknowledge support for the research reported here from the National Science Foundation (to Blau: SOC782516, SOC7919935). We are also grateful to the Center for the Social Sciences at Columbia University for making its facilities available for our research. We are indebted to many graduate students at Columbia University and at the State University of New York at Albany for helping us with the research at various stages, especially to Terry C. Blum, Linda A. Cranor, and Hilary Silver at Columbia University; and Carolyn Beeker, Kevin M. Fitzgerald, and Reid Golden at SUNY–Albany, some of whose coauthored papers are incorporated in different form in this volume. Blau received advice about statistical problems from Richard Alba and Steven L. Rytina, for which he is thankful. Judith R. Blau read the entire manuscript and made many invaluable suggestions, for which we owe her much. Finally, we thank Norma E. Fuentes for getting the manuscript ready for the publisher.

CHAPTER 1

Macrosociological Theory: Design and Test

One of Simmel's (1955) profound insights is that social structure comprises crosscutting social circles that create a web of group affiliations for individuals. Particularly in modern communities and societies, a multitude of crosscutting differences among people produce an intricate network of partly overlapping social affiliations. Individuals are located at the intersection of numerous social circles, so that their ingroup members along any one dimension are not the same as their ingroup partners along other dimensions. Simmel's imaginative analysis of intersecting circles draws attention to their significance for various aspects of contemporary culture—the diverse human personalities, the individualized situations of people, the lesser domination by social norms and pressures, the potential for subjectivity and departure from conformity, and the greater individual freedom.[1]

The fruitful concept of intersecting social circles can serve as the central theoretical term of a deductive macrosociological theory of social structure. To be sure, developing axiomatic theory was not Simmel's style. His perceptive reflections on crosscutting circles convey original ideas and suggest new implications, but he was not interested in formulating these ideas in a deductive system. The objective of this book is to present such a theory, subject major parts of it to empirical tests, and refine it accordingly. The original version of this theory (Blau, 1977) aimed to indicate its wide applicability by deriving many implications and corollaries from the major theorems. Instead of following this procedure, the analysis here is confined to the major theorems. Starting with definitions of primitive terms and postulated assumptions as premises, theorems logically implied by definitions and premises are formulated to refer to the

[1]Bendix (Simmel, 1955:125), the translator, substitutes for Simmel's title, *Die Kreuzung sozialer Kreise*, another term (*The Web of Group Affiliations*) because, he explains, "literal translation of this phrase, 'intersection of social circles,' is almost meaningless." It surely is no longer meaningless since network analysis has made the idea familiar.

1

influences of a community's structural conditions on intergroup relations. Specific empirical predictions deducible from the theorems—for example, how ethnic heterogeneity affects ethnic intermarriage—are tested on the basis of quantitative data from the 125 largest metropolitan areas in the United States. Furthermore, the theory is extended by examining the status-attainment processes that generate structural differences among communities and by inferring implications of these differences for conflictual as well as integrative social relations.

Metasociological Principles of Theorizing

There is no general consensus among social scientists as to what proper social theories are. Still greater is the diversity of opinion about what is meant by structural theory, ranging from Marxian to Lévi-Straussian to Parsonian conceptions of it. It is, therefore, advisable to start by presenting the view of theorizing adopted and to go on to explicate the conceptual scheme in terms of which social structure is defined, a scheme that constitutes the framework for the macrostructural theory formulated.

In discussing the principles of theorizing, concern is with the interface between the philosophy of science and a given discipline's subject matter—in this case, sociology's. Two principles of the philosophy of science are accepted as fundamental postulates of systematic theorizing. The first is that rigorous theories are scientific explanations (R. B. Braithwaite, 1953) in the sense that they constitute deductive systems of propositions in which the less general statements are explained by showing that they are logically implied by more general ones. The second principle is that scientific theories must be falsifiable (Popper, 1959), which requires that theorems make empirical predictions that are testable through research and that, if contradicted, falsify the theorem in its present form. This hypothetical–deductive view of theorizing differs from both the inductive view of positivists and the emphasis on interpretative meaning and understanding of social philosophers. But how does one come to construct such a logical system of interrelated and testable propositions? In an endeavor to answer this question, the building blocks used in theory construction will be outlined, largely on the basis of dissecting what some successful theorists in sociology and other disciplines have done.

At the foundation of systematic theories is a clear conception of the subject matter, notably what is being explained—the *explicandum*—and in which terms one wants to explain it—the *explicans*. At an early stage, this may merely be a general orientation to the subject matter (Merton, 1968:142), indicating the most important factors to be taken into account, as illustrated by Freud's focus on sex drive, Marx's focus on class conflict, and Durkheim's focus on social facts. Further clarification involves specifying the connection between explicandum and explicans. Thus, Durkheim discussed at length external constraints as distinguishing criteria of social facts and stressed that social facts must be explained in terms of other social facts. Freud explained a variety of nonrational behavior—dreams, neurotic symptoms, slips of the tongue—in terms of sexual and aggressive drives and their repression. Darwin's objective was to explain the variety of species on the basis of the struggle for existence in nature. Simmel was concerned with social forms abstracted from their substantive content, such as the distinction between competition and conflict in any area, or the significance of size and number of collectivities of all kinds.

Another prerequisite for constructing systematic theory is empirical knowledge. To be sure, deductive theory is not built from the ground up, starting with narrow empirical findings and accumulating more and more to widen the empirical base: this is inductive theorizing. Axiomatic or deductive theories are constructed from the top down, starting with primitive terms and postulated assumptions and deriving their logical implications, theorems and empirical predictions. However, scientific theories cannot be built in a vacuum, in complete ignorance of empirical research on the subject matter. The postulates assumed as given, for instance, must not be contradicted by available evidence. Indeed, all propositions in the system must be compatible with existing research findings, and empirical knowledge is needed to ensure that this is the case. The nature and rigor of the empirical information used in developing theories differs greatly. Durkheim pioneered in the quantitative analysis of social data to derive a systematic theory of suicide rates. Freud used largely clinical observation and therapy experience in the development of psychoanalytic theory. Darwin devoted many years to the study of breeding and the observation of the distribution of various species in different areas before formulating his deductive theory of natural selection. Simmel, in contrast, did not conduct quantitative research but relied largely on perceptive impressions from everyday life to gain his theoretical insights.

What makes a theory original and fruitful and constitutes its most important building block is a profound new theoretical insight, which is typically embodied in its central theoretical term. Although it is essential to use rigorous methods in scientific theorizing as well as in research, our emphasis on this requirement has sometimes led us to slight the crucial importance of the most creative part of the scientific enterprise—the inspiration to advance a profound new concept that provides a novel perspective on empirical reality and throws fresh light on empirical observations, thereby stimulating new discoveries. The analysis of empirical data often provides the initial clues for theoretical insights that result from an imaginative reconceptualization of apparently diverse research findings. Thus, in seeking to discern a common factor in such disparate phenomena as Catholicism, war, and family life—which all are inversely related to suicide rates—Durkheim discovered the principle that explains egoistic suicide.

This core concept may be called the theory's *operator,* which supplies the connections among elements on both the theoretical and the empirical level. It is the mechanism that links and unites many of the propositions in the theoretical system, and it is the underlying force that accounts for the dynamic interrelations among elements in the empirical structure under investigation. These are not two concretely distinct levels, of course, but two sides of the same coin because the interrelated theoretical terms and propositions are designed to explain the interconnections and their dynamics in the subject matter being studied. Thus, Durkheim's concept of *social integration* or *solidarity* is the link of most of his theories and also a basic social fact in terms of which many empirical observations can be explained. Freud's concept of *unconscious motivation* is a corresponding central term in his theory: it is a main element implicit in virtually all psychoanalytic concepts—repression, superego, dream work, hysteria, neuroses, projection, and other psychological dynamisms; and it is the principle underlying the dynamics of personality development and human behavior generally. *Natural selection,* too, operates as the underlying principle linking the various parts of Darwin's theory of evolution (which will be illustrated by a citation from Darwin presently) and as the natural force producing the diversity of species and the complexity of the most advanced ones. We show in this book that Simmel's concept of *intersecting social circles* can be looked at from the same two perspectives: as the central theoretical term of the theory to be presented and as the structural force that accounts for many patterns of social relations in communities.

A profound idea gives original meaning to a subject and provides a new way of seeing things that have been looked at all along. But a brilliant insight is not enough. Building scientific theories involves disciplined creativity, which requires three further steps: conceptually clarifying the ideas and transforming them into precise theoretical terms with operational implications; constructing a deductive system of propositions incorporating these concepts; and confronting the predictions implied by the theory with empirical data.

Conceptual refinement entails more than the elaboration of a conceptual scheme by expanding the number of categories and subcategories in various ways. Conceptual elaboration can easily become a sterile exercise in ingenuity. For conceptual refinement to provide the framework for constructing a deductive theoretical system of propositions, it must specify the links between concepts, not only between those on the same level of abstraction but also between those on different levels. Theoretical terms must be abstract and general, which gives them their explanatory power, and yet precise enough to imply empirical variables that have operational measures. A useful strategy for accomplishing this is to analyze the original insight to discern the different aspects of it that have to be taken into consideration in empirical studies. Thus, the concept of crosscutting social circles raises a number of questions of what the several ideas implicit in it specifically mean. What is the criterion of a social circle? Does it require social contacts of all members with one another, is a we-feeling necessarily involved, is sharing any social attribute sufficient, or is there still some other criterion? What difference does it make if various social circles are hierarchically ordered, as social classes are? Social differences do not necessarily divide people into categories or circles but may involve continuous gradations, as exemplified by income or years of schooling. Can one speak of crosscutting in these cases, and what difference does it make that there are no distinct circles? Are all social circles crosscutting? Are some more crosscutting than others? What does *more crosscutting* mean? What are its implications for social life? These questions are addressed when presenting the theory's conceptual framework in the next section of this chapter.

The fundamental requirement for constructing a scientific theory is to formulate a deductive system of propositions in which definitions of primitive terms and postulated assumptions logically imply less general synthetic propositions, which are the theorems and, on a still less general level, empirical predictions of the theory. Propositions are said to be explained by more general ones from which they are deducible, although many social scientists do not consider deducibility a sufficient criterion for adequate explanation. Deductive theorizing is still quite rare in the social sciences, but there are some cases of it (for instance, Blalock, 1967; Homans, 1961). Most theories in the natural sciences take this form, often expressed in mathematical equations. Darwin's theory of natural selection is a beautiful example, not formulated in mathematical terms, which Darwin (1958:128) summarizes, after developing the deductive arguments in more than one hundred pages, in a brief paragraph. This is worth quoting in full because it is a concise summary of deductive theorizing and because it shows how Darwin refines his broad conception of life in nature as a struggle for existence by drawing on relevant empirical information to yield the central term of his deductive theory, natural selection:

> If under changing conditions of life organic beings present individual differences in almost every part of their structure, and this cannot be disputed; if there be, owing to their geometric rate of increase, a severe struggle for life at some age, season, or year, and this certainly cannot be disputed; then, considering the infinite complexity of the relations of all organic beings to each other and to their conditions of life, causing an infinite diversity of structure, constitution, and habits, to be advantageous to them, it would be a most extraordinary fact if no variations had ever occurred useful to each being's own welfare, in the same manner as so many variations have occurred useful to man. But if variations useful to any organic being ever do occur, assuredly individuals thus characterized will have the best chance of being preserved in the struggle for life; and from the strong principle of inheritance, these will tend to produce offspring similarly characterized. This principle of preservation, or the survival of the fittest, I have called Natural Selection. It leads to the

improvement of each creature in relation to its organic and inorganic conditions of life; and consequently, in most cases, to what must be regarded as an advance in organization. Nevertheless, low and simple forms will long endure if well fitted for their simple condition of life.

The requirements of deductive theory can be subsumed, in somewhat simplified form, under four main principles. First, a deductive theory is composed of propositions, mostly synthetic ones. Analytic propositions are definitions and thus are not subject to empirical testing (e.g., *social integration* means a dense network of friendships). Synthetic propositions refer to the relationship between two (or more) independently defined terms (e.g., social integration reduces suicide rates) and hence are subject to empirical testing. Whereas the premises of a deductive theory often include both analytic and synthetic propositions (the definitions of terms and the assumptions made about their relationships), the theorems, corollaries, and empirical predictions deduced from them must all be synthetic propositions.

Second, the propositions constitute a hierarchical logical system in which all lower-level propositions are deducible from higher ones. Any proposition not so deducible is a premise in the logical system—an assumption, postulate, axiom, or definition. Levels of abstraction and generality are a matter of degree, and one often cannot draw a clear line between more abstract theoretical and less abstract empirical generalizations. Nevertheless, there is an important difference, at least between extremes, and the other two principles refer to this difference.

Third, the highest-order generalizations of the deductive theory must contain some purely theoretical terms that cannot be empirically measured. This is a central thesis of R. B. Braithwaite's (1953:50–87), who emphasizes that unless the theoretical propositions contain terms that go beyond any empirical data, they merely summarize the empirical generalizations (findings) logically implied by them and do not provide new ideas that explain them. In his own words (1953:76): ''A theory which it is hoped may be expanded in the future to explain more generalizations than it was originally designed to explain must allow more freedom to its theoretical terms than would be given them were they to be logical constructions out of observable entities.''

Yet these theoretical terms must be sufficiently precise to have implications for empirical variables, lest the fourth principle is violated, which requires that the lowest-level propositions contain only terms that can be translated into operational variables for research. Otherwise, the theory would not make testable predictions and hence not be falsifiable. Testable predictions are part of the body of theory and deducing them is part of the theorist's job. Theoretical terms that go beyond empirical data are usually vague and are rarely precise enough to imply testable propositions. But precise theoretical concepts are not unknown. Natural selection is an example. It is not operational; there is no empirical measure by which it can be represented. But it has implications that are testable—that reproduction produces more offspring than can survive, that later generations are better adapted to their environment than earlier ones, that species become more complex over many generations, and so forth.

Although not all social scientists agree that explaining generalizations involves demonstrating that they can be deduced from higher-order generalizations, many—quite possibly most—do. However, there is much controversy about whether such deduction is sufficient for a satisfactory explanation or whether it is possibly necessary but certainly not sufficient for it. Philosophers of science as well as social scientists are in disagreement on this issue. R. B. Braithwaite (1953:343) takes the first position that empirical laws are explained simply when they logically follow from a more general theory: "It is scarcely too much to say that this is the whole truth about the explanation of scientific laws." Campbell (1952:82–83) disagrees: "When we say that the theory explains the laws we mean something additional to this mere logical deduction. . . . What else do we require? . . . We require that it shall add to our ideas and that the ideas it adds shall be acceptable."

Whereas these two positions appear diametrically opposed, they are actually reconcilable. R. B. Braithwaite claims that logical deduction from a theory is all there is to explanation, yet he noted earlier (in the first passage quoted from him) that the theory must include abstract terms that go beyond any known empirical data. Such original theoretical concepts that, jointly with others, logically imply various empirical observations that could not heretofor be explained constitute precisely new insightful ideas, and their logical implications for empirical generalizations make them acceptable to experts in the field. Thus, Braithwaite's emphasis on theoretical terms that go beyond any empirical evidence implicitly endows his conception of theory with the fresh ideas that Campbell makes an explicit requirement of explanatory theory, which suggests that the two approaches to theorizing are not in fundamental disagreement.[2]

The final building block of theory construction is confronting the theory with empirical evidence. Even before genuine tests of new predictions derived from the theory are made and while still in the process of developing the theory, the propositions are given a preliminary screening on the basis of available empirical evidence. It obviously is a waste of effort to devise a logically tight system of propositions if some of them are incompatible with existing empirical knowledge. To avoid this danger, the astute theorist will deliberately search for negative evidence and modify the theory accordingly. But this very adjustment of the theory on the basis of empirical data indicates that such use of research findings

[2]Weber's principle of *Verstehen* has been variously interpreted as referring to intuitive understanding, empathy, taking psychological factors into account, or interpretation in terms of cultural values which give meaning to conduct. But one can interpret his principle more narrowly as referring to fresh ideas that provide new meaningful explanations, in short, as essentially similar to Campbell's requirement.

is part of theory construction and cannot be considered theory testing. Only new empirical predictions derived from the theory can test it. A main purpose of this book is to present a number of tests of the core of a macrosociological theory of social structure previously advanced.[3]

Conceptual Framework

The simple definition of *sociology* as the study of social relations is not inaccurate, though it fails to convey the complexity of the subject matter concealed by the common words. Explaining people's relations is, indeed, a main objective of sociology, whether in microsociological analysis of marriage, friendships, or social networks in work groups and neighborhoods, or whether in macrosociological analysis of the pattern, organization, or institutionalization of social relations in entire communities and societies. People's relations with one another involve, of course, human behavior and thus can be analyzed from the standpoint of this behavior, that is, by explaining why people establish certain relations with others on the basis of their personality traits, attitudes, and motives. But this psychological or sociopsychological task is not the one undertaken here. Our macrosociological objective is to examine how patterns of social relations in a community are affected by the social environment because the other people in their environment determine the options people have in establishing social relations. We cannot have Buddhist friends if there are no Buddhists around. The relations between persons belonging to different groups or occupying different positions are of special interest because these intergroup relations connect and integrate the diverse segments of a large population.

In short, patterns of social relations in a community or society are the explicandum. The aim is not to explain these patterns in terms of the motivated behavior implicit in them, that is, by the motivations to enter them and maintain them. These motivations, such as ingroup preferences, are taken as prior assumptions (supported by empirical evidence). The question is raised of how the community structure, given these psychological tendencies, influences social relations, especially those that link various groups and positions. *Social structure*, as here defined, refers essentially to the extent of differentiation of a population along various lines, this being the explicans of our scheme. But this concept requires clarification.

---

[3]Ideally, the aim of empirical tests of theorems should be to falsify them because theories are corroborated by repeated unsuccessful attempts to falsify them. The best persons to perform such tests are sociologists biased against the theory. Since one of us is the theory's author, we can hardly be expected to have such a bias. We can only hope that our protheory bias does not distort our endeavor to conduct fair tests and present the evidence they supply, whatever it is.

Social structure reflects the differences among people, specifically, the differences in social position among them. The concept of *social position* is interpreted broadly. Social positions are indicated by attributes or affiliations that distinguish people and that they themselves take into account in their social life and use as criteria for making social distinctions in their social intercourse. In other words, not the distinctions the investigator makes a priori but the distinctions community members themselves make are the criteria of differences in position. Whether some attribute does influence social interaction and thus is considered a social position in a society can be empirically ascertained. Since position is, accordingly, defined on the basis of its influence on social relations, theorems that stipulate such an influence would be tautological and true by definition. However, the theory is not concerned with the influence of an individual's position on his or her social life but with the influence of a population's differentiation among positions for the pattern of relations among its members. These influences are not the same; indeed, they are often in the opposite direction, as we shall point out. By *differentiation* we mean a population's size distribution among different positions; for example, a society's distribution among different religious denominations or its income distribution. Simmel's concern with size and numbers is thus extended to size distributions. Of course, every person occupies many positions simultaneously—each person has a religion and an income and other attributes defining positions. Size distributions, and hence, forms of differentiation exist along all these lines.

Taking the various lines of differentiation into account, social structure can be defined by the distribution of a population among positions in a multidimensional space. The axes in this social space are dimensions of social differences, such as race or wealth, and a point represents a joint position on two or more dimensions, such as black and earning $1234 a month. The concept of social structure is an abstract theoretical term, in Braithwaite's sense. It cannot be represented by an empirical measure, yet it is sufficiently precise to imply numerous operational variables that can be used to make empirical predictions. Specific forms of differentiation—in education, in occupation—can be empirically measured, and their theoretically predicted influences on social relations can be investigated in research, which indirectly tests the theory. Since the theory is concerned with the influence of a community's structural features on patterns of social relations in it, not with the influence of an individual's position on his or her social relations, empirical tests require comparing communities with varying structural conditions, not merely comparing a sample of individuals whose social positions differ.

The population distribution in any one dimension is a property of the social structure. Social structures are circumscribed by parameters that characterize their distributions. One type of structural parameter refers to the extent of differentiation of a population with respect to a given dimension, that is, the degree of variation among the population's members in this dimension. Illustrations are an economy's industrial diversity, a nation's concentration of wealth, a state's division of labor, a city's uneven income distribution, and a neighborhood's racial admixture. The various dimensions of social structure are not necessarily orthogonal. Differentiation along two or more dimensions may be closely related or virtually independent. In other words, the population distributions in several dimensions can exhibit more or less concomitant variations. For instance, education, occupational status, and income exhibit much covariation because they are substantially related to one another. On the other hand, variations in national descent are related very little to variations in age. The degree of covariation of several dimensions, which indicates how similar the various population distributions are and thus how parallel the corresponding forms of differentiation are, can also be considered a structural parameter.[4] Hence, social structure refers here to the joint distribution whose main parameters are univariate variations and multivariate covariations.

There are three generic forms of parameters, which subsume a large number of specific forms of differentiation. Two forms of differentiation refer to variation in a single dimension, whereas the third refers to covariation of several dimensions. The distinction between the first two rests on whether the dimension divides the population into unordered nominal groups, such as religious denominations or ethnic groups, or classifies people on the basis of a status gradation, such as wealth or education.[5] The resulting two forms of differentiation are heterogeneity and inequality.

Heterogeneity is a population's differentiation among nominal groups in a single dimension. The division of labor is a form of heterogeneity; so is ethnic diversity. A criterion of heterogeneity—whether in a small neighborhood or an entire society—is the chance expectation that two randomly selected persons belong to different groups. The larger the number of groups and the more even the population's distribution among them, the higher is this expectation and the greater is the heterogeneity. An empirical measure exactly representing this

---

[4]The concept of *parameter* is given a slightly different meaning now than it had been originally (Blau, 1977:6). Then it was used for the dimensions themselves (e.g., age), whereas now it is used for characteristics of the distribution in a given dimension (e.g., the age distribution or variation in age). The reason for the change is to make the usage more similar to that in statistics, in which a *population parameter* refers to the quantitative properties of a population (such as means or variances). However, our set of structural parameters does not include every statistical property of a population but only those that are indicative of the population structure, specifically, variations and covariations, because these are indicative of structural differentiation.

[5]The theoretical concept of *status gradation* is assumed to refer to a continuum, even if no ratio measures for concrete manifestations of it are available. Another assumption is that ranked classes— owners and workers, slaves and slaveholders—are the result of nominal categories that are highly related to graduated dimensions.

criterion is the index used by Gibbs and Martin (1962) for industrial diversification, which is equally suitable for measuring other forms of heterogeneity.[6]

Inequality is a population's differentiation in terms of a status gradation. The concentration of wealth and of power are forms of inequality. The more uneven the distribution of a resource, the greater the inequality. A criterion of the degree of inequality is the mean difference in status or resources between any two persons relative to the mean status or resources for all persons. (This is the same as the chance expectation of the resource difference between any pair of persons relative to the chance expectation of a person's resources.) For example, the larger the average difference in income between all possible pairs proportionate to the average income of the population, the greater is the income inequality. This substantive criterion of inequality is precisely reflected in the Gini coefficient, which is, therefore, the preferred measure for testing the inequality theorems.[7] An inherent paradox of inequality is that the concentration of a resource, such as wealth, in a few hands, which the criterion defines as pronounced inequality, implies that many people have hardly any of it and are thus roughly equal. To distinguish inequality, as defined (here and usually), from the proportion of the population who are more or less equal, variations in the latter are designated as *status diversity,* which is the graduated-dimension equivalent of heterogeneity for a nominal dimension. Graduated dimensions are distinguished from nominal ones on strictly technical grounds: whether the variate refers to an ordered gradation or to unordered categories. Most social rank orders or gradations reflect differences in resources: wealth, power, income, or education. But some do not: age is a case in point. Ordered social differences based on resources and those not so based have some parallel implications, but the former also have implications that are characteristic only of variations in resources. For instance, age differences and educational differences probably have similar implications for the likelihood of social association, whereas only differences in resources tend to engender distinctive conflicts of interest.[8]

Consolidation–intersection refers not to variation in a single dimension but to concomitant variations of several dimensions. If social differences along various lines are closely related, they consolidate group boundaries and class distinctions and strengthen the barriers between insiders and outsiders. An illustration is that

[6]Lieberson (1969) discusses this measure and notes that it was used already in 1912 by Gini and has been published in Simpson (1949).

[7]There are numerous measures of inequality and much controversy about their respective limitations and advantages (Atkinson, 1970; Allison, 1978; Schwartz and Winship, 1979). Despite some justified criticisms of it, the Gini coefficient is the preferred measure because it corresponds so well with the conceptualization of inequality in the theoretical scheme. (Specifically it is the mean difference in score values between all pairs of persons divided by twice the mean for all persons.)

[8]There may be a conflict of interest between young and old over social security taxes and benefits, but this is rooted in resource differences associated with age and not in age differences as such.

race in many countries, including ours, is closely related to education, occupation, income, prestige, wealth, and power. These reinforcing social differences consolidate the superior position of some and the inferior position of others, increasing the social distance between members of different races. The inverse or complement of consolidation is intersection. Its polar extreme is that social differences along various lines are unrelated. Such orthogonal dimensions mean that lines of differentiation intersect, thereby weakening social distinctions and affiliations owing to the counteracting influences of other social distinctions and affiliations. In this situation, a person's outgroup in one dimension contains many individuals who are members of his ingroups in other dimensions (Merton, 1972). Complete intersection of all social differences is an impossible extreme, just as complete consolidation is, but it is possible to ascertain how strongly differences in one respect are related to differences in others, which indicates consolidation and, in reverse, intersection.[9] Intersecting social differences, which are indicated by the degree to which various dimensions approximate orthogonality and hence by the reverse of the strength of their association, are essentially Simmel's crosscutting circles.[10] The degree to which social differences intersect is of prime significance for intergroup relations and a community's integration. Intersection is the central concept of the theory under consideration.

Social integration is often interpreted as resting on strong ingroup bonds. But this is a microsociological view, which looks at integration from the standpoint of the individual. Whatever benefits ingroup bonds may have for individuals, from the macrosociological perspective they are a disintegrative force because, far from integrating the diverse segments of a society or community, they fragment it into exclusive groupings. The social integration of the various segments of a large population depends not on strong ingroup ties but on extensive intergroup relations that strengthen the connections among segments and unite them in a distinctive community, notwithstanding their diversity. Value consensus is not sufficient for the social integration of an entire society or large community, and neither is functional interdependence. Although both may contribute to social integration indirectly by promoting intergroup relations, the social integra-

----

[9]The relationships between nominal differences and between them and graduated differences have no sign and cannot be negative (although a high eta of sex with SEI, for example, may mean that males are either higher or lower than females in average SEI). The correlation between two status gradations can be negative, but this is empirically very rare. None of the correlations used as measures of consolidation–intersection have a negative sign in any of the 125 SMSAs, except some associations with age, which are *only* used in the regression analyses in Chapter 5.

[10]Simmel's concept has been altered in two ways: our concept refers to graduated differences (ratio variables) as well as nominal ones (whereas *circle* implies a nominal category), and it takes into account variations in degree of intersection.

tion of a large population depends on the actual connections among its various groups and strata, connections established by the direct associations between members from different groups and strata. Extensive casual intergroup associations, as well as the necessarily rarer lasting and profound ones, further social integration, and the theory applies to all of them from the most superficial to the most intimate (but is restricted to the frequency and duration of actual *dyadic* associations). However, rates of intermarriage are especially relevant for indicating the integration of diverse subpopulations. Integration on a large scale requires that no group is looked upon by the rest of the population as so alien and beyond the pale that intimate relations with its members are virtually inconceivable or taboo. As marriage is one of the most lasting and intimate human relations and intermarriage has important consequences for the population, rates of intermarriage and their responsiveness to structural conditions are particularly good indications of the acceptability of different groups and of social integration. Another advantage of using marriage as an indicator of social relations is that it pertains to enduring behavior, not merely to interview responses.

Not all social interaction is cordial; some involves conflict, possibly violent conflict. The primary concern in this book is with congenial social relations. The bulk of the book is devoted to presenting the core of the deductive theory of the influences of structural conditions on cordial intergroup relations, testing the implications of major theorems for intermarriage, and analyzing the processes of status attainment underlying the structural conditions observed. But then we extend the analysis to conflict and attempt to infer from the theory what conditions in social structures engender conflict. Two major sources of conflict are suggested, and some relevant data are presented.

Précis of Structural Theory

People's cultural values and psychological preferences affect, of course, with whom they establish social relations, particularly profound and lasting relations like marriage. But these are not the only factors that affect social bonds: the constraints and opportunities of the environment do too. Physical, biological, technological, and economic conditions limit one's options, and so does the social environment, the population composition in the place where people live. To be sure, people can migrate to another place, but this merely alters and does not eliminate the constraints the population structure imposes on their choices. The issues of free will and voluntarism are quite beside the point. We are entirely free to refrain from becoming friends with any type of person—black, poor, fat, or whatever—but we are obviously not free to become friends if there are no opportunities for such friendships in our surroundings. We cannot have an American Indian as a friend if there are none in any place we have ever been. But structural constraints are more severe than this example of individual choice implies. Although about one-tenth of the population is black, most whites cannot have a close friend who is black because this would require that every black have at least nine close friends who are white, and friends are not close if one has so many.

A domain assumption (Gouldner, 1970:31–35) underlying the theory is that the structural constraints and opportunities resulting from the population composition and population distributions in a place exert a dominant influence on social relations that partly counteracts, and may suppress, the influences of cultural values and psychological preferences. The major theorems reflect this assumption, and empirical evidence corroborating the theorems provides indirect support for the structural assumption. At this point, only three core theorems are briefly summarized. They are explicitly deduced from higher-order premises, empirically tested, and supplemented by additional theorems, corollaries, and extensions of the analysis in the rest of the volume.

A basic assumption—supported by much existing empirical evidence as well as by our own data—is that people tend to associate with others located close to them in social space, which means that associates tend to belong to the same group and are similar in status, whatever dimension is under consideration. This assumption implies that group and status differences inhibit social relations. Group differences are naturally more prevalent in heterogeneous than in homogeneous communities. Nevertheless, one of the main theorems is that heterogeneity promotes intergroup relations. Although this seems paradoxical, it follows from the assumption made and the definition of heterogeneity. (As is shown in the next chapter, strict logical deduction requires one additional assumption.) Since the defining criterion of heterogeneity is the chance expectation that two randomly chosen persons belong to different groups, the chance that any encounter involves members of the same group decreases and the chance that it involves members of different groups increases with increasing heterogeneity. Hence, increasing heterogeneity reduces opportunities for ingroup choices and increases the constraints to make outgroup choices, thereby enhancing the probability of intergroup associations.

The inequality theorem originally inferred was that inequality reduces the likelihood of association between status-distant persons (Blau, 1977:55), but the research findings and further reflection prove this proposition to be false. The original reasoning was that because status distance inhibits associations—by assumption (which is empirically supported)—and because inequality is defined in terms of average status-distance, a plausible inference is that mean status-distance, just as status distance, has the effect of discouraging associations. But this argument looks at associations completely from the standpoint of the individual and ignores the constraints the social structure imposes on the individual's choices of associates.[11] Just as an increase in heterogeneity makes it more likely that chance encounters involve persons of different groups, an increase in inequality makes it more likely that chance encounters involve persons whose status is further apart. Hence, increasing inequality constrains individuals to modify their tendencies to associate with peers and find associates who are somewhat less close to them in status. The accordingly revised theorem is: Inequality increases the status distance of associates.

Many intersecting social differences promote intergroup relations. This is the central theorem, from which numerous others will be derived, and which incorporates Simmel's idea of crosscutting circles. It is a slightly revised version of theorems originally formulated. Aside from combining several theorems and simplifying the wording, the only change made is adding *many*, a change required by empirical findings. Although the original formulation of the theorem did not explicitly specify that the stipulated effect depends on the intersection of numerous social differences, the discussion preceding it did note that this is the case (Blau, 1977:86–87). The multiform heterogeneity resulting from many crosscutting lines is what exerts structural constraints to establish intergroup relations, for multiple intersection implies that many ingroup associations in any one dimension involve intergroup associations in other dimensions. This theorem can explain the influences on intergroup relations of segregation, of within-group and between-group differences, and of penetrating differentiation.

To test these theorems and some others, data on the 125 largest standard metropolitan statistical areas (SMSAs) in the United States in 1970 are used. Measures of heterogeneity, inequality, multiple intersection, and other structural features were constructed for every SMSA. Thus, indexes on nine forms of heterogeneity—such as racial, industrial, and occupational heterogeneity—were derived, as were indexes of five aspects of inequality and 10 kinds of multiple intersection. A subsample of young married couples was selected in every SMSA, which served as the basis for constructing rates of intermarriage along various lines in each SMSA. Published data on violent crimes provide the dependent variables for analyzing the influence of structural conditions on conflict. The 125 SMSAs are the units of analysis. However, the internal processes within SMSAs are also analyzed to discern how the processes of status attainment generate the existing variations in structural conditions.

Data on rates of intermarriage in SMSAs provide severe tests of the theory and its structural assumptions. The domain assumption is that structural conditions limit options and influence social relations even in the face of opposite influences exerted by cultural values and psychological preferences. This assumption is most plausible for casual acquaintances in small places, inasmuch as one would

----

[11]It is ironic that Blau, despite his structural orientation, overlooked structural constraints and viewed associations only from the standpoint of the associating individuals.

expect opportunities of chance meetings to influence such superficial contacts greatly whereas values and preferences have little significance for them. Marriage, in contrast, is a profound and enduring relation that people do not enter into lightly as the result of their chance encounters and that is undoubtedly much more influenced, than casual acquaintances are, by people's values and preferences, such as religious beliefs and ethnic bias. Moreover, in a large metropolis with many thousands or millions of people, it should be relatively easy to escape the constraints imposed by the population composition and find a spouse of one's choosing. If marriage in large metropolitan areas is subject to the structural constraints implied by the theorems, less intimate social relations in smaller places in all likelihood are too.

Testing Procedures

The major data source for the empirical tests of theorems is the one-in-a-hundred public-use sample of basic records of the 1970 U.S. Census, specifically, the data from the 15% county-group file that pertain to the 125 American SMSAs with a population of more than 250,000.[12] The SMSA is the unit of analysis, and the 125 cases range in size from 250,000 to 11,000,000. The total number of persons in the sample is 1,223,000. The average number sampled in an SMSA is 9941, and the range is from 2483 to 116,384 for the 125 cases. (A full description of the sample and all items included on the original data tapes is found in U.S. Bureau of the Census, 1972.)

The initial phase of the research involved aggregating the data on the sample of individuals in each SMSA to construct a large number of measures of metropolitan structure, designed to represent the empirical manifestations of the theoretical concepts under study. This was a time-consuming task, entailing complicated computer programming, because in effect it constituted carrying out 125 quantitative case studies. For example, six measures of income inequality were computed for every SMSA[13] and so were several measures of other forms of

---

[12]In New England, the only region where SMSAs cut through county lines, SMSAs are approximated in the public-use sample, and hence in our research, in terms of entire counties. In Hawaii, Honolulu is distinguished from the rest of the state. For a list of the 125 SMSAs and their boundaries, see U.S. Bureau of the Census, 1972:123–126, 135–137.

[13]The six measures of income inequality are family income, personal income (both including income from all sources), and earnings (including only wages, salaries, and self-employment compensation), each measured by the Gini coefficient and the coefficient of variation. These two indexes are highly correlated for the same substantive variable (.94 for family income, .87 for individual income, .85 for earnings, 1.00 for education, and .99 for Duncan's [1961] socioeconomic index).

inequality. In addition, bivariate correlations between most available pairs of attributes were computed in each SMSA.

These procedures, which are usually part of the substantive analysis of a study, are for our purposes merely preliminary steps in index construction. The goal is not to find out how much income inequality, for instance, there is in one metropolitan area or another. Although this information is of substantive interest, in the present study it is simply a measure of one case to be used together with other data to test the theoretical prediction that inequality has a certain effect on intermarriage. The bivariate correlation coefficients are not even the final measures for our research but are merely preliminary steps to construct indexes of multiple intersection and consolidation. Thus, one variable's measures of association with several others are combined into a score, which is then inverted to yield an index of multiple intersection. In addition, the correlations within SMSAs are used as items in a factor analysis of the 125 SMSAs to ascertain whether there are underlying dimensions of overall consolidation that distinguish places where various lines of differentiation are highly related from those where they are less related to each other.

The measures of structural conditions in an SMSA are based on the entire sample, children as well as adults, for variables referring to ascribed positions, like race or national origin, but only on the relevant members of the sample for achieved-position variables. Thus, industrial and occupational heterogeneity includes only persons in the civilian labor force, as does inequality in occupational status; educational inequality excludes persons under 25 and those still enrolled in school; and the three income variables exclude those without income (who are not identical for the three). The smallest number of cases on which any measure is based is 559, for family income in the smallest SMSA.

Three types of variables refer to social differences in a single dimension: a certain group's proportionate size in an SMSA, an SMSA's heterogeneity in a given respect, and an SMSA's inequality along some line. In all cases, comparisons are made among the 125 SMSAs. The measure of a group's relative size is the proportion of its members to the SMSA's entire population or total labor force. Examples are the proportion of the population who are nonwhite, the proportion who are of foreign stock, the percentage of migrants from another region, or the proportion of the labor force working in manufacturing or that in professional and technical occupations.

The measure of heterogeneity, which represents the expectation that a random pair belongs to two different groups is $H = 1 - \Sigma p_i^2$, where p_i is the fraction of the population in a given category (group) and the sum is taken over all categories (groups). Nine forms of heterogeneity, so measured, are analyzed: (1) detailed race, with 9 categories; (2) white–nonwhite dichotomy; (3) national origin, with 12 categories; (4) mother-tongue dichotomy (English–other); (5) ethnic background, with 15 categories (a combination of race and national origin); (6) region of birth, with 9 categories; (7) major industry, with 16 categories; (8) major occupation, with 13 categories; and (9) detailed occupation, with 444 categories. The number of categories affects the degree of heterogeneity observed. Hence, it makes little sense to compare heterogeneity for major and for detailed occupations. But since the same number of categories for any specific form of heterogeneity is used for every SMSA, comparisons accurately reflect SMSA differences in heterogeneity.[14]

For each form of inequality, two measures are computed: the Gini coefficient and the coefficient of variation. Both are indexes of relative inequality. Although they are readily transferable into measures of absolute inequality, relative measures are generally preferable because they refer to proportionate rather than absolute differences and are independent of the mean and the unit of measurement. If everybody's income is taxed 10%, measures of absolute inequality decrease, which is misleading, whereas measures of relative inequality remain the same. Although one of us has criticized it for being insensitive to certain changes in the distribution of resources (Schwartz and Winship, 1979), the Gini coefficient has the advantage that it most accurately represents the theoretical conception of inequality under consideration, and it is used for this reason in the test of the theory. Five types of inequality are examined: educational inequality, three aspects of economic inequality (in family income, total personal income, and earnings from jobs), and inequality in occupational status, based on Duncan's (1961) socioeconomic index (SEI).[15]

Intersection and consolidation are complementary terms. Measures of association indicate the strength of the relationships between lines of differentiation, and their reverse indicates how close to orthogonal the lines of differentiation are and hence the degree of their intersection. As a start, bivariate measures of association are computed (for each SMSA): Cramer's V for two nominal variables; the correlation ratio (eta) for one nominal and one interval variable; and the Pearsonian correlation coefficient (r) for two interval variables. The bivariate measures are combined to generate indexes of multiple intersection of one factor with several others. Then an average was computed of a given variable's measures of association with all other available variables after eliminating those bivariate associations that did not fit with the rest (according to a criterion that is discussed in Chapter 4). The resulting score is reversed (subtracted from 1.0) to produce an index of intersection of a given social position with several others. These indexes

[14]Of course, if an SMSA has no person in a certain occupation (or any other category), it lowers the index of heterogeneity, but this accurately reflects the lesser heterogeneity of the labor force distributed among fewer occupations.

[15]Using the Gini index is only justified for ratio variables with a meaningful zero point (Allison, 1978). Contrary to Allison, we consider this assumption justified for occupational status, and a fortiori for the other graduated variables.

are computed separately for every SMSA, as noted. Thus, the index of multiple intersection of race shows how weakly race is related to education, occupation, income, and other factors in some SMSAs compared to others.

The dependent variables for the major tests of the theory are rates of intermarriage. These rates must be based on marriages that were contracted just prior to the 1970 census in the metropolitan area for which the structural conditions are measured because the theorems stipulate that these conditions affect marriage. Unfortunately, the census source contains no information on date or place of marriage. As a substitute, we selected couples for whom it is most likely that their marriage occurred just prior to 1970 in the SMSA of their present (1970) residence. The specific criteria of selection were that the woman was currently married, was under 25 years of age, and had been living in the same county 5 years earlier. Nearly all these couples got married in the late 1960s in the SMSA of their 1970 residence. The subsample so selected consists of 17,341 couples. The number of couples in an average SMSA is 138.7 and ranges from a minimum of 30 to a maximum of 1235. Raw marriage rates were computed first, and these were then refined to take differences in sex distributions into account. All marriage rates are computed separately for every SMSA.

The raw outmarriage rate of a group is the proportion of its members whose spouse is not a member of the same group.[16] To compute intermarriage rates for nominal variables, a matrix is generated for each SMSA with the group affiliations of wives in the rows, those of husbands in the columns, and the number of marriages in the appropriate cells. The major diagonal represents ingroup marriages, and the proportion of couples not in the major diagonal is the raw rate of intermarriage; for example, the proportion of couples whose ethnic affiliation differs. For interval variables, the raw (relative) rate of intermarriage (status-distant marriage) is the mean absolute difference in status between couples divided by twice the mean status in the subsample (this division makes the measure relative and comparable to the Gini index of relative inequality). For instance, education intermarriage is the mean absolute difference in years of education between spouses divided by twice the mean years of education in the SMSA's subsample of recently married couples.

To take the differences in sex distribution on a given variable into account, constrained intermarriage rates were computed, based on the assumption that the excess of the larger sex over the smaller one in a category is constrained to intermarry (e.g., the excess of female nurses exerts such an outmarriage constraint) and, therefore, should not be included in the constrained intermarriage measure. Thus, the constrained outmarriage rate for a group is one minus the ratio of the number of inmarried couples to either the number of husbands or the

---

[16]If an SMSA's subsample contains either no wife or no husband in a group, the outmarriage rate of that group is assigned a missing value.

number of wives in the group, whichever is smaller. The same principle is applied to compute the constrained intermarriage rates for a nominal variable. After constructing the matrix, the number outside the major diagonal is divided not by the grand total but by the sum of the smaller of the two corresponding marginals (which is the same as dividing by the grand total minus the sum of the absolute differences between males and females in the same category).[17] Finally, the constrained intermarriage rates for interval variables subtracts the absolute difference between the male and the female mean from the mean absolute difference of the subsample, before dividing by the subsample mean.[18]

The marriages on which these rates are based occurred mostly prior to 1970, when the structural conditions assumed to influence them are measured. This is the reverse temporal sequence from the causal order posited by the theory. To be sure, it is not plausible to assume that the causal sequence is in the opposite direction and that the marriage patterns of a small fraction of the population influence the structure of the entire population in a metropolitan area. Nevertheless, attempts are made to provide some direct tests of the assumption of causal direction. For this purpose, some measures of heterogeneity, inequality, and

[17]However, for racial intermarriage the constrained index would not effect an improvement but reduce the validity of the analysis. The reason is that the constrained measure further reduces (to less than $\frac{1}{4}$%) the number of intermarried couples, which is already small (1% of the young couples in the average SMSA), because the constraint equalizes the two sex distributions by eliminating some intermarried but no inmarried couples (whose elimination would not alter the sex distributions). As a result, most SMSAs have no racial intermarriages, as indicated by the constrained measure, leaving very little variation in the dependent variable to be explained. Hence, the unconstrained measure is preferable, and it is the one used for intermarriage based on either detailed race or the race dichotomy.

[18]The formula for constrained outmarriage is

$$1 - \frac{\text{number of inmarried in category}}{\text{smaller of the male or female marginal in the category}}.$$

The formula for intermarriage for a nominal variable is

$$1 - \frac{\sum d}{N - \frac{1}{2}\sum \text{AD}},$$

where $\sum d$ is the sum of couples in the diagonal (inmarried), $\sum \text{AD}$ is the sum of the absolute difference between numbers of males and females in a category, and N is the number of couples in the SMSA matrix.

The formula for intermarriage for a graduated dimension is

$$\frac{(1/N)\sum |(Xm_i - \overline{X}m) - (Xf_i - \overline{X}f)|}{(\overline{X}m + \overline{X}f)/2},$$

where Xm_i refers to values for males, Xf_i to values for females, and N to the total number of couples.

intersection in 1960 were derived from published sources (U.S. Bureau of the Census, 1963). These make it possible to ascertain whether corresponding 1960 and 1970 measures of metropolitan structure are substantially correlated and whether intermarriage rates reveal parallel relationships with 1960 structural measures as with corresponding 1970 ones.

The study of the significance of the metropolitan structure for conflict uses as dependent variables the four major types of violent crimes against persons: murder, aggravated assault, forcible rape, and robbery. This information was obtained from the Uniform Crime Reports (F.B.I., 1971). Several other factors, such as the prevalence of divorce and the SMSA's population size, are used as control or intervening variables in this analysis and in others.

No claim is made that marriage patterns are not influenced by any condition other than those specified in the theorems. Besides, sometimes two theorems stipulate different variables that both have parallel influences on intermarriage. For example, both heterogeneity and intersection are posited to increase inter-marriage. All this means that the theorems must be qualified by ceteris paribus.[19] However, there is a great danger that this qualification is used to discount negative empirical results or hunt around until acceptable findings are dis-covered. Although most generalizations in the social sciences need to be qualified by ceteris paribus, this qualification should be interpreted to mean ''unless unusual disturbances interfere, this principle holds,'' and not ''this is one of many, partly unknown, influences and is, therefore, frequently not ob-servable.'' In accordance with these strictures, we report negative as well as positive results and initially test the theorems with simple correlations, on the assumption that their implications should usually be manifest without controls. One exception to this rule is made if an influence stipulated by one theorem is parallel to that stipulated by another theorem. In this case, the correlation is suspect of being spurious unless the other influence is controlled. Another excep-tion is occasionally made if a predicted relationship is found to be too weak to be statistically significant. In such situations, we explore whether controlling an-other antecedent strengthens the relationship. But this procedure is admittedly not ideal and should be resorted to only in exceptional cases, notably when most

---

[19]Such a qualification would not be required for a strictly deterministic theory, which permits only empirical predictions that follow in strict logic from the theoretical premises. No theory in the social sciences has this perfectly logical structure, and one can hardly imagine one that would not also be tautological. The empirical tests of the theorems to be conducted include inferences that are not purely logical consequences of the theoretical premises, which means that, granted the theorem, negative cases of the empirical inferences are logically possible though empirically improbable. An illustration (examined in the next chapter) is that the tautology of how the relative size of *two* groups in *one* community affects their comparative outmarriage rates serves as a basis to infer how the relative size of *many* groups in *different* communities affect their outmarriage rates, which is not a logically inevitable conclusion, but which yields an empirical inference whose confirmation strength-ens confidence in the theoretical premises.

predictions of a theorem are confirmed in research and only one or two fail to be. However, the procedure is completely justified when the control introduced conforms to other parts of the theory.

The correlation and regression analyses with marriage rates as dependent variables use weighted-least-squares (WLS) procedures. The reason is that the number of couples in an SMSA's subsample, on which these rates are based, varies greatly, producing differences in standard errors and heteroskedasticity that violate the assumptions of ordinary-least-squares (OLS). As increasing sample size reduces the standard error and increases the reliability of the measures, smaller SMSAs are given less weight than larger ones.[20] A variety of other procedures are used in special cases. Thus, odds ratios or their logarithms are calculated to investigate the relationship between observed and expected rates of mobility and intermarriage between pairs of groups. The block-modeling techniques are also employed in analyzing the relationship between social mobility and intermarriage. Principal-component analysis or maximum-likelihood factor analysis serves to look for underlying dimensions of covariance matrixes. Path analysis explicates the process of status attainment underlying metropolitan structures. Nested analysis of variance furnishes measures of penetrating differentiation.

A description of the variables used, together with their means and standard deviations for the 125 SMSAs, is in Appendix A.

Brief Overview

In the next chapter, two basic assumptions are introduced, and the significance for social life of size differences and distributions in one dimension are analyzed. After deducing theorems about the influences of group size, heterogeneity, and inequality on intergroup relations, the implications of these theorems for specific forms of these structural features are tested with data on rates of intermarriage in SMSAs. Chapter 3 is devoted to social mobility. Theorems about the relationships of social mobility to intergroup relations and to changes in structural differentiation are discussed, followed by an empirical investigation of the relationship between occupational mobility and intermarriage and the underlying dimensions accounting for the similarity in the two social processes. The theory's central concept of crosscutting social circles is the focus of the fourth

---

[20]Most of the weights are simply the number of couples in the SMSA's subsample. But when intermarriage is based on a dichotomy—intermarriage (or outmarriage) versus inmarriage—a more refined weight used is $(n - 1)/pq$, where n is the number of couples in an SMSA's subsample, p the fraction of inmarried, and q the fraction not inmarried. This is the inverse of the squared estimate of the standard error of the rate.

chapter. After deriving theorems about the consequences of intersecting social differences for intergroup relations and testing empirical predictions implied by them, theorems about the unexpected influences of intersection and structural change on each other are analyzed. Finally, an empirical inquiry is presented of the conditions that make metropolitan structures consolidated and resistant to change.

The structural features primarily treated as independent variables heretofore are considered as dependent variables in Chapter 5, which dissects the processes of status attainment that produce these structural conditions and examines differences in these processes among SMSAs. Chapter 6 analyzes the principle that the component parts of social structures are themselves social structures in terms of the theoretical scheme. Societies have social structures, so do their communities, and so do the neighborhoods within communities. Society's differentiation—its various forms of heterogeneity, inequality, and consolidated social differences—can be decomposed into the amount of differentiation within and among communities, and the same is true for neighborhoods within communities and for any other type of subdivision: for example, detailed occupations within major occupational groups. The analysis shows that the intersection theorems imply a series of theorems about (1) the influences on intergroup relations of differentiation within and differentiation among subunits and (2) the significance of the penetration of differentiation into successive subunits for intergroup relations. Two major sources of conflict suggested by the theory are analyzed in Chapter 7, and empirical data on violent crimes are shown to lend support to the inferences. The last chapter summarizes the theory, indicates the revisions made as the result of the empirical tests, points out the extensions of the analysis introduced, and ends with some conjectures about further implications.

CHAPTER 2

Size Distributions

The idea of crosscutting social circles is one of Simmel's significant theoretical contributions; another is his emphasis on the importance of the quantitative dimension of social life. The two conceptions have a closer underlying connection than may at first be apparent. Both refer to strictly formal aspects of social life abstracted from the diverse empirical contents in which the forms necessarily find expression, which is, of course, Simmel's explicit criterion of sociological inquiry. Both also are purely structural social facts pertaining to social affiliations and distributions, as distinguished from cultural aspects underlying social life, such as the nature of ethical standards, anomie, the implicit meaning of symbols, or consensus on common values. To be sure, Simmel's focus is on the microsociological study of the consequences of these and other structural conditions for individuals—for example, for their greater individuality and freedom from domination by the community and for their strategies in social relations—which differs from the macrosociological orientation adopted in this book. A major aim in this chapter is to extend Simmel's microsociological concern with the size and number of small groups to a macrosociological concern with size distributions in large populations.

Size distributions, considered singly and jointly, indicate the extent of a collectivity's differentiation in various respects and thus delineate its social structure. The three generic forms of differentiation, which in their various specific manifestations constitute the social structure, have already been distinguished. The first is heterogeneity, which refers to people's distribution among different groups with relatively distinct boundaries and without any inherent rank order. A society's division of labor, a city's religious diversity, and a neighborhood's ethnic admixture are illustrations. The second type is inequality, which indicates how uneven the distribution of resources or of status in a population is, as exemplified by the concentration of wealth, differences in education among people, and the centralization of authority over many others. Heterogeneity and inequality in a single dimension are analyzed in this chapter. But social differences in one dimension are not necessarily or usually independent of those in others. Hence, theorems about the significance for social life of differentiation in one dimension must be complemented by theorems about the social significance of the extent to which various differences are related. Do strongly interrelated differences along several lines consolidate group boundaries and social positions and distinctions, or do intersecting lines of differentiation act as countervailing forces on people's social relations? The question is naturally one of degree— depending on how much various social differences consolidate or crosscut one another. These problems are examined in Chapter 4.

Two Basic Assumptions

Microsociological network analysis and macrosociological structural analysis both center attention on the nexus between people's social positions and their social relations. But the two approaches treat this nexus somewhat differently. Network analysis defines the social positions or roles of individuals in terms of their social relations. This is the case for Moreno's (1934) original sociometry of positions in a clique linked by choices; for applications of graph theory (Harary *et al.*, 1965) that analyzes the social balance in configurations of direct links; for network analyses (Mitchell, 1969) of the various aspects of social ties that distinguish network positions; and for blockmodels and studies of structural equivalence (White *et al.*, 1976; Burt, 1976), which conceptualize positions not on the basis of direct links but on that of having similar links to third persons. Such studies that use the linkages between individuals, however defined, as starting points are confined to small populations, usually a few dozen and, at most, a few hundred individuals, because potential linkages increase exponentially with population size, which makes it impossible to analyze the social relations of several hundred thousands or millions of persons without first classifying them into a limited number of categories (except by considering total societies as *actors*).

This is precisely what macrosociological structural analysis does. It first classifies the population of a large community or an entire society into a limited number of categories of a dimension presumed to be socially relevant. (In the research reported here, the number of categories used varies from 2 to 444.) A matrix is constructed with the same categories in both rows and columns—for instance, ethnic groups or occupations—and the number of relations between members of two categories, whatever the criterion of relation decided upon, are entered into the cells.[1] If no consistent pattern of social relations is observed for

[1] For ratio variables, the procedure is different but conceptually equivalent. Instead of distinguishing to which categories the two partners in a relation belong, the status or resource difference between two related persons is determined, and the differences are then averaged (ignoring sign).

any type of social associations examined, the dimension has no discernible influence on social life, which means that no basis has been found to claim that it distinguishes social positions.

Thus, social relations are taken into consideration as criteria of social positions, but in the second rather than the first step of the procedure employed. Although people initially are classified by their attributes, the procedure has the result that only those characteristics that exert a consistent, patterned influence on the social relations of many people are treated as social positions in the macrostructure.[2] Of course, there are thousands of small networks of friendship cliques that are ignored because these are not of macrosociological significance. Theoretical as well as methodological reasons demand that we abstract from these minutiae of social ties some broader patterns in order to obtain a meaningful image of the structure of social positions and relations in a large population. The social relations of interest are actual dyadic associations, not merely choices or verbal preferences, but they may range from such superficial contacts as greeting acquaintances to such basic bonds as marriages. People's distributions in various dimensions of social positions that influence their relations describe a community's or society's social structure.

Assumptions, postulates, and *axioms* are largely synonymous terms, although a difference in emphasis is sometimes apparent. All three refer to synthetic propositions about the relationships between two (or more) independently defined terms (the greater x is, the greater y will be), and all three are propositions that cannot be deduced from any others in the theoretical system. They are distinguished from both *analytic propositions,* which define the primitive and other terms of the theory, and *theorems,* which are deducible from other propositions in the theory. The premises from which the theorems are derived include analytic propositions that define its primitive terms—in our case, structural concepts—as well as *synthetic propositions* postulated as assumptions. The difference in emphasis is that axioms tend to be considered the central principles of a theory, whereas assumptions or postulates are more frequently thought of as the conditions that must be treated as given for the theory to be applicable, but they are not the theory's explanatory principles. For example, although economic theory rests on the assumption of rational behavior, its objective is not to explain why or when people behave rationally. Similarly, the assumptions of the present theory are not its central principles but the exogenous conditions that are postulated as given (such as people's prevailing preferences) in order for the derived theorems, which do embody its central principles, to be correct.

The first assumption made is that *social associations are more prevalent between persons in proximate than those in distant social positions* (A-1). The distinct implications of this assumption for nominal and graduated dimensions,

---

[2]It is possible that no pattern of social relations will be discovered while unexamined kinds of relations would reveal patterns.

respectively, can be specified. For nominal population distributions, it implies that ingroup associations are more prevalent than intergroup or outgroup associations. For graduated distributions, it implies that the prevalence of associations between persons declines with their status distance.[3] The underlying idea is the familiar one that people prefer associates like themselves or at least similar to themselves. The psychological questions are why individuals have these tendencies, what motivates them, and which personality characteristics influence them. The sociological questions raised here are entirely different: accepting such tendencies as given, why do people often establish intergroup relations and have associates whose status differs from their own, as is evidently the case? Do we have to explain these patterns by assuming that some people do not have ingroup but outgroup preferences? Or can we explain them in terms of structural conditions that counteract ingroup preferences? Before trying to demonstrate an affirmative answer to the last question, which is the aim of the theory, we briefly examine empirical evidence that justifies postulating the assumption.

Numerous empirical studies report that disproportionate numbers of marriages involve spouses with the same group affiliations, particularly with respect to ascriptive groups, such as race, religion, and national origin (Kennedy, 1944; Hollingshead, 1950; Carter and Glick, 1970; Abramson, 1973; Heer, 1974; Alba, 1976). Shared achieved positions exert parallel, though possibly less pronounced, influences. Similarity in education, occupation, and social class increases the likelihood of marriage (Centers, 1949; Hollingshead, 1950; Blau and Duncan, 1967; Carter and Glick, 1970; Tyree and Treas, 1974; Rockwell, 1976). In other words, status and class differences inhibit marriage. They also inhibit friendships (Hollingshead, 1949; Athanasiou and Yoshika, 1973). Indeed, Warner and Lunt's (1941) famous study of Yankee City made extensive intimate associations and marriages the criterion of social class and barriers to them the criterion of class boundaries. Although there is much empirical evidence that many shared affiliations encourage marriage and other social associations, this does not prove, of course, that all the social differences in our research also do. In short, whether the data under investigation satisfy the assumption or not must be empirically tested.

A-1 is treated here as a testable assumption, but with a slight modification it turns into a definition, which illustrates the narrow line of distinction between analytical propositions (definitions) and synthetic ones (specifying the relationship between two factors). If the criterion of *social position* is that an observed difference in attributes exerts some influence on social relations, not necessarily that it effects a preponderance of ingroup relations, the ingroup assumption is a synthetic proposition that can be empirically tested. But if social position is defined more narrowly as entailing an influence on the tendency to establish ingroup relations, the assumption is transformed into a defining criterion of

---

[3]Prevalence refers to an excess of social associations over chance expectations.

social position and parameter. In this case, negative empirical evidence would simply indicate that the differentiation in a given variable should not be considered a structural parameter. For practical purposes, however, it would make little difference which of the two views is adopted.

The same empirical data that indicate whether certain social differences foster ingroup tendencies also reveal how strongly they influence ingroup relations. The extent to which ingroup relations exceed chance expectations is an indication of the *salience* of the dimension of social affiliation under investigation. To be sure, this is not the only possible measure of salience. The salience of group differences could also be ascertained with attitudinal measures. For example, expressions of group identification and loyalty could be obtained, the Bogardus social-distance scale could be administered, or respondents could be asked what sacrifices they would be willing to incur or what obligations they would be willing to assume for a group. The two kinds of measures are undoubtedly related. The overt expression of the salience of social differences in marriage and friendship rates may be more reliable than attitudinal measures, but a limitation of the former is that they do not reveal whether low intergroup rates are the results of strong ingroup feelings of all parties or of strong prejudices of some groups against others. There are naturally great differences in salience among structural parameters, which the data indicate, with some forms of intermarriage being very rare and other forms being quite common.

The second assumption postulated is that *rates of social association depend on opportunities for social contact* (A-2). It is virtually self-evident that people cannot become friendly unless they have an opportunity to meet. However, the postulate implies more than that. It posits that the extent of contact opportunities governs the probability of associations of people, not merely of casual acquaintances but even of intimate relations, like those of lovers. A clear implication of this assumption, which can serve as a means for testing, is that *spatial propinquity*, because it increases the chances of fortuitous contacts, enhances the probability of friendship and even of marriage. There is much research on this subject, that is, on the effects of propinquity on both friendship and marriage.

One of the earliest studies on the influence of propinquity on marriage selection is Bossard's (1932), which concludes that the likelihood of marriage decreases with physical distance. This suggests the interpretation that the similarity in cultural background of people living in the same neighborhood may be responsible. Other research confirms the finding that residential propinquity is positively related to marriage (Abrams, 1943) and also to friendships (Merton, 1948; Festinger *et al.*, 1950; Caplow and Forman, 1950). Some of these authors warn that the observed influences of propinquity may be confined to or contingent on the homogeneity of the community or neighborhood. Gans (1970), particularly, stressed the importance of background homogeneity for close relations.

The criticism advanced is that the relationship between propinquity and friendship or marriage may be spurious, owing to the segregation of groups in different neighborhoods and the influence of group affiliation—race or class or religion—on marriage and friendship. But empirical studies that controlled such group affiliations found that propinquity still exerts on influence on mate selection and friendship with these controls (Ramsoy, 1966; Athanasiou and Yoshika, 1973), although there is some indication that the influence of propinquity on marriage depends on similarity in background (Peach, 1974). The general conclusion is that propinquity increases the probability of friendship and marriage, albeit most strongly for persons with similar backgrounds. These empirical results support the assumption that greater opportunity for contact resulting from spatial proximity increases the likelihood of social associations, even intimate ones.

The two assumptions introduced refer to cultural, psychological, and physical influences on social life. These are not the operators of the theory, that is, its basic explanatory principles. They are, rather, social processes assumed to be given, and the question raised is how social life is affected by variations in structural features, which constitute the primitive terms of the theory and its conceptual framework. (Of course, other social scientists could—and do—treat the effects of structural conditions on social life as given and study how cultural values or sociopsychological processes affect it.) The explanatory principles are contained in the theorems, which stipulate how heterogeneity, inequality, intersection, and related structural features influence social relations; that is, how variations in several aspects of the social structure affect patterns of social relations under the assumption that the exogeneous influences postulated are universal conditions.

Unless the assumptions are satisfied—people do tend to make ingroup choices and their contact opportunities do affect their social relations—the theorems cannot be logically deduced, but these assumptions are not enough to explain variations in the patterns of social relations. Only variations in the structural features that constitute the primitive terms of the theory can. Since social positions are defined on the basis of their influences on social relations, theorems that would stipulate such influences would be tautological (or close to tautological). The theorems do not deal with effects of social positions on relations at all, however. They specify effects of variations in social positions among individuals within communities. Thus, concern is not with the significance for social relations of the race of individuals but with that of the racial heterogeneity in a place; it is not with the impact on social life of people's class position but with that of the economic inequality in societies or communities.

Group Size

When only two groups are under consideration, the rate of outgroup relations of the smaller group must exceed that of the larger, whatever kind of actual dyadic associations are examined. For example, the proportion of a group's members who are married to an outsider—a member of the other group—must be greater for the smaller group. Specifically, the ratio of the percentage of outmarried people is an inverse function of the ratio of group size. The reason is that the number of group members married to an outsider must be the same for each group, so that their proportion is completely determined by the denominator, which is the group size (number of members). For two groups, this is an arithmetic tautology. But it implies a probability proposition which is not tautological for many groups. The proposition applies to comparisons of the relative size of different groups (in a given dimension) in the same community—for instance, the different religious denominations in the city. From it one can further infer a parallel effect of differences in relative size of the same kind of group in different communities—for instance, the percentage of Catholics in different cities. These considerations provide a basis for the first theorem.

As group size increases, the probable rate of outgroup relations decreases (T-1).[4] The theorem does not claim that there is a perfect inverse correlation between group size and outgroup relations, only that there is an inverse correlation.[5] If there are substantial differences in salience among groups, small groups with exceptionally strong ingroup salience would depart from the regression line and have lower outgroup rates than predicted.[6] On the other hand, if salience properly operationalized is constant (that is, the same for all groups), the rank correlation would be perfect and the theorem would be a deterministic rather than a probabilistic one. The theorem can be derived from the tautology for two groups. Considering only its relation with any group that is larger, a group's rate of outgroup relations must exceed that of the other group, and similarly in its relation with any group that is smaller, a group's outgroup rate must be lower than that of the other groups. Since this is the case for all groups, the probability is that group size and extent of outgroup relations are inversely related.[7]

---

[4]If there are no relations between group members, all rates are zero and the theorem does not apply. But such a condition is extremely unlikely, and if it does occur, the aggregate can hardly be called a single community or coherent collectivity. For example, the theorem requires only some interracial associations, not that there be interracial marriages. Actually, there are such marriages in our society, despite profound racial prejudices.

[5]The term *outgroup* relations refers to one group's social associations with members of other groups; the term *intergroup* relations refers to all associations in a population between members of different groups (and when reference is to both concepts). In this theorem, in contrast to subsequent ones, groups (not entire SMSAs) can be the unit of analysis.

[6]In cases of extreme variation in salience among groups, it is even logically possible to obtain positive relationships between group size and outgroup marriage. Artificial examples of such cases can be constructed, but the theory predicts that this is not likely to occur in the real world.

[7]The original derivation of this theorem contained an error (Blau, 1977:23–24). It stated that "the average rate of [outgroup] associations of all small groups must exceed that of all large ones," but this is only true if salience is constant. Otherwise, the rates of two large groups can far exceed that of either with smaller groups, contradicting the quoted statement.

Alternatively, the theorem can be deduced from the assumption that associations depend on contact opportunities (A-2). The smaller one's group is, the lower are the chances of finding a congenial mate or associate among its members. By congenial we include not only feelings of attraction but also other shared social affiliations and attributes, other than the one under consideration. In other words, the opportunities for meeting a compatible associate in one's own group are much better in large than in small groups. The resulting structural constraints raise the probability of outmarriage with declining group size.

However, group differences in salience also affect outmarriage, which implies that this proposition admits exception. It is predicted to be true in most cases but not in all. As a matter of fact, there is a well-known exception (and the existence of this negative case demonstrates, incidentally, that the theorem is not tautological). If the American population is divided into the three major religious groups, Jews, who are by far the smallest group, have traditionally had the lowest outmarriage rates (Kennedy, 1944; Yinger, 1968), contrary to the theorem's implications. However, religious intermarriage is increasing, and it is increasing faster for Jews than for members of the two Christian denominations. Using the religion of spouse's parents as a criterion (so that results are not distorted by conversion), Bumpass (1970) shows that the outmarriage rate of Jews, which used to be lowest in the 1930s, was in the 1960s higher than that of Protestants and exceeded only by that of Catholics. One could even suggest that we are witnessing here the process in which structural constraints overcome the influence of cultural bias on social relations. If this is true, we can anticipate that Jewish outmarriage rates will exceed Catholic ones in the not-too-distant future.

The theorem (as well as all others) applies to the actual number of dyadic associations per group member. It does not apply to unilateral choices or preferences, nor to one person's speaking to a whole audience or being watched by them in some performance. Neither does it indicate anything about the content of the association—whether it entails love or subordination or hate—although the nature of the dependent variable often gives some indication of this. But the theorems do apply to four types of dyadic associations and all their specific forms. The first is the proportion who are intermarried or have some other exclusive association (of which a person can have only one at a time) with an outsider, such as mutual best friend. Second, the theorems apply to the mean number of intergroup *associates* of any kind; for example, coworkers who belong to different groups, intergroup mutual friends, or greeting acquaintances who belong to different groups. A third type is the mean number of intergroup *associations* of any kind; for instance, how often the average member of an ethnic group has kissed someone from a different ethnic group or how many times the average Catholic has played tennis with a non-Catholic. Finally, the theorems also apply to the average amount of time involved in intergroup associations, such as the amount of time per person the people in a neighborhood spend in interracial associations or the average amount of time the inhabitants of a city are engaged in social interaction between members of different religious denominations.

The deduction of the first theorem does not depend on the assumption that ingroup relations are more prevalent than intergroup relations (A-1), but its meaningfulness does depend on this assumption. If there were no ingroup tendencies, the theorem would be true but vacuous. To illustrate, we consider an attribute of individuals that they are unaware of and that consequently cannot influence whom they choose or who chooses them. Say that it is whether a person can or cannot taste PTC, a genetic trait that most people are not aware of. The likelihood that a person who can taste it marries someone who cannot (a member of the outgroup) would be completely determined by chance, that is, by the proportions of the population who can and cannot taste it. The theorem's prediction would be confirmed empirically—the smaller the proportion of tasters in a city, the greater the probability that tasters marry nontasters—but this empirical finding would be entirely trivial, since nothing but chance can influence people's pairing with respect to attributes unknown to them. The theorem on size differences (T-1) and those on size distributions that are later discussed are substantively meaningful only if the first assumption is satisfied, because then they imply that size differences and distributions exert structural constraints that counteract the influences in ingroup tendencies and pressures.

In order for the tests of the first assumption to apply to the heterogeneity as well as to the size theorem, they are performed on the entire size distribution among all groups in each of eight dimensions in all 125 SMSAs, except for 34 missing cases,[8] yielding 966 [(8 × 125) − 34] chi-squares. After collapsing each of the 966 matrixes into two cells—inmarriage and intermarriage, chi-squares with one degree of freedom are computed (as illustrated in Table 2.1). The results are in Table 2.2. The distribution of chi-squares by their critical values for a one-tailed test (with signs of the differences between observed and expected scores preserved) ranges from highly significant in the predicted to slightly significant in the opposite direction. The inmarriage test is significant in the predicted direction in the majority of cases; it is in the predicted direction in more than 80% of the cases. Only two tests have negative results that are significant at the .05, but not at the .04 level (one-tailed), with no negative result that is significant at a higher level.[9]

[8]Cases are designated as missing if one group (e.g., nonwhites) has no representative in the subsample. Although the heterogeneity theorem is tested with 9 dimensions, including detailed occupation, which has 444 categories, considerations of cost led to the decision not to compute chi-squares for the 444 categories in each of the 125 SMSAs.

[9]The empirical analysis in the rest of this section appeared, in different form, in a paper written in collaboration with Terry C. Blum (Blau et al., 1982). As the chi-square of a matrix takes differences in the two-size distributions of the marginals into account, these tests are performed with uncon-

TABLE 2.1
Fictitious Illustration of Ingroup Marriage Tendencies Test

Proportion of ingroup marriage tendencies

		Observed proportions					Expected proportions				
		Husband's birth region					Husband's birth region				
		North	Mid-west	South	West	Total	North	Mid-west	South	West	Total
	North	.19	.05	.03	.03	.30	.09	.09	.06	.06	.30
Wife's	Midwest	.06	.18	.04	.02	.30	.09	.09	.06	.06	.30
birth	South	.02	.03	.12	.03	.20	.06	.06	.04	.04	.20
region	West	.04	.02	.03	.11	.20	.06	.06	.04	.04	.20
	Total	.30	.30	.20	.20	1.00	.30	.30	.20	.20	1.00

Total of inmarriage and outmarriage proportions

	Observed proportions	Expected proportions
Inmarriage[a]	.60	.26
Outmarriage[b]	.40	.74
Total	1.00	1.00

Chi-square tabulation of results

$$\chi^2 = \frac{(.60-.26)^2}{.26} + \frac{(.40-.74)^2}{.74} = 60.08$$

If the observed proportion of inmarriages is less than the expected proportion, then we report the χ^2 statistic as negative.

[a] Inmarriage is the sum of the diagonal cells.
[b] Outmarriage is the sum of the nondiagonal cells.

strained measures of intermarriage (which has the advantage that there are fewer missing cases owing to zero marginals). It can be shown that the procedure of summing the diagonal cells of the observed and expected intermarriage matrixes—and, correspondingly, the off-diagonal cells—yields a conservative test of the tendency toward ingroup associations. Since the results in Table 2.2 are conclusive, and because more refined log-linear approaches to testing this hypothesis would be considerably more complex, time-consuming, and expensive, the latter testing procedures were deemed unnecessary.

TABLE 2.2
Ingroup Marriage Tendencies

| | Critical values[a] of X^2 | | | | | | | |
	Above +9.55	+9.54 to +2.71	+2.70 to 0	0 to -2.70	-2.71 to -9.54	Below -9.55	N	z-value[b]	Salience[c]
Race	71	26	16	2	0	0	115	54.1	.89
Race dichotomy	71	26	16	2	0	0	115	53.4	.89
National origin	8	16	60	34	0	0	118	11.9	.15
Mother tongue	35	17	48	20	0	0	120	24.4	.31
Ethnic background	67	33	20	4	0	0	124	51.7	.58
Birth region	11	20	65	28	0	0	124	12.8	.14
Industry	20	44	45	15	1	0	125	19.4	.09
Occupation	6	36	68	14	1	0	125	13.3	.06

[a] A critical value of 9.55 is significant at the .001 level and one of 2.71 is significant at the .05 level (one-tailed). The sign indicates whether the deviations of observed from expected proportions are in the predicted direction.

[b] This z-value is the Mantel–Haenszel statistic (Snedecor and Cochran, 1967:254) for pooling the results of N independent chi–square tests (each with one degree of freedom) of the same one-tailed null hypothesis. After creating a signed chi–statistic (the square root of X^2, with a positive value if the observed proportions differ from the expected proportions in the predicted direction and a negative value otherwise), the z–statistic equals $(\Sigma x / N^{.5})$. Under the null hypothesis that the observed inmarriage rates do not exceed the expected rates, the Mantel–Haenszel z–statistic has a standard normal distribution; for z greater than 3.291, the null hypothesis is rejected at the .0005 level.

[c] Our indicator of salience for each SMSA is $1 - (O_i/E_i)$, where O_i is the observed and E_i is the expected intermarriage rate; the mean for the SMSAs, reported in this column is $\Sigma^i [1 - (O_i/E_i)]/N$, where N is the number of SMSAs.

It is informative to combine the data for SMSAs to obtain an overall indication of the prevalence of inmarriage. For this purpose, a Mantel–Haenszel z-test (Snedecor and Cochran, 1967:254) is computed for each of the eight dimensions of the pooled difference in all SMSAs between observed and expected inmarriage rates. The null hypothesis is that the mean difference does not exceed zero. The results, in the penultimate column, show the z-statistics: they are significant beyond the .0005 level for all eight inmarriage rates (within SMSAs). The null hypothesis is clearly rejected and the assumption that ingroup tendencies prevail (A-1) is strongly supported for every group difference examined.

But the salience of various group affiliations, as manifested by their inhibiting effect on intermarriage, differs greatly. The measure of salience in the last column of Table 2.2 indicates these differences.[10] Race is most salient in our society, which makes interracial marriages very rare. Although only 1% of young metropolitan couples are racially intermarried, 10% of the nonwhite persons are, which reflects the small proportionate size of the nonwhite group. At the other extreme, occupation has little salience for marriage, and most couples both of whom work have different occupations. Nevertheless, the proportion of those with the same occupation does exceed chance expectation. Generally, ascribed affiliations are more salient than achieved ones (compare the first six with the last two rows). The great differences in salience make it particularly reassuring that the ingroup assumption is met by each dimension of group affiliations.

To test the theorem about group size (T-1), variations in the proportionate size of a given group, such as nonwhites, among the 125 SMSAs are related to their outmarriage rates for 10 kinds of groups. Despite the huge size of the total sample, the number of young couples on whom outmarriage rates are based is as low as 30 in the smallest SMSA, and even lower for variables (like occupation) restricted to couples who both are in the labor force. If these are further divided into several groups for computing outmarriage rates, the rates are based on too few cases to furnish reliable estimates. Hence, only large groupings are used in these tests, some dividing an SMSA's sample into a dichotomy, others dividing it into a few groups.[11] We use 10 categories: three broad ethnic groups (nonwhite, white of native stock, and white of foreign stock), a dichotomy of birth region (born in region of residence or born elsewhere), an industry dichotomy (manufacturing versus other), and three of eight major occupational groupings (professional and technical workers; sales and clerical workers; and operatives and transportation workers). The other five (managers and proprietors, craftspeople, service workers, laborers, and farm workers) are eliminated by the criterion described in Note 11.[12]

Table 2.3 presents the average of a group's proportion in the 125 SMSAs (Column 1), the average of its unconstrained (Column 2) and its constrained

---

[10]Salience can be measured in a variety of ways, the substantive implications of which differ. The measure in Table 2.2 is based on relative deviations of the observed from expected frequencies.

[11]To be included, a group (or category) has to have at least 10 wives and 10 husbands in 20 or more SMSA subsamples. If this criterion is met, all SMSAs are analyzed, the difference in reliability being taken account of by WLS. The weight used in this chapter is $(N - 1)/pq$, where N is the number of couples in the SMSA on which the marriage rate is based, and p and q are the fraction inmarried and outmarried, respectively.

[12]Pairs of groups that encompass the entire population do not furnish independent tests of the predictions, but neither are the results for them completely determined by and dependent upon each other. The reason is that the outmarriage rates for the two groups (e.g., manufacturing and other

TABLE 2.3
Relative Size and Outmarriage[*]

	Size[a]	Mean outmarriage rate in SMSAs		WLS correlation
		Unconstrained	Constrained	
Broad ethnic group				
Nonwhite[b]	.12	.10		-.33
Native stock	.73	.07	.05	-.57
Foreign stock	.15	.79	.67	-.78
Birth region				
Born in region	.76	.15	.11	-.82
Born elsewhere	.24	.69	.60	-.23
Industry				
Manufacturing	.26	.65	.47	-.51
Other	.74	.25	.15	-.73
Occupation[c]				
Professional and technical workers	.15	.76	.61	-.33
Sales and clerical workers	.26	.72	.33	-.15
Operatives and transportation workers	.17	.74	.52	-.22

[*] All correlation coefficients are significant at the .05 level (one-tailed).

[a] Size is the mean percentage in the SMSAs.
[b] Based on 124 cases, excluding the outlier, Honolulu, and using the unconstrained measure (see Note 17 in Chapter 1).
[c] The outmarriage rates are based on eight occupational groups, but five of them had too few SMSAs with a sufficient subsample for reliable estimates (see Note 11). The five excluded groups are managers and proprietors, craftspeople, service workers, laborers, and farm workers.

industries) are neither identical nor perfectly correlated across SMSAs despite the fact that the denominators of the groups' outmarriage rates are perfectly negatively correlated and the numerators are identical. The resulting correlation among the outmarriage rates will not be perfect and can in fact be positive or negative. Using Pearson's approximation formula for the correlation between two ratio variables, one finds the sign of r (X/Y, $X/1 - Y$,) depends on the sign of

$$V_x^2 + r_{xy} (V_{1-y}V_y) - V_yV_{1-y},$$

where V is the coefficient of variation across the 125 SMSAs.

(Column 3) outmarriage rates,[13] and the WLS correlation between its proportion and constrained outmarriage rate in the 125 SMSAs (Column 4).[14] All correlations are negative, all but one are significant at the .025 level (one-tailed), and even the weakest (sales and clerical workers) is significant at the .05 level (one-tailed). Although these do not constitute 10 entirely independent tests of the theorem (see Note 12), it is not easily determined how much the tests affect one another. In any case, the available evidence, comprising several independent tests, corroborates the theorem that group size and outmarriage are inversely related.

But the results raise a methodological issue that is nearly a century old, namely, whether it is legitimate to use ratio variables with a common term in correlation and regression analysis. Pearson (1897) warns that such correlations are likely to be spurious. Yule (1910) points out that they are not spurious if the theoretical terms in a causal argument refer to ratios. Many articles on both sides of the controversy have recently been published. Freeman and Kronenfeld (1973), Schuessler (1974), and Fuguitt and Lieberson (1974) admonish us about the pitfalls of using ratio variables. Kasarda and Nolan (1979) and Macmillan and Daft (1979, 1980) justify their use.

Two points need to be made about this issue. First, although the empirical hypotheses entail ratios with a common term—size—substantive reasons make this unavoidable because the theory's primitive terms are size differences, size distributions, and the probability of social association determined by them. Ratios are an integral part of the theorems and therefore are appropriate for empirical analysis (Bollen and Ward, 1979). The very ratios that may produce definitional dependency are, in terms of the theory, structural constraints of size distributions that affect the chances of social relations. This illustrates Yule's argument that theoretical causal reasoning based on ratios legitimates the use of ratio variables in empirical analysis. Second, there is the issue of possible correlation between errors of ratio variables with a common term. But this potential problem is substantially circumvented in the present research because the variables on the two sides of the equations are based on different samples—the independent variables on the total sample and the dependent variables on the subsample of young couples.

---

[13]The unconstrained intermarriage rate presents an accurate picture of the amount of outmarriage (or intermarriage). The constrained one does not because all outmarriages for which a difference in the two corresponding marginals is responsible are eliminated whereas no inmarriages are eliminated. This makes the rates too low. But this conservative estimate of intermarriage is used in the correlations (except for the racial variable; see Note 17 in Chapter 1).

[14]The correlations here and in Table 2.4 differ some from those presented in the earlier paper reporting a parallel analysis (Blau *et al.*, 1982) because unconstrained intermarriage measures were used there and mostly constrained ones are used here.

For those who, like Bollen and Ward, accept the legitimacy of using ratio variables when the substantive hypothesis is formulated in terms of ratios but who are, nonetheless, concerned that definitional dependence may lead to artifactual results, we have investigated the possible spuriousness of our results via an adaptation of the WLS methodology. In addition to estimating an equation of the form $(Y/X) = a + bX + e$, where X appears on both sides of the equation and might negatively bias the estimate of b, we have also estimated the functionally equivalent equation $Y = aX + bX^2 + e'$, where $e' = eX$. Although these two equations differ in their appearance—the first is a simple regression whereas the second is a multiple regression with no intercept—their parameters a and b are substantively identical. Therefore, conclusions based on the estimate of b and its significance in the second equation, where there is no definitional dependence between the dependent and independent variables, also apply to b in the first equation. The results for the second equation, which are not presented to save space, are virtually identical to the WLS results for the first equation presented in Tables 2.3 and, below, 2.4. (In modifying the equation to eliminate definitional dependency, we may have introduced heteroskedasticity among the residuals. Whereas this would be unfortunate because it would increase the standard errors of the parameters, it should not bias the estimates of a and b. Hence, this procedure sacrifices some efficiency in the parameter estimates—increasing the probability of Type II error—in exchange for eliminating definitional dependency.)

Some inferences of the first theorem may be briefly pointed out. Members of small minorities, on the average, inevitably have more relations with majority members than the latter have with them. Thus, Williams (1964:245) found that none of the blacks but two-thirds of the whites in Elmira had no social contacts with the other race. The claim blacks sometimes make that they know whites better than whites know them has considerable factual basis. Most members of a large majority are isolated from any association with small minorities. There are simply too few of the latter to associate with most majority members. Accordingly, most people have never associated with anybody in the *elite*, whatever elite is under consideration, as long as it is defined as a small fraction of the population. The larger the difference in size between two groups, the greater is the discrepancy in the rates of intergroup associations between their members. As group size decreases, there is a linear increase in the probability of intergroup relations but an exponential increase in the probability of dense networks of ingroup relations. (*Density* refers to the proportion of all possible social ties in a group that actually occur; it applies only to nonexclusive social relations of which persons can have more than one; the denominator for ingroup density is $n(n-1)$, whereas that for rate of intergroup relations is n, which accounts for the growing difference in probabilities with changing size.) Hence, chances are that both ingroup cohesion and outgroup connections are more pronounced for small than large groups, despite the fact that the time devoted to either kind of social relations infringes on the time available for the other kind.

The Paradox of Structural Differentiation

Social differences between individuals reduce the likelihood of marriage and other social relations between them. There is much empirical evidence in support of this proposition, which is incorporated in the first assumption of the theory, postulated as a given condition. Empirical tests supporting the assumption with respect to the social differences under investigation have been presented. Notwithstanding these tendencies, however, *structural differentiation* enhances the likelihood of intermarriage and other intergroup relations, whether one examines persons who belong to different groups or those who differ in hierarchical status. This is the paradox: structural differentiation and individual differences have opposite effects on social relations.

Of course, more differentiation implies that there are more or greater differences between individuals. Much heterogeneity entails more boundaries separating people than exist in a homogeneous population. Much inequality in a society implies that the average status distance between persons is greater than in societies with less inequality. How can the very differences that inhibit social relations also promote them? They can and do because they impose limits and constraints on options that differ from and counteract the influences of preferences on choices. The joke sometimes made that sociology is wholesale psychology completely misunderstands the nature of sociology. Sociology does not simply aggregate the influences of personality traits, attitudes, and preferences on behavior. Doing this and explaining the results is the task of psychology. Sociology's task, in contrast, is to analyze how people are influenced by the social conditions in their environment, particularly the other people among whom they live and the attributes of these others. Doing so does not involve aggregating the choices and decisions of the members of a population but, on the contrary, investigating how the population composition governs the opportunities of individuals and limits the choices they can make. Any one individual can probably escape these limits on opportunities for social relations imposed by the population structure, but most members of the population cannot, which means that the community structure exerts inevitable constraints on the patterns of social relations in it. Although there are few X's in a city, any individual can search until he finds one or migrate to another place where there are more, but the few X's in that city make it unavoidable that most people there are not married to an X and do not have an X as a friend.

The structural influences on social relations do not mean that individuals do not seek to satisfy their preferences in their friendships and marriages, but they must do so as best they can in the context of the limitations the social structure imposes. The data in Table 2.2 show that group differences inhibit marriage and that people exhibit ingroup preferences in their selection of mates. However, the fact that people do manifest cultural ingroup values in their choices of associates must not be interpreted to imply that structural influences merely mitigate cultural and psychological influences and become apparent only if these other factors are controlled. The argument advanced is that structural differentiation exerts overwhelming influences on social relations, including marriage. To justify this claim that the effect of structural differentiation on important human relations overwhelms other influences on these relations, the two theorems about the implications of differentiation for social life are initially tested with simple correlations, which reveal only influences that are not overshadowed by other influences.

Heterogeneity promotes intergroup relations (T-2). This second theorem follows from the assumptions and the definition of the primitive term, heterogeneity. Since heterogeneity is defined as the chance expectation that any random meeting involves members of different groups, and since people's tendencies are to associate with members of their own group (A-1), homogeneous communities provide little basis for intergroup associations. But since associations depend on contact opportunities (A-2) and since growing heterogeneity entails more fortuitous contacts between members of different groups, much heterogeneity reduces the opportunities for ingroup associations and increases the probability of intergroup relations. Of course, most random meetings do not lead to lasting social relations, let alone marriage. Yet casual contacts are a necessary, though not a sufficient, condition for more intimate relations to develop, and some of them are likely to grow into lasting acquaintances, friendships, and even marriage. Heterogeneity increases the opportunity for members of different groups to get to meet and to know each other well enough for intimate relations between them to possibly develop. As already mentioned, the theorem is of substantive interest only for dimensions of social differences for which ingroup tendencies exist (just as is the case for the size theorem) because otherwise chance expectations naturally exert the dominant influence on social ties, making the theorem true but trivial.[15]

[15]It is implied, here and throughout, that heterogeneity, operationally defined as the chance expectation that two random persons belong to different groups, is the same as the chance expectation that the two have social contact. This is, indeed, correct for all social associations whose partners can be anybody—for handshakes, meeting at a party, mutual friendship—but it is not strictly true for marriage unless the social attribute under consideration, for instance race, has the same distribution for men and women. For an attribute whose distribution differs by sex, such as occupation, actual chance expectations would be computed by summing the products of the number of men and of women in all relevant category combinations.

The greater the inequality, the greater is the probability of status-distant social relations (T-3). This theorem has been completely revised on the basis of empirical and theoretical analysis. As a matter of fact, the original version of the inequality theorem does not have clear implications because its wording is ambiguous, which probably reflects Blau's (1977:55) lack of confidence in the inferences he drew, but the wording suggested that a decline in inequality reduces barriers to social relations, which implies the opposite of the reformulated theorem. The reasoning was that if status distance discourages social relations, the greater status distance implied by greater inequality should also do so. But this argument ignores the counteracting structural influence. The revised theorem is deducible in the same manner as the heterogeneity theorem. If people tend to associate with others in proximate status (A-1), if inequality is defined in terms of mean or expected status distance, and if associations depend on contact opportunities (A-2), it follows that the greater mean distance resulting from increased inequality increases the status distance of random meetings and thus the opportunities for and probabilities of associating with more status-distant persons. In short, if people prefer proximate associates, the greater the mean status distance (the criterion of inequality), the less proximate are the closest associates they are likely to find.

Inequality and heterogeneity are two generic forms of differentiation, but they entail entirely different population distributions. Much inequality is manifest in a highly skewed distribution, with large proportions of poor or powerless and very few owning great riches or having much power. Much heterogeneity, on the other hand, involves an even distribution among the different categories. A paradox of inequality, mentioned earlier, is that if there is much of it, then most people are roughly equal, that is, evenly distributed among all but the top categories. A status continuum can be divided into strata, and one can determine how even the distribution among the various strata is, which is the graduated-dimension equivalent of heterogeneity (for a nominal dimension) and which has been termed status diversity. If there is no inequality then there is also no status diversity because all people are equal, but maximum inequality—one person has all the wealth or power—is near-minimum status diversity. The operational criterion of status diversity is the uniformity of the status distribution, with a uniform distribution indicating maximum diversity and the degree of divergence from the uniform distribution indicating decreasing diversity (or diversity in reverse).[16] Inasmuch as status diversity can be considered a special case of heterogeneity, a corollary of the heterogeneity theorem is that status diversity promotes intergroup relations.

---

[16]A possible measure of diversity would be the measure of heterogeneity weighted by number of categories, weighted because the categories are not real groups but arbitrary divisions of a continuum. The equation is

$$D = (1 - \sum p_i^2)\left(\frac{c}{c-1}\right),$$

Testing the Heterogeneity and Inequality Theorems[17]

The heterogeneity theorem (T-2) rests on the influence of size distributions among nominal groups on social relations. These distributions govern the chance expectation of social contacts between members of different groups, in terms of which heterogeneity is defined and on which associations are assumed to depend (A-2), so that the theorem logically follows from these premises. Since heterogeneity determines the chances of fortuitous meetings between strangers with different group affiliations, it is hardly surprising that casual intergroup associations are more likely the more pronounced the heterogeneity. Empirical evidence that this is the case would not constitute very impressive support for the theory. If structural conditions can only explain greeting acquaintances, they contribute little to our understanding of social life. But patterns of marriage and intermarriage constitute important relations that shape the nature of the population in future generations. If structural conditions can explain these patterns, it demonstrates their significance for knowledge of society and its development. This is a significant advantage of testing the theory with data on rates of marriage. Empirical support for the theorems also strengthens confidence in the structural scheme underlying them, that is, the claim of the pervasive significance of population structures.

The relationships of nine forms of heterogeneity with intermarriage in an SMSA are analyzed to test the heterogeneity theorem. The same classification of groups is always used for the heterogeneity and the intermarriage measure. For instance, if heterogeneity is defined on the basis of major occupational groups, spouses (including only couples who both work) in different detailed occupations in the same major group are counted as inmarried, but if heterogeneity is defined on the basis of detailed occupations, they are defined as intermarried. Because some of the dependent variables are closely related, there are not nine but six independent tests of the theorem: race (two measures), ethnic group (three measures), birth region, industry, major occupation, and detailed occupation.[18]

Table 2.4 presents the results of the analysis of the 125 SMSAs. The first column shows the average heterogeneity in the 125 metropolitan areas, and the

---

where p_i is the number of persons in a category and c the number of categories. A preferable measure could be constructed based on the cumulative frequencies of the uniform distribution as reference standard for maximal diversity and computing departures from it as indications of decreasing status diversity.

[17]The research reported in this section was conducted jointly with Terry C. Blum, and a paper based on it was jointly published (Blau et al., 1982).

[18]The intermarriage rates, the dependent variables, are highly correlated for the two (unconstrained) indicators of race (.94); and (now referring to constrained measures) for ethnic background (which is a combination of race and national origin) with national origin (.99) and with mother tongue (.65); and for national origin with mother tongue (.65). All other correlations for the two dependent variables are less than .30 except for one—that between industry and detailed occupation (which is .39).

TABLE 2.4
Heterogeneity and Intermarriage

	Mean 1970 hetero- geneity	Mean intermarriage		WLS 1970 correla- tion	WLS 1960 correla- tion
		Unconstrained	Constrained		
Race (detailed)[a]	.19	.01		-.03[*]	
Race dichotomy[a]	.19	.01		-.05[*]	-.09[*]
National origin	.27	.11	.07	.86	.81
Mother tongue	.31	.13	.09	.76	
Ethnic background	.43	.12	.07	.65	
Birth region	.38	.25	.18	.84	
Industry	.87	.81	.66	.32	.29
Occupation (major)	.87	.84	.60	.13	.19
Occupation (detailed)	.99	.97	.95	.08[*]	.10[*]

[*] Not significant at the .05 level (one-tailed); all others are significant.

[a] Based on 124 cases, excluding the outlier, Honolulu, and using the unconstrained measure (see Note 17 in Chapter 1).

second, the average fraction of young couples who are intermarried. Since heterogeneity also indicates the chance expectation of intermarriage (but see Note 15), the finding that the means in the second column are always smaller than those in the first furnishes a rough indication of the prevailing ingroup tendencies that depress intermarriage below the rate expected by chance, as already shown by the much more detailed analysis in Table 2.2. There is little racial heterogeneity in most metropolitan areas, which are still predominantly white, in contrast to many inner cities. Other ascribed positions exhibit more heterogeneity in SMSAs. But heterogeneity is far more pronounced with respect to industry and occupation, which reflects the advanced industrialization and division of labor in the contemporary American metropolis. Major occupational groups, which indicate heterogeneity among broad socioeconomic strata, are not a good indication of the division of labor because they fail to take into account the extensive specialization within major groups. Thus, the group of professional and technical workers has by now expanded beyond its proportionate share of the labor force, with the result that its recent and future expansion reduces the major-occupation index of heterogeneity. This ignores that the many specialized professional and technical occupations continue to contribute to the division of labor, which is taken into account by the index based on detailed occupations.[19]

Only 1% of young couples in metropolitan America are racially intermarried, as shown in the second column of Table 2.4, and only a little more than a quarter of the interracial marriages are black–white marriages, although blacks constitute the largest racial minority. Other ethnic intermarriages, whichever measure is used, are not that rare but also fairly infrequent. In contrast, nearly all spouses that are both in the labor force work in different industries and have different occupations, though the small fraction who have the same occupation (3%) still exceeds chance expectation. The constrained measures in Column 3 are not accurate indications of the extent of intermarriage because numerous intermarriages but no inmarriages have been excluded from them. However, they are the ones used in most correlations because they usually produce more reliable indexes of voluntary intermarriages by eliminating any distorting effects of differences in sex distributions. An illustration can clarify this point: most nurses are married to someone in a different occupation, and so are most craftsmen, the reason obviously being that there are very few male nurses and few females in crafts occupations. The procedure used on account of these extreme cases (see Notes 17 and 18 of Chapter 1) deletes so many intermarriages that it becomes an unreliable measure of racial intermarriage because there are very few in each SMSA; therefore, the unconstrained measure for racial intermarriage (for which the two sex distributions do not differ much) is used.

The WLS correlations in the fourth column of Table 2.4 indicate that most forms of heterogeneity are positively related to intermarriage, as the theorem implies.[20] The heterogeneity of an SMSA in national descent, mother tongue, ethnic background, and birth region has pronounced positive correlations with intermarriage along these lines. The positive correlation of industrial heterogeneity and intermarriage is not so strong, and those for the two forms of occupational heterogeneity and intermarriage are quite weak, with that for detailed occupations not being significant on the .05 level. However, racial heterogeneity and interracial marriage are not positively related, regardless of which measure is used. The two kinds of group affiliation that fail to support the theoretical prediction are, interestingly enough, at opposite extremes in terms of salience: race, which is most salient, and detailed occupation, which is least salient for marriage, are negative cases. We investigate these negative results after first examining the issue posed by the assumption about causal sequence.

Metropolitan structures are measured in 1970, but most of the marriages

[19]The two measures of occupational heterogeneity—based on major groups and detailed occupations, respectively—are uncorrelated for the 125 SMSAs ($r = .03$).

[20]The results using unconstrained intermarriage rates are largely similar to the ones reported using constrained ones, though there are minor differences (see Blau et al., 1982:54).

assumed to be influenced by them occurred before 1970. The assumption made in testing the heterogeneity theorem is that the variations in heterogeneity among SMSAs in 1970 reflect parallel variations in the 1960s when the couples under study decided to get married.[21] To test this assumption, data for 1960, abstracted from published census sources, are used. These data, which are available for five of the nine dimensions for all but four of the SMSAs, make it possible to ascertain whether SMSA differences in 1960 parallel those in 1970 and whether the 1970 intermarriage rates exhibit parallel correlations with 1960 as with 1970 heterogeneity measures.[22]

Three of the five correlations between 1960 and 1970 heterogeneity are very high—that for the race dichotomy (.98), for national origin (.97), and for industry (.93)—but two are low—that for major occupation (.42) and especially that for detailed occupation (.18). The reason for the two low correlations is undoubtedly in large part the methodological one that the measures for 1960 and 1970 occupational heterogeneity are not the same, as just mentioned in Note 22. The five WLS correlations of 1960 heterogeneity with 1970 intermarriage largely replicate the results obtained with the corresponding 1970 measures, as a comparison of the last two columns in Table 2.3 shows. Intermarriage in 1970 is positively related to three forms of 1960 as well as 1970 heterogeneity—in national origin, industry, and major occupation—but it is not positively related to either 1960 or 1970 heterogeneity in race or in detailed occupation. These two negative cases must be more closely examined.

Heterogeneity with respect to detailed occupations is very high everywhere because it is based on 444 categories, which means that a ceiling effect may well dampen the possible variation among SMSAs (note how near the mean is to the maximum). This distorting influence can be removed by logit transformation for both independent and dependent variables (substituting the logarithm of the odds ratio for the percentage), which increases the possible range from plus to minus infinity. The logit transformations raise the correlations to .25 for 1970 heterogeneity and .22 for 1960 heterogeneity, both being significant beyond the .025 level. These data support the theorem (T-2) and leave racial heterogeneity as the only case failing to do so.

This negative case can be explained in terms of another component of the theory, according to which the consolidation of group differences by correlated economic or other status differences inhibits intergroup relations (as mentioned earlier but fully discussed only later in Chapter 4). Racial differences in the

[21]The causal assumption does not require that the SMSA compositions did not change during the decade, only that the variations among SMSAs remained largely the same.

[22]It should be noted that two of the five heterogeneity measures are not the same for 1960 and 1970 (the other three are). The two measures of occupational heterogeneity are based on the entire labor force for 1970 but only on the male labor force in 1960 because the published source presented them separately for men and women, and combining the two would have entailed excessive cost.

TABLE 2.5
Weighted Regression of Racial intermarriage[*]

	b	SE	β	R^2
Racial heterogeneity	.012	.007	.17	.12
White-nonwhite SEI ratio (log)	-.041	.010	-.40	

Note: Based on 124 cases (excluding Honolulu).

[*]Both coefficients are significant at the .05 level (one-tailed).

United States are strongly related to differences in income, occupation, prestige, and numerous other aspects of status. If socioeconomic differences between groups have a negative effect on intergroup relations while heterogeneity has a positive one, as the theory implies, such group differences may well suppress the influence of heterogeneity, and controlling them would reveal its influence. To investigate this inference, a regression analysis of racial intermarriage on racial heterogeneity and the log ratio of white to nonwhite mean socioeconomic status (Duncan's SEI) is carried out. A large ratio means that occupational differences consolidate racial ones. The results of the regression analysis are in Table 2.5.[23] The greater the socioeconomic superiority of whites over nonwhites, the rarer are interracial marriages. But if this indicator of the consolidation of racial by economic status differences is controlled, racial heterogeneity and intermarriage are positively related, just as other forms of heterogeneity and intermarriage are. Thus, the data on racial as well as those on eight other forms of heterogeneity corroborate the theorem (T-2).

Turning now to testing the implications of the inequality theorem (T-3) for intermarriage, it must be acknowledged at the outset that the data available for doing so are less adequate than those used for testing the heterogeneity theorem's predictions. Although several, reliable indexes of various forms of inequality in SMSAs can be constructed, two of the four measures of status differences between spouses are of questionable validity as indicators of the difference between them at the time of mate selection, which is the basis of the dependent variable of interest. The four social differences under consideration are those in education, occupational status (SEI), income, and earnings.[24]

[23]The racial measures are based on detailed race, but the results are essentially the same for the race dichotomy. The unconstrained intermarriage rate is used and the case base is 124 SMSAs, excluding the outlier (Honolulu). Both coefficients are significant at the .05 level (one-tailed). There is little multicollinearity; the correlation for the two independent variables is .48.

[24]The constrained intermarriage rates for income and earnings are correlated .90; none of the other rates constituting the dependent variables exhibit a correlation as high as .30.

TABLE 2.6
Inequality and Intermarriage

	Mean 1970 inequality	Mean intermarriage		WLS 1970 correla- tion	WLS 1960 correla- tion
		uncon- strained	con- strained		
Education	.17	.13	.12	.65	.59
Socioeconomic index	.32	.50	.49	.36	.13[*]
Income	.49	.91	.61	.14[*]	
Earnings	.46	.90	.61	.23	-.01[*]

[*] Not significant at the .05 level (one-tailed).

Two of them are acceptable, though not perfect, indications of differences between spouses at the time of mate selection. Most people have completed their education at that time, and while many have not, they are far enough along to estimate fairly well what their final education will be, and these estimates are what may influence, consciously or unconsciously, the decision to get married. Occupational status is perhaps somewhat more likely to change but can also be pretty accurately anticipated a few years in advance. The situation is different for income and earnings, which are liable to change considerably for young people. Although young people may discount their economic standing at the time of marriage and consider only economic prospects, these expectations can be mistaken. Moreover, the very earnings of one spouse may negatively affect the other's because the higher earnings of one decrease the need for income from the other, and vice versa. Hence, income and earnings are not very good indexes of status difference at the time of mate selection.[25]

The correlations between the Gini coefficient of inequality and intermarriage (as indicated by the constrained mean status distance between spouses) for 1970 are presented in the fourth column of Table 2.6. The positive relationship between the two implied by the inequality theorem is observed for all four forms of status differences, and it is significant far beyond the .025 level for three of the four. An SMSA's inequality in education, occupational status, and earnings is

[25]The inequality measure is the Gini coefficient. The constrained intermarriage measure is computed in three steps: (1) subtracting husband's score from male subsample mean and wife's score from female subsample mean; (2) taking mean absolute difference of results in Step 1 between spouses for SMSA; (3) dividing by mean for entire (both male and female) SMSA subsample (see equation in Note 18 of Chapter 1). Education is confined to those over 25 years of age who have completed their education. Occupational status is based on those couples who both work; income on those who both have an income; and earnings on those who both have earnings.

substantially related to the status distance between spouses in these respects, though income inequality is not significantly related to income differences between spouses.[26] These results lend considerable support to the theorem (T-3). For three of the four forms of inequality, corresponding measures for 1960 were derived from published sources,[27] but only two of the 1960 and 1970 measures are the same, those for education and earnings. Duncan's socioeconomic index is based on the occupations of the entire labor force for 1970 but on those of the male labor force only for 1960, which makes the two measures of inequality in SEI very different. Indeed, their correlation is only .11, whereas the 1960–1970 correlation for educational inequality is .87 and that for inequality in earnings is .67. Table 2.6's last column shows that educational inequality in 1960 exhibits about as pronounced a positive correlation with educational differences between spouses as does 1970 educational inequality. For inequality in SEI, however, the 1960 correlation is positive but insignificant, and for inequality in earnings, it is essentially nil. In sum, the empirical data on SMSAs give some qualified support to the implications of the inequality theorem for intermarriage.

A possible reason for the lack of consistency in findings is that the original idea that inequality has adverse consequences for status-distant associations, though flawed, is not entirely incorrect. It is flawed because it ignores the dominant influence of inequality on the structure of opportunities, which increases the probable status distance between associates. But the notion that inequality also strengthens barriers to social intercourse may well be correct because much inequality probably increases the salience of status, and the greater the salience of status, the greater is the inhibiting effect of status differences on associations. According to these conjectures, inequality has a direct positive effect on the opportunities and probabilities of status-distant associations, but it also has a negative indirect effect, mediated by status salience, on the likelihood of these associations. Rytina and colleagues (1982) analyzed this model and showed that the direct positive effect in most circumstances overwhelms the indirect negative one. This conclusion is reflected in our finding that six of seven correlations examined are positive (though two of the six are not statistically significant). But the opposite indirect influence, though rarely strong enough to produce a negative overall effect, may be responsible for reductions in the positive correlations, making two of them too small to be statistically significant and completely neutralizing the positive effect of a third. However, another

[26]If absolute measures of inequality and intermarriage are substituted for the relative ones generally used (by using the numerator of the Gini index of income inequality and the numerator of the constrained measure of mean income difference between spouses, without dividing by mean income), the resulting measures of absolute income inequality and mean absolute constrained income difference between spouses exhibit a substantial positive correlation (.53).

[27]No measure for total income of individuals, including public assistance and other income as well as earnings, is available for 1960.

reason for these findings is the counteracting influence of consolidated status-differences, which are briefly noted in the conclusions, and for which empirical evidence is supplied in a later chapter.

Conclusions

Two basic assumptions of the theory are introduced in this chapter: that people associate disproportionately with others in proximate social positions (A-1) and that social associations depend on contact opportunities (A-2). Empirical evidence is provided in support of the assumption that ingroup tendencies prevail not only for group memberships that are highly salient but also for those with very little salience. Next, the theorem that a group's small size reduces opportunities for ingroup relations and, therefore, promotes intergroup relations (T-1) is tested with data on the proportionate size of several kinds of groups in 125 SMSAs. All marriage patterns observed conform to the theorem's implications.

A fundamental sociological paradox is that structural differentiation exerts an influence on social relations that is in the opposite direction from the influence of individual differences. Whereas individual differences in social affiliations inhibit social relations, structural differentiation promotes social relations between persons with different affiliations. Two theorems expressing this paradox are deduced from primitive terms and assumptions: that heterogeneity promotes intergroup relations (T-2) and that inequality promotes status-distant relations (T-3). Five of six independent tests of the heterogeneity theorem corroborated it outright, and the sixth also confirmed its prediction once another condition that, according to the theory, should inhibit intergroup relations is controlled. The empirical findings also support the underlying assumption about causal sequence. The implications of the inequality theorem are not so unequivocally supported. Although most forms of inequality and intermarriage are found to be positively related, as theoretically predicted, one is not and two of the relations are not significant. One reason for the lack of clear-cut support for the theorem may be that inequality tends to increase the salience of status, which inhibits status-distant associations. The consequent indirect negative effect of inequality on status-distant marriage counteracts or weakens its direct positive effect. Another possible reason is that several forms of inequality usually are related, and such consolidated status-differences inhibit social relations. As a matter of fact, in Chapter 4, where the influences of consolidation and intersection are discussed, it is observed that forms of inequality that are seen in this chapter to exhibit no simple correlation with status-distant marriage do exhibit a positive relation with it when consolidation–intersection is controlled.

In sum, heterogeneity generally promotes intermarriage, and so does inequality, unless the counteracting effects of consolidated group or status differences suppress this influence. Controlling these counteracting influences of consolidation reveals the predicted effects of heterogeneity and inequality. This is illustrated for racial heterogeneity in this chapter, and it is illustrated for inequality in Chapter 4. Before analyzing the significance of consolidation and intersection, social mobility is discussed in the next chapter.

CHAPTER 3

Social Mobility

Two important social processes that are closely connected with a social structure and its dynamics are processes of association between people and processes of mobility of people. *Social associations* are channels of communications, while *social mobility* entails channels of movements of people from one social position to another. The processes of social association and mobility influence each other directly, and mobility also exerts an indirect influence on rates of associations between groups by usually altering their relative size.

Social mobility typically results in structural change, that is, in changes in population distributions, whatever the ultimate exogenous conditions that created the demands for the redistribution of people. Whether technological or economic or political developments are the basic cause of the required redistribution, it is the movement of people that brings the redistribution about—their occupational or economic or educational or industrial mobility. Although differences in fertility among groups or strata alter population distributions even in the absence of social mobility, the very population changes so produced generally precipitate mobility as a needed adjustment to economic conditions. An illustration is the high birth rate of farmers which engenders pressures to move out of farming into other lines of work.

The next three chapters deal with the dynamics of social mobility and structural change. The relationships of mobility with social associations and with changes in structural differentiation in any one dimension are examined in this chapter. The intersection and consolidation of multiple dimensions of social differences and how mobility is related to change in these structural conditions are analyzed in the next chapter. The processes of status attainment within the metropolitan structure that help shape that structure are the topic of Chapter 5.

Social Association and Mobility

Mobile persons occupy two positions in terms of the classification system under consideration, a position of social origin and a destination position. Thus, the socioeconomic stratum in which they were raised differs for the mobile from their current socioeconomic position. According to the first assumption, both positions encourage mobile persons to associate with others in the same or proximate positions. They will continue to associate with their relatives and old friends and neighbors, and they will establish associations with others in their new social position. This is the case whether the mobility considered constitutes movements between regions, neighborhoods, occupations, or social classes. But given their current position, the association of mobile persons with members of their former groups or strata constitute intergroup relations.

Mobility promotes intergroup relations (T-4).[1] This fourth theorem can be derived from the first assumption and the definitions of social position and of social mobility. If people tend to associate with persons in proximate social positions (A-1), and if positions are defined as attributes that influence people's relations, and if *mobility* is defined as involving two positions that exert such influences, it follows that mobile individuals tend to associate more than others with persons not in their present position, namely with those with whom they maintain associations because they have common social origins. (The term *intergroup* is used broadly, here and throughout, to include also interstratum, interclass, and generally status-distant associations.)

A corollary of the fourth theorem is that high rates of social mobility in a community or society lead to extensive intergroup relations there. A complementary corollary is that barriers to social mobility reduce intergroup relations. One implication of these corollaries is that the rate of occupational mobility and the rate of association among persons in different occupational positions are positively related. We test this implication with data on occupational intermarriage.

Initially, the high rates of intergroup relations in communities with high rates of mobility are entirely the result of the higher rates of the many mobiles there, which raise the average for the community. But the relatively frequent intergroup relations of the mobile are likely to spread to the nonmobile. One reason is that

[1] In the original formulation (Blau, 1977:38), this theorem was considered to require the assumption that "established role relations resist disruption." Further reflection suggests that this assumption is not needed. Having common social origins is undoubtedly a social attribute that influences social relations (and thus qualifies as a social position by the criterion adopted). Not only do some of the relations established when the origin position was occupied persist, but new relations often develop when people discover that they have background attributes in common (e.g., two Southerners meeting in New York). The assumption that origin positions influence social relations is, of course, testable.

the mobile, who tend to have friends in their former as well as their present group, are likely sometimes to bring their two kinds of friends together, providing an opportunity for them also to become friendly, despite initial resistance to associate with outsiders. (This inference can be deduced in strict logic only if one makes the additional assumption that strangers who have a common associate disproportionately often become associates themselves.)

There is another reason for this development as well. Rare intergroup relations imply group pressures that discourage them. The more frequent intergroup relations are, the weaker are these anti-outgroup pressures because an increasing number who themselves have outgroup friends indicates that such friendships are more widely accepted in a group. For example, as more Jews get married to Christians, disapproval of marrying non-Jews becomes less widespread among Jews. Indeed, there are two ways in which extensive outmarriage reduces group pressure against it: there are fewer persons who manifest in their conduct a taboo against marrying non-Jews, and this, in turn, weakens the taboo among those who themselves are married to Jews. Thus, mobility has cumulative effects on the likelihood of intergroup relations. First, since mobile persons have more intergroup associates than nonmobile persons (T-4), many mobiles raise the group's average. Second, they sometimes introduce their friends from the two groups, initiating intergroup relations between these. Third, the consequent high rates of intergroup relations in communities with many mobiles indicate weakened ingroup pressures and wider acceptance of associations with outsiders, encouraging still others to establish intergroup relations.[2] Finally, the relatively frequent intergroup relations lessen ingroup salience, even among those who themselves are not involved in intergroup associations, further facilitating intergroup contacts in the future. The inference is that extensive mobility promotes intergroup relations of a population's nonmobile as well as its mobile members.

Ingroup salience is defined on the basis of the low prevalence of intergroup relations. Another corollary of the theorem that mobility increases the likelihood of intergroup relations (T-4) is that social mobility reduces the salience of group boundaries and social differences. For example, high rates of residential mobility in a city reduce the salience of neighborhoods and increase the associations among people living in different areas. This corollary can explain the higher salience of ascribed than acquired positions usually observed, as we have seen illustrated in Table 2.2. Since there is no, or virtually no, mobility among ascribed positions, it follows from T-4 that there would be lower rates of intermarriage and other intergroup relations between members of ascribed than those of achieved positions.

---

[2]Although some individuals who succeed in moving into an elite may attempt to keep others out in order to gain social acceptance, if there are many mobile persons in a group they do not need such defense mechanisms and undoubtedly weaken ingroup pressures.

T-4 applies to vertical as well as horizontal mobility. Thus, it implies that if more and more professionals originated in the lower-middle or working class, as a practically inevitable result of the expansion of professional occupations, the inhibiting effect of class differences on social intercourse is reduced. It also helps explain why economic growth tends to weaken class barriers. Two more corollaries referring to vertical mobility can be formulated. Extensive mobility between *two* hierarchical strata or social classes increases the likelihood of social associations between their members. Generally high rates of vertical mobility in an entire society engender extensive associations among the members of various social classes or strata. These principles are expected to find expression in hierarchical differences of any kind. For example, high promotion rates in a firm should increase social interaction between different ranks; little circulation of the elite should reduce the elite's contacts with the rest of the population; the chances of poor people to improve their relative economic standing should affect the extent of social association among persons whose economic resources and standard of living differ; and intergenerational occupational mobility should be positively related to marriage between persons whose socioeconomic origin, as defined by parental occupation, differs.

In addition to its direct influences, mobility also often exerts indirect influences on rates of intergroup associations by altering the relative size of groups or strata. For a change in the relative size of groups affects their rates of intergroup relations, as size and the probable rate of outgroup relations are inversely related (T-1). For instance, rural–urban mobility has reduced the size of the rural and increased that of the urban population. One result of this migration is that many people in cities have relatives and friends in rural areas, and many rural people have relatives and friends in cities, which is expected directly to increase the amount of social association between rural and urban people. But a second result of the same migration is that it contracted the size of the rural and expanded the size of the urban population, thereby altering the denominators of the rates and, of course, indirectly affecting the rates. As a consequence of these changes in population size, the rate of association of rural with urban people has been increased more by the migration and is larger than the rate of association of urban with rural people. In accordance with these considerations, a fifth theorem is deducible jointly from T-1 and T-4. If the proportionate size of groups is inversely related to the probability of outgroup relations (T-1); and if net mobility in one direction changes the proportionate size of groups; and if mobility increases the likelihood of intergroup relations (T-4); it follows that *net outmobility from a group promotes outgroup relations more than net inmobility to it does* (T-5).[3]

Social mobility and intergroup relations undoubtedly exert mutual influences. So far, the discussion has been confined to the influences in one direction, those

---

[3]The theorem does not contradict the possibility that inmobility on a large scale may actually increase the rate of intergroup relations.

of social mobility on intergroup relations. But outgroup contacts also affect the likelihood of mobility. People often get jobs in a firm by hearing about them from acquaintances who work there. Migrants to a city tend to move to neighborhoods where they already have friends who can ease their adjustment to the new situation. The chances to learn about the opportunities in a certain occupation and the requirements for it are best for those persons in the labor market who know somebody in that occupation. People are most likely to join a political movement or party if they have associates who belong to it and perhaps recruit them for it. All these illustrations indicate that having associates in a group to which one does not belong frequently makes it easier to move there rather than to a group where one has no connections. It seems plausible that friends and relatives who belong to another group encourage and facilitate mobility to that group. We shall assume that this plausible inference is correct and introduce it as the third assumption formally postulated in the theory: *Associates in other groups or strata facilitate mobility to them* (A-3).

Intergroup relations increase the probability of social mobility (T-6). This theorem is directly implied by the assumption just made. If associates in other groups or strata facilitate mobility there (A-3), it follows that high rates of intergroup relations promote high rates of mobility. T-6 is intended to apply to the relations between any two groups or strata (except, of course, those defined by unalterable, ascribed attributes), to those of one group with all others in the collectivity, and to the relations among all groups or strata (in a given dimension) of a community or society. Thus, if there is a disproportionate number of friendships between two Protestant denominations, many conversions from either denomination to the other are expected (religious conversions being in our terms a form of mobility). Firms whose members have most occasion to associate with members of other firms are expected (when employment conditions are held constant) to have high labor turnover because many of their employees move to jobs in other firms. As class barriers in a society weaken and marriages between members of different social classes become more frequent, the chances of vertical mobility are expected to increase.

The combination of the last two theorems, T-5 and T-6, raises a problem. If there is an initial change either in intergroup relations or in social mobility and the influences stipulated by the two theorems are the only ones, the change would set off a reciprocal chain reaction that could wipe out all group boundaries. More intergroup relations increase mobility, which increases intergroup relations, which further increases mobility. If these two reciprocal influences are sufficiently large, the chain reaction will continue until there are no group differences, which makes it meaningless to speak of mobility. Once in a while this happens and some group differences do disappear, such as that between aristocrats and commoners after a revolution or ethnic differences as the result of intermarriage and assimilation. But because this is very rare, one can infer either that the reciprocal influences are not jointly large enough to set off an explosive social change or that other structural conditions restrain these influences. The very social processes that generate structural change also create conditions that limit it, as is seen in the next chapter.

The last theorem (T-6) in conjunction with two earlier ones (T-2, T-3) implies two new theorems. If heterogeneity makes intergroup relations more probable (T-2), and if intergroup relations make mobility more probable (T-6), the implication is that *heterogeneity is positively related to social mobility* (T-7). For example, one would expect that extensive division of labor—much occupational heterogeneity—fosters frequent shifts of workers from one occupational specialty to another. Furthermore, if inequality makes intergroup relations more likely (T-3), and if intergroup relations make mobility more likely (T-6), the implication is that *inequality is positively related to mobility across greater status distances* (T-8).[4] It appears paradoxical that status inequality should further vertical mobility, but this is not quite what the theorem specifies. What it does stipulate is that status-distant mobility is more likely under conditions of more than under those of less inequality.

The effects of historical changes in inequality may be very different from those of cross-sectional variations in it because a great increase in inequality, for example, may raise the salience of status. The raised salience reduces status-distant moves. In extreme cases this indirect negative effect of greater inequality could outweigh the direct positive effect, as noted by Rytina and colleagues (1982) and in the preceding chapter. But there are good grounds for expecting a positive relationship between the condition of inequality and status-distant moves. To illustrate: Assume that exogenous conditions in technology and in the economy reduce the need for jobs in farming (which are poorly paid) and increase the need for professional jobs (which are well paid). We are asking how income inequality would affect economic mobility given this development. If income inequality is great, the above change in distribution of jobs would produce a greater difference in income than if inequality is not so great. Hence, although subsequent repercussions may alter the situation, inequality and mobility are positively related when subject to the same condition.

Change in Heterogeneity

Social mobility plays an important part in structural change. However, it is not the ultimate source of changes in macrostructures, nor is it a necessary condition for all changes in population distributions. These two qualifications are briefly

---

[4]Several authors (e.g., Costner and Leik, 1964; Blalock, 1969) stress the danger of deducing theorems from a long chain of propositions that refer to one influence among several (probability or ceteris paribus propositions). But deriving a theorem from a short chain of only two theorems, as is done here, is not likely to lead to a false conclusion, assuming there is no counteracting direct effect and provided that the theorems used as premises refer to substantial probabilities, that is, to influences unlikely to be entirely suppressed by other influences.

examined before turning to the consequences of social mobility for structural differentiation—first for heterogeneity and then for inequality.

New conditions that are exogenous to the population structure itself are the basic source of changes in that structure. For example, technological innovations, economic developments, political revolutions, and religious rebellions are changed exogenous conditions to which society adjusts by redistributions of its population. What generally implements such pressures for structural change is social mobility. The technological and economic improvements that greatly raised agricultural productivity in the nineteenth century created a more urbanized and industrialized society, but these changes were actually realized by the social mobility of many people from rural to urban areas and from farm work to jobs in factories. When peasant revolutions expropriate large plantations and redistribute land, drastic downward mobility of a few and some upward mobility of many is what affects the economic redistribution. For new religious sects that rebel against the traditional churches to be successful, many persons must leave their old denomination to join the new religious movement. In short, whatever the exogenous cause of structural changes, they are usually effected by social mobility.

Whereas most changes in population distributions depend on mobility among physical locations or social positions, not all do. The major exception is *differential fertility* of various groups or strata, which also alters the population distribution, independent of any mobility. (Reference here is to *net fertility*, which is birth rates minus death rates.) Thus, the higher birth rates of the Catholic minority than the Protestant majority has increased religious heterogeneity in the United States. The comparatively high fertility of Puerto Ricans has increased ethnic heterogeneity in many American cities. On the other hand, the higher fertility of blacks than whites has not raised ethnic heterogeneity in this country because it was more than compensated for by the large number of white immigrants.

Migration is a form of social mobility because the change in physical location involves a change in social (as well as economic and political) environment that is no less great, and often greater, than that entailed by other changes in group affiliation and social position. However, these similarities apply largely to internal migration because both it and social mobility refer to changes in positions and distributions within the collectivity under consideration. The cases of immigration and emigration are quite different because they do not involve internal processes that alter the society's structure but exogenous influences on that structure. Net immigration is in this respect more similar to net fertility than to internal migration. The ethnically rather homogeneous American society two centuries ago was transformed into a very heterogeneous one by large streams of immigrants from diverse countries. Because the immigrants spoke a variety of languages linguistic heterogeneity was also increased. Sweden, where one out of eight people is an immigrant, is a contemporary example.

In-migration to SMSAs from different places in the nation is an equivocal case. It is naturally internal migration in the United States; but from the perspective of SMSAs, which are the units of analysis here, it is an exogenous force that alters the population distributions. *Net in-migration* (in-migration minus out-migration) is of distinctive significance for another reason as well. Internal migration can only change the population structure in regard to acquired positions, but not in regard to ascribed ones which are inborn. Net in-migration, however, can, and often does, change the population composition and thus the SMSA structure with respect to ascriptive social differences. An SMSA's net in-migration and a society's net immigration are in many ways equivalent. Small towns grow into cities and cities into metropolitan centers because economic opportunities attract outsiders from many places, which produces a minimum of heterogeneity, at least in terms of place of origin.[5] The different economic opportunities in a large metropolis, its initial heterogeneity, and its large size as such make it attractive for a variety of people, ranging from artists to alcoholics. Many of these would be deviants in homogeneous small towns but fit into a metropolis, where one can find unusual jobs and companions with rare attributes. Accordingly, heterogeneity breeds more heterogeneity, or rather, heterogeneity on a large scale does because the heterogeneous large metropolis provides an opportunity to form homogeneous friendship networks for a great variety of people.[6]

The impersonality of the heterogeneous metropolis is often decried and contrasted with the friendliness of people in small towns. Although this contrast is not entirely false, it is misleading. In a small place where one knows most others, it is natural to be friendly to anybody one meets. If one lives in the same place with millions of people, it is impossible to exchange even a greeting or a smile with everybody one sees. Such impersonal demeanor is only maintained toward strangers, however, not between individuals who have a personal relation. Neither small-town nor big-city people are friendly with millions of others, but this fact is more conspicuous in the large metropolis where strangers live together in the same city, not in different small towns, and one sees thousands of people every day. Indeed, the diverse big city enables more people to have congenial associates than the homogeneous small town. Persons with unusual interests or preferences, who are treated as outcasts or at least oddballs in homogeneous small places, can usually find a group of compatible friends in a heterogeneous metropolis, be they fellow violists or bums or lesbians or sociologists. The large size of a collectivity, be it a city or an organization (Blau and Schoenherr,

[5]For this reason, it is hardly surprising that net in-migration and birth-region heterogeneity in an SMSA are substantially correlated for the 125 cases (.51).

[6]The greater heterogeneity of larger places is illustrated by the findings that SMSA size (log) is correlated .48 with ethnic heterogeneity and .35 with division of labor (detailed-occupation heterogeneity).

1971:63–67), increases the chances of both suitable ingroup and intergroup relations.

Turning finally to internal social mobility, its main macrosociological significance is as the process implementing most structural change. When exogenous conditions engender pressures for social change, processes of social mobility are usually the means by which the change is effected. Not all social mobility is accompanied by a change in population distribution, which is the criterion of changing structural differentiation, but most mobility is.[7] Unless the same number of people move in both directions, the mobility alters the distribution among groups and, thereby, heterogeneity. Whether mobility increases or decreases heterogeneity depends on whether the net migration is from larger to smaller groups or from smaller to larger ones. The definition of heterogeneity in terms of an even distribution of the population among different groups implies the ninth theorem. If heterogeneity depends on the degree to which a population distribution approximates a uniform distribution, it follows that *net mobility from larger to smaller groups increases heterogeneity* (T-9). A corollary of this theorem is that net mobility from smaller to larger groups increases homogeneity.

A few illustrations may give the ninth theorem more concrete meaning. The mobility of farmers to work in factories increased industrial heterogeneity in the nineteenth century, but the same mobility decreases industrial heterogeneity nowadays. The reason is that a century ago the agricultural sector was larger, while now it is much smaller than the manufacturing sector, so that moves of people from agriculture to manufacturing made the distribution of the labor force more even in the nineteenth century and more uneven in recent decades. The movements of the labor force out of manufacturing into various service industries, which we observe now, increases industrial heterogeneity again because it expands several small service industries and shrinks the large manufacturing industries, thereby making the distribution of the labor force among industries more even, the criterion of heterogeneity. If subgroups split off from a larger one, it is equivalent to mobility by the members of the subgroup to new groups, as far as its effect on heterogeneity is concerned. In other words, such splits increase heterogeneity. Thus, growing specialization of jobs and the progressing division of labor increase occupational heterogeneity. When a third party splits off from a major one, political heterogeneity increases. When firms are bought by conglomerates, the heterogeneity of the economy declines and with it, economic competition. When major religious denominations lose members to small

---

[7]So-called exchange mobility, which strictly speaking requires that the same absolute numbers move in opposite direction from the same origins to the same destinations, does not alter the population distribution or the social differentiation indicated by that distribution. However, most social mobility does not involve such equal exchanges but does involve a change in population distribution. Moreover, even mobility that does not alter the shape of a distribution, as exemplified by the circulation of the elite, produces structural changes, which is discussed in the next chapter.

sects, religious heterogeneity increases. Success of ecumenical movements and mergers of denominations decrease it.

Change in Inequality

Status distributions that rest on differences in resources tend to be positively skewed, with the majority of the population below the mean and ever smaller numbers further and further above the mean. (An exception is education in the United States.) There are many poor people and very few very rich ones, many who are powerless and minute fractions in whose hands more and more power is concentrated. However, this is not the case if status is conceptualized purely as relative standing based on percentiles. The percentage distribution of a population is not skewed but uniform because every percentage rank contains necessarily the same number of persons. The number in the 12th percentile is the same as that in the 98th and as that in any other percentile. Percentile distributions ignore how great the difference in resources (or status scores) between two given percentiles is; for example, they ignore whether the income difference between the 5th percentile and the median is $5000 or $25,000, or whether it is a quarter or three-quarters of the average income. Percentile distributions cannot be used to analyze inequality because there are no variations in inequality for these distributions.

The skewness of the status distribution implies that if resources or other status measures are divided into equal intervals, the modal category will be below the mean and the size of categories will, more or less gradually, decline as the values of the measures increase (beyond the mode). For the size distribution to remain roughly the same, it is necessary that upward and downward mobility be about the same in absolute numbers. (Specifically, the number of persons times the number of categories moved must be the same upward and downward.) But if the numbers are the same, the rate of downward mobility exceeds that of upward mobility owing to the size difference. The case is most extreme for the elite, defined as the top category. The risk of downward mobility of elite members is much greater than the chance of upward mobility of others, simply because the elite is such a small fraction of the population. This principle helps explain endeavors of economic elites to secure their positions in perpetuity by acquiring aristocratic titles or emphasizing family lineage as a criterion of elite membership. It can also explain why studies of mobility based on samples of entire populations discover few, if any, persons who have moved up into the elite; whereas studies of elite members find many who originated in lower socioeconomic strata. For other strata above the modal category, the decline in numbers with increasing status produces the same effect, though in considerably milder form; for example, between any two categories above the modal category, the chances of downward mobility are greater than the chances of upward mobility. The only condition under which this is not true is if the size distribution among categories changes substantially. Such a change is precisely what occurred in the American occupational distribution, as professional and technical work expanded and farm work contracted, with the expected result of an excess of upward over downward mobility.[8]

Automation eliminates the most routine jobs because the more tasks have become routinized, the more easily can machines be invented to perform them. Let us optimistically assume that most very routine and, consequently, low-status jobs will have been eliminated in the near future and the laid-off workers will have been retrained and absorbed in occupations entailing higher skills. This would reduce inequality in occupational status. Yet at the same time, it would lower the relative standing of semiskilled workers. The paradox is real. It illustrates the difference in perspective between conceptualizing status on the basis of an independent criterion for scoring it and viewing it strictly as relative standing in a rank order. If everybody poorer than us disappears, for whatever reason, we do not lose anything, with one exception, we lose relative standing.

Changes in inequality are usually precipitated by social mobility, but not always. Differential fertility, as it alters the size distribution, also changes inequality. If lower socioeconomic strata have more children than higher ones, as is generally the case, the resulting change in the socioeconomic distribution of the population increases inequality. A further result may be that the failure of the higher strata to reproduce themselves, owing to their low birth rates, provides opportunities for the offspring of the strata below them to move up in the occupational hierarchy, compensating for the earlier increase in inequality and restoring it to about what it was before.[9] These considerations could explain the apparently contradictory findings of research that there has been much upward mobility in this country for many decades, yet very little decline in economic inequality (except for a short period just before and during World War II; see H. P. Miller, 1966, and Taussig and Danziger, 1976). Immigration to the United States probably had similar short-run and long-range effects on inequality in opposite directions. Immigrants worked disproportionately in low-status and

---

[8]Hauser et al. (1975) have emphasized that mobility research has been too preoccupied with finding measures of mobility that are independent of the marginal distributions of occupations and that more attention should be paid to the larger amount of social mobility that is related to changes in the occupational distribution.

[9]Actually, the middle, not the highest, socioeconomic strata have the lowest birth rates (see, for instance, Blau and Duncan, 1967:371–88). Fertility differences, consequently, foster mobility into the middle and not into the highest strata.

low-paid occupations, so that their influx must have initially increased inequality, but the expanding population raised opportunities for upward mobility that counteracted the initial increase in inequality.

Historically, however, it is internal social mobility that most often translates a need for structural adjustments to new technological or economic conditions into changes in inequality that meet the need. Thus, when technological improvements demanded a literate and otherwise better trained labor force, free secondary schooling enabled large numbers to move up the educational ladder, thereby diminishing inequality in education.[10]

Economists conceptualize changes in inequality, not as the result of moves by people, but as the consequence of transfers of resources from some to others. Any transfer from a richer to a poorer person reduces inequality. But this conception seems unrealistic, unless one refers to employer–employee relations or those between taxpayer and welfare recipient. Although changes in people's socioeconomic positions could be translated as such transfers, doing so involves an artificial and meaningless conception when concern is with inequality in education, for instance. In any case, the sociological conception is that inequality entails a population distribution in a *status hierarchy*—including but not confined to economic hierarchies—and the distribution changes when people move up or down.

How do various movements of people alter inequality? To answer this question, we must remember that the criterion of inequality is a ratio: the expected or mean difference in status or resources for a pair randomly selected from the population, divided by (twice) the expected status or resources of a member of the population. Hence, all mobility of persons below the median has an unequivocal effect on inequality: upward mobility reduces it, as it diminishes the average absolute status distance and increases the average status; and downward mobility increases inequality, as it increases the numerator and decreases the denominator. But the case is not so clear-cut for mobility above the median because down moves decrease and up moves increase both the mean difference in the numerator and the mean in the denominator. Of course, downward mobility from the very top reduces inequality, but the case is not straightforward for the upper-middle strata, nor is it simple to determine where the top ends.

To deal with this issue, we must first answer the question of how a unit increase in a person's income or other status—provided it can be expressed in a ratio scale—affects the operational criterion of inequality, the Gini coefficient. Differential calculus makes it possible to answer this question as well as some

[10]Inequality in education is much less in the average SMSA (.17) than inequality in occupational status (SEI; .32) or in personal income (.49). The values in parentheses are Gini coefficients.

related ones. Specifically, it involves computing the first derivative of the Gini coefficient, taken with respect to X_k (where k is the person under consideration and X her income or other status).[11] This is the computation of the first partial derivative of X_k:

$$\frac{\delta}{\delta X_k} \text{Gini} = \frac{\delta}{\delta X_k} \frac{\sum_i \sum_j |X_i - X_j|}{2N \sum_i X_i}$$

$$= \frac{1}{2N} \left\{ \frac{\frac{\delta}{\delta X_k}(\sum_i \sum_j |X_i - X_j|)}{\sum_i X_i} - \frac{(\sum_i \sum_j |X_i - X_j|)\frac{\delta}{\delta X_k}(\sum_i X_i)}{(\sum_i X_i)^2} \right\}$$

$$= \frac{1}{2N} \left\{ \frac{\frac{\delta}{\delta X_k}\sum_{j \neq k}|X_k - X_j| + \frac{\delta}{\delta X_k}\sum_{i \neq k}|X_i - X_k| + \frac{\delta}{\delta X_k}|X_k - X_k|}{\sum_i X_i} \right.$$

$$\left. - \frac{(\sum_i \sum_j |X_i - X_j|)1}{(\sum_i X_i)^2} \right\}$$

$$= \frac{1}{2N} \left\{ \frac{[(r_k - 1) - (N - r_k)] + [(r_k - 1) - (N - r_k)] + 0}{\sum_i X_i} \right.$$

$$\left. - \frac{\sum_i \sum_j |X_i - X_j|}{(\sum_i X_i)^2} \right\}$$

$$= \frac{2(2r_k - N - 1)}{2N \sum_i X_i} - \frac{\sum_i \sum_j |X_i - X_j|}{2N(\sum_i X_i)^2}$$

$$= \frac{2r_k - N - 1}{N \sum_i X_i} - \frac{\text{Gini}}{\sum_i X_i}$$

$$= \frac{1}{N\overline{X}}(2\frac{r_k}{N} - 1 - \frac{1}{N} - \text{Gini}) = \frac{1}{N\overline{X}}[(P_b - P_a) - \text{Gini}].$$

Let us examine the substantive implications of the final equation. The larger the population, the less effect does one person's mobility have on inequality. The

[11]Definitions of symbols: X is any resource or status measure (e.g., income); i is the ith individual, j the jth, but i and j are not the same individual; k is the individual whose income or status change is under consideration; r_k is this person's numerical rank, which is an integer between 1 and N; N is the number of persons in the population; P_b is the fraction of the population with less income than person k, P_a the fraction with more income than k. The formula used in this calculation for the Gini index is

$$\text{Gini} = \frac{\sum_i \sum_j |X_i - X_j|}{2N^2 \overline{X}} = \frac{\sum_i \sum_j |X_i - X_j|}{2N \sum_i X_i}.$$

higher the average status, the less effect does a one-unit move in status have, which implies that the effect of any change in status on inequality depends on its ratio to mean status. The most important result is that the effect of people's mobility on inequality depends on their percentile rank, specifically on whether the difference between the percentage of the population below and that above them is greater or less than the Gini coefficient. This complex matter requires clarification. For anybody below the median, the difference between the fraction below and that above them is negative, a value that is necessarily less than the Gini coefficient, which cannot be below zero. For anybody below the median, therefore, upward mobility reduces and downward mobility increases inequality, which accords with our earlier conclusion. Although the difference between the two fractions is positive for all persons above the median, it may not be as large as the Gini coefficient. How large it has to be in order to be that large depends on the degree of inequality in the population, because the greater the inequality the larger is the Gini coefficient. In fact, the boundary is located at that person for whom the fraction below is .5(1 + Gini). Thus, the upward mobility of a member of the upper-middle class—say, someone in the 75th percentile of the income distribution—will increase inequality unless there is much of it, in which case it will reduce it (in the example, it will reduce inequality if the Gini coefficient is more than .50). The lower the status of persons who are upwardly mobile a given distance, the greater is the reduction in inequality.[12] Downward mobility has the opposite effects of those of upward mobility, but only if the distances from the median as well as distances moved are identical.

A line can be drawn in every status hierarchy at which the effects of mobility on inequality become reversed. Below that line, upward mobility diminishes and downward mobility enhances inequality; above that line, upward mobility increases and downward mobility decreases inequality. (These statements refer to mobility that does not cross this line.) Where this line is depends on the existing extent of inequality. The greater the inequality, the larger is the proportion of the population below and the smaller is the proportion above the line; in other words, the higher is the point in the status rank order where the line is drawn. Let us call this line the *upper–lower boundary,* to remind us that below it people's status is low enough so that their upward mobility reduces inequality, whereas above it status is sufficiently high so that downward mobility reduces inequality. A theorem about mobility and inequality can be derived from this definition, keeping in mind the considerations leading up to it: *Mobility toward the upper–lower boundary in a status hierarchy diminishes inequality* (T-10). The corollary evi-

[12]Upward mobility may, of course, cross the line below which it reduces inequality and start increasing it again, and the same, mutatis mutandis, is true for downward mobility. No attempt to formulate equations for these complex cases (crossing this line) is made.

dently is that mobility away from the upper–lower boundary intensifies inequality.[13]

Occupational Mobility and Intermarriage

The census source on which most empirical tests in this book are based does not include data on social origins or early careers, which precludes its use for the study of social mobility. Data on occupational mobility and intermarriage are available from another source, however, though only for the United States as a whole and not for SMSAs separately. The relevant information was collected on a representative sample of adult men in 1962. Occupational mobility is based on a matrix crosstabulating father's and respondent's current occupation. Intermarriage in terms of occupational origins of the two spouses is based on a matrix crosstabulating father's and father-in-law's occupation (Blau and Duncan, 1967:496, 511). The 17-category mobility matrix (p. 496) is collapsed into the same 12 categories used in the intermarriage matrix (p. 511). The marriage matrix excludes unmarried men and couples for whom both occupations are not reported, which results in a substantially smaller number of cases than in the mobility matrix. These data are analyzed to ascertain (on the level of occupational groups) whether mobility and intermarriage reveal similar patterns and whether a few underlying dimensions can be discovered that account for these patterns. Since the following analysis is based on the two macrolevel matrixes (and we have not reanalyzed the individual, microlevel data on which these matrixes are based), no attempt is made to infer whether mobile men are the most likely to intermarry, intermarried persons tend to be mobile, or whether the two social processes are entirely independent at the individual level.

The raw data of the 12 × 12 mobility and the 12 × 12 marriage matrixes are in Tables 3.1 and 3.2. In the rows of both tables, respondents are classified by *social origin,* defined as the occupation of their fathers when they were 16 years old. The order is the occupational group's mean status (SEI). In the columns of the mobility table, men are classified by their current occupation in 1962. In the columns of the marriage table, they are classified by the occupation of their wife's father when she was 16 years old. Hence, the criterion of intermarriage is the difference in socioeconomic origins, as indicated by father's occupational group.

As a first step in the analysis, the raw data were transformed into log odds ratios (LORs), the natural logarithms of the ratio of two odds, based on the entries in four cells generated by crosstabulating two rows with the *same* two

---

[13]The theorem is based on the premise that inequality is measured by the Gini coefficient.

Table 3.1
Occupational Mobility: Frequencies

Husband's social origin[a]	Occupation of husband in 1962												
	1	2	3	4	5	6	7	8	9	10	11	12	Total
1 Self-employed professionals	83	158	49	22	54	20	30	21	9	13	10	4	473
2 Salaried professionals	40	388	157	58	93	93	112	147	41	19	10	2	1160
3 Salaried managers	50	320	275	111	104	108	196	93	21	27	7	2	1314
4 Self-employed proprietors	106	390	522	455	259	175	360	248	80	49	32	11	2687
5 Sales workers	37	229	260	149	205	84	162	142	44	28	23	2	1365
6 Clerical workers	28	295	141	64	90	111	195	106	70	35	16	0	1151
7 Craftspeople	62	753	567	469	297	487	1843	1098	323	302	50	23	6274
8 Operatives	46	566	295	345	230	348	1250	1358	311	395	49	49	5242
9 Service workers	13	151	128	103	93	154	341	340	180	102	17	4	1626
10 Laborers	6	124	96	81	80	177	498	582	201	313	27	25	2210
11 Farmers	64	439	421	677	235	447	1871	1946	499	808	1896	405	9508
12 Farm laborers	2	20	30	42	19	37	197	250	78	129	60	98	962
	537	3833	2941	2576	1759	2241	7055	6331	1857	2220	1997	625	33972

[a] Occupation of father when he was 16 years old.

Table 3.2
Occupational Origin Intermarriage: Frequencies

Husband's social origin[a]		Wife's social origin[a]												
		1	2	3	4	5	6	7	8	9	10	11	12	Total
1	Self-employed professionals	22	40	34	66	35	20	73	30	12	6	57	2	397
2	Salaried professionals	57	100	82	132	57	39	207	125	42	26	110	6	983
3	Salaried managers	51	72	107	122	86	72	200	160	60	35	131	2	1098
4	Self-employed proprietors	106	135	102	334	141	85	418	319	108	76	358	11	2193
5	Sales workers	32	69	78	134	128	54	266	151	57	55	130	18	1172
6	Clerical workers	28	53	48	98	62	30	196	129	55	55	142	19	915
7	Craftspeople	73	255	223	358	208	207	1464	1074	226	377	785	77	5327
8	Operatives	44	132	105	244	173	120	997	1313	183	315	800	75	4301
9	Service workers	22	65	64	96	45	54	343	208	93	100	168	24	1282
10	Laborers	24	49	28	72	62	52	273	358	81	297	237	81	1614
11	Farmers	59	166	157	323	151	123	894	895	184	392	4174	219	7737
12	Farm laborers	8	18	12	18	20	12	112	102	23	80	161	148	714
		526	1154	1040	1997	1168	868	5443	4864	1124	1814	7053	682	27733

[a] Occupation of subject's father when subject was 16 years old.

columns (for instance, the 2×2 crosstabulation of Categories 1 and 6). Thus, two of the four cells of each LOR are in the main diagonal and indicate either no mobility or inmarriage, while the other two cells indicate mobility or intermarriage between two occupational groups (in the illustration, between Groups 1 and 6).[14] Every LOR represents the excess of occupational inheritance (or inmarriage) over mobility (or intermarriage) in the comparison of two groups. The results yield a matrix that is symmetric about the main diagonal, one for mobility and another for intermarriage. At this stage, the data do not take into account the population distributions outside the two categories being examined for a given LOR, but the next step in the procedure does take their influence into account. (Our use of LORs is consistent with contemporary log-linear modeling procedures. The entire analysis has been replicated using a more traditional measure for mobility or intermarriage that is based on the ratio of observed to expected frequencies in a cell and thus does take the population distributions into consideration at the outset.[15] Because the results using either procedure are very similar, only those using the LOR are presented.)

The matrix of these LORs for occupational mobility appears in Table 3.3 and the matrix for the marriage LORs is in Table 3.4. The values in the cells indicate how much occupational inheritance disproportionately exceeds mobility and how much inmarriage exceeds intermarriage in the comparison between every pair of groups; they indicate the strength of the barrier to mobility (or intermarriage) between the pair of occupational groups. Thus, for Categories 1 and 6, the LOR for immobility of 2.8 and that for inmarriage of 1.6 imply that the barrier to mobility is greater than for intermarriage between self-employed professionals and clerical workers. The zeros in the diagonal simply reflect the fact that there is no barrier between an occupation and itself. Occupational groups are listed by Duncan's socioeconomic index for occupations, as already mentioned, and the

[14]The formula for the log odds ratio is

$$\ln\left(\frac{f_{ii}f_{jj}}{f_{ij}f_{ji}}\right)$$

where f_{ii} and f_{jj} refer to two different immobility or inmarriage cells, and f_{ij} and f_{ji} to the two other cells in the 2×2 tabulation. The LOR in the sixth row of column one in Table 3.3 thus equals $\ln(83 \cdot 111/20 \cdot 28)$ or 2.790.

[15]The formula is

$$\ln\frac{O_{ij}}{E_{ij}} = \ln\frac{Nf_{ij}}{R_iC_j},$$

where O_{ij} and E_{ij} refer to observed and expected cell values, respectively, R_i to the sum of frequencies in the ith row and C_j to the sum in the jth column. This measure has been criticized because it depends on the marginal distribution it presumably controls and because it is impossible to observe no change in mobility with this measure whenever there are substantial differences in the two marginal distributions (see, for example, Blau and Duncan, 1967:90–97).

Table 3.3
Mobility Log of Odds Ratios

Husband's social origin [a]		Occupation of husband in 1962										
		1	2	3	4	5	6	7	8	9	10	11	12
1	Self-employed professionals	0.000	1.626	2.228	2.778	2.137	2.790	4.404	4.750	4.821	5.771	5.376	6.807
2	Salaried professionals	1.626	0.000	0.753	2.052	1.316	0.451	2.136	1.845	2.419	3.933	4.994	6.771
3	Salaried Managers	2.228	0.753	0.000	0.769	0.734	0.695	1.517	2.609	2.906	3.496	5.041	6.024
4	Self-employed proprietors	2.778	2.052	0.769	0.000	0.882	1.504	1.602	1.976	2.294	3.576	3.568	4.553
5	Sales workers	2.137	1.316	0.734	0.882	0.000	1.100	2.060	2.142	2.195	3.348	4.157	6.184
6	Clerical workers	2.790	0.451	0.695	1.504	1.100	0.000	0.768	1.407	0.616	1.721	3.261	7.474
7	Craftspeople	4.404	2.136	1.517	1.602	2.060	0.768	0.000	0.601	1.103	1.344	3.506	3.679
8	Operatives	4.750	1.845	2.609	1.976	2.142	1.407	0.601	0.000	0.838	0.615	3.181	2.383
9	Service workers	4.821	2.419	2.906	2.294	2.195	0.616	1.103	0.838	0.000	1.010	3.574	3.995
10	Laborers	5.771	3.933	3.496	3.576	3.348	1.721	1.344	0.615	1.010	0.000	3.186	2.247
11	Farmers	5.376	4.994	5.041	3.568	4.157	3.261	3.506	3.181	3.574	3.186	0.000	1.921
12	Farm laborers	6.807	6.771	6.024	4.553	6.184	7.474	3.679	2.383	3.995	2.247	1.921	0.000

[a] Occupation of subject's father when he was 16 years old.

Table 3.4
Intermarriage Log of Odds Ratios

Husband's social origin[a]	Wife's social origin[a]											
	1	2	3	4	5	6	7	8	9	10	11	12
1 Self-employed professionals	0.000	-0.034	0.307	0.053	0.921	0.163	1.802	3.084	2.036	3.789	3.309	5.224
2 Salaried professionals	-0.034	0.000	0.593	0.628	1.178	0.372	1.020	2.073	1.223	3.141	3.129	4.886
3 Salaried managers	0.307	0.593	0.000	1.054	0.713	-0.073	1.256	2.123	0.950	3.470	3.077	6.401
4 Self-employed proprietors	0.053	0.628	1.054	0.000	0.816	0.187	1.184	1.728	1.096	2.894	2.489	5.497
5 Sales workers	0.921	1.178	0.713	0.816	0.000	0.138	1.220	1.861	1.531	2.407	3.303	3.948
6 Clerical workers	0.163	0.372	-0.073	0.187	0.138	0.000	0.083	0.937	-0.061	1.136	1.973	2.953
7 Craftspeople	1.802	1.020	1.256	1.184	1.220	0.083	0.000	0.585	0.564	1.441	2.164	3.221
8 Operatives	3.084	2.073	2.123	1.728	1.861	0.937	0.585	0.000	1.166	1.240	2.323	3.232
9 Service workers	2.036	1.223	0.950	1.096	1.531	-0.061	0.564	1.166	0.000	1.225	2.530	3.205
10 Laborers	3.789	3.141	3.470	2.894	2.407	1.136	1.441	1.240	1.225	0.000	2.591	1.912
11 Farmers	3.309	3.129	3.077	2.489	3.303	1.973	2.164	2.323	2.530	2.591	0.000	2.863
12 Farm laborers	5.224	4.886	6.401	5.497	3.948	2.953	3.221	3.232	3.205	1.912	2.863	0.000

[a] Occupation of subject's father when subject was 16 years old.

LORs in the tables reflect this. The further apart in socioeconomic status two occupational groups are, the more occupational inheritance exceeds mobility and inmarriage exceeds intermarriage between these two groups, as revealed by the fairly regular increases in LORs as one moves away from the main diagonal. The values in Table 3.3 are generally higher than the ones in the corresponding cells of Table 3.4, which implies that the tendency of men to remain in the same socioeconomic stratum as their fathers is stronger than their tendency to marry someone with the same socioeconomic background. What is most impressive, however, is that the patterns in the two tables are so similar. It appears that the processes of social mobility versus immobility and the processes of intermarriage versus inmarriage reflect the same underlying dimensions and are governed by parallel social forces. The barriers to mobility are very similar in form, albeit consistently somewhat more rigid, than barriers to intermarriage.

A brief glance at Tables 3.3 and 3.4 reveals that the average LOR (across a row or down a column) is highest for those occupations at either extreme of the status spectrum. This is not surprising because the greatest barriers to mobility and intermarriage are between those occupations at opposite ends of the spectrum; individuals from the middle occupations cannot experience as extreme forms of mobility or intermarriage and, therefore, the mobility (intermarriage) barriers to or from the middle occupations are less severe. In comparing the pattern of barriers between one category and all others with the pattern of barriers between a second category and all others, we do not want the comparison to be affected by differences in these average strengths of barriers; rather, we want to compare the two occupations' patterns of deviations of barrier strength from the respective occupation's average. Therefore, the LORs are modified by removing row and column effects. Procedurally these deviations can be computed by (1) subtracting the grand mean of all LORs in a matrix from each individual LOR; (2) calculating the average for each row and each column of the remaining matrix (these are the row and column effects); and (3) subtracting the corresponding row effect and column effect from each cell in the result of step one. In summary, our modified LORs are

$$\text{LOR}_{modified} = \text{LOR} - (\text{grand mean} + \text{row effect} + \text{column effect}).$$

Each modified LOR reflects the strength of the barriers to mobility (or intermarriage) between two occupations, adjusted for the overall average barrier strengths of both occupations.

To assess the degree of structural equivalence (White *et al.*, 1976; Burt, 1976) of two occupational categories, we investigate how closely any one occupational category's pattern (vector) of modified LORs with all other occupations resembles the pattern for a second occupation. Two different comparisons between all possible pairs of the twelve occupational groups are analyzed, based on the values of the modified LORs derived from Tables 3.3 and 3.4. For any two occupations, we ask how closely the first's pattern of mobility to and from every other occupation resembles the second's pattern to and from the same other occupations; and for any two, we also ask how closely the first's pattern of intermarriage with every other occupation resembles the second's pattern. In short, we ask what the correlations are between any pair of rows (or columns, since the matrices are symmetric) of the modified LORs derived from Table 3.3 and between any pair of rows (or columns) of the modified LORs derived from Table 3.4.[16]

The correlation matrixes of the modified LORs for mobility and intermarriage are in Tables 3.5 and 3.6. High positive values indicate that the two occupational groups (identified in the row stub and column heading) are structurally quite similar ($r = 1$ implies that they are structurally equivalent), which means that the members of the two groups have similar patterns of mobility (or intermarriage) to the members of the various other occupations. Negative correlations mean that the mobility (intermarriage) links with third occupations are very different for two occupational groups. It is important to note the difference between the data in Tables 3.5 and 3.6, which refer to structural equivalence (similarity), and those in Tables 3.3 and 3.4, which refer only to direct connections between the two occupations in question. Since occupational categories are presented in order of average socioeconomic status, the low values near the diagonal and the high ones far from it in Table 3.3 and especially Table 3.4 show that for occupations close in socioeconomic status, intermarriage is nearly as prevalent as inmarriage, and mobility is not much rarer than occupational inheritance, whereas both intermarriage and mobility are infrequent between socially distant occupations. Tables 3.5 and 3.6 do not refer to these direct links between occupations. Their high positive values near the diagonal and negative ones distant from it indicate that two occupations close in socioeconomic status have similar patterns of prevalent and rare connections, through careers and marriages, to *other* occupations; similarly, the two patterns of connections to various third occupations differ greatly (as indicated by substantial negative correlations) for occupations that are far apart in socioeconomic status. It is this similarity of two groups to third parties that defines structural equivalence, whether or not there are many direct linkages between the two. Nevertheless, the correspondence of the findings in Tables 3.5 and 3.6 with those in Tables 3.3 and 3.4 suggests that social

---

[16]As the matrixes are symmetric, rows and columns (for the same categories) are the same, as are correlations between pairs of them. For the data based on observed to expected ratios (see Note 15), the matrixes are not symmetric—pairs of rows and the corresponding pairs of columns differ and produce different correlations. A single measure of similarity can be computed by stacking the transpose of the matrix of modified logs of observed-to-expected ratios on top of the untransposed matrix (creating a 24 × 12 matrix) and then correlating pairs of columns (which now also contain rows). The results of the analysis of these stacked matrixes are very similar to those reported for the separate analyses of each matrix.

Table 3.5
Correlations between Pairs of Rows of Modified Mobility Log Odds Ratios

Husband's social origin[a]							Occupation of husband in 1962					
	1	2	3	4	5	6	7	8	9	10	11	12
1 Self-employed professionals	1.000	0.768	0.729	0.586	0.746	0.285	-0.789	-0.890	-0.791	-0.885	-0.403	-0.562
2 Salaried professionals	0.768	1.000	0.885	0.520	0.852	0.723	-0.333	-0.692	-0.410	-0.813	-0.799	-0.911
3 Salaried managers	0.729	0.885	1.000	0.773	0.917	0.614	-0.261	-0.737	-0.528	-0.856	-0.798	-0.874
4 Self-employed proprietors	0.586	0.520	0.773	1.000	0.787	0.236	-0.346	-0.716	-0.636	-0.817	-0.435	-0.524
5 Sales workers	0.746	0.852	0.917	0.787	1.000	0.657	-0.423	-0.802	-0.503	-0.884	-0.729	-0.864
6 Clerical workers	0.285	0.723	0.614	0.236	0.657	1.000	0.063	-0.413	0.081	-0.467	-0.722	-0.857
7 Craftspeople	-0.789	-0.333	-0.261	-0.346	-0.423	0.063	1.000	0.724	0.737	0.629	-0.128	0.105
8 Operatives	-0.890	-0.692	-0.737	-0.716	-0.802	-0.413	0.724	1.000	0.771	0.909	0.316	0.603
9 Service workers	-0.791	-0.410	-0.528	-0.636	-0.503	0.081	0.737	0.771	1.000	0.763	0.048	0.159
10 Laborers	-0.885	-0.813	-0.856	-0.817	-0.884	-0.467	0.629	0.909	0.763	1.000	0.501	0.696
11 Farmers	-0.403	-0.799	-0.798	-0.435	-0.729	-0.722	-0.128	0.316	0.048	0.501	1.000	0.830
12 Farm laborers	-0.562	-0.911	-0.874	-0.524	-0.864	-0.857	0.105	0.603	0.159	0.696	0.830	1.000

[a] Occupation of subject's father when he was 16 years old.

TABLE 3.6
Correlations between Pairs of Rows of Modified Intermarriage Log Odds Ratios

Husband's social origin[a]		Wife's social origin[a]											
		1	2	3	4	5	6	7	8	9	10	11	12
1	Self-employed professionals	1.000	0.943	0.845	0.870	0.766	0.646	-0.564	-0.847	-0.403	-0.944	-0.581	-0.826
2	Salaried professionals	0.943	1.000	0.894	0.894	0.681	0.712	-0.377	-0.754	-0.313	-0.942	-0.672	-0.873
3	Salaried managers	0.845	0.894	1.000	0.897	0.703	0.694	-0.254	-0.638	-0.156	-0.903	-0.664	-0.953
4	Self-employed proprietors	0.870	0.894	0.897	1.000	0.640	0.600	-0.379	-0.647	-0.359	-0.903	-0.556	-0.915
5	Sales workers	0.766	0.681	0.703	0.640	1.000	0.689	-0.416	-0.613	-0.305	-0.683	-0.762	-0.657
6	Clerical workers	0.646	0.712	0.694	0.600	0.689	1.000	-0.291	-0.552	-0.003	-0.634	-0.709	-0.700
7	Craftspeople	-0.564	-0.377	-0.254	-0.379	-0.416	-0.291	1.000	0.803	0.625	0.436	-0.020	0.153
8	Operatives	-0.847	-0.754	-0.638	-0.647	-0.613	-0.552	0.803	1.000	0.458	0.756	0.364	0.508
9	Service workers	-0.403	-0.313	-0.156	-0.359	-0.305	-0.003	0.625	0.458	1.000	0.422	-0.174	0.086
10	Laborers	-0.944	-0.942	-0.903	-0.903	-0.683	-0.634	0.436	0.756	0.422	1.000	0.496	0.875
11	Farmers	-0.581	-0.672	-0.664	-0.556	-0.762	-0.709	-0.020	0.364	-0.174	0.496	1.000	0.654
12	Farm laborers	-0.826	-0.873	-0.953	-0.915	-0.657	-0.700	0.153	0.508	0.086	0.875	0.654	1.000

[a] Occupation of subject's father when subject was 16 years old.

Table 3.7
First Three Eigenvectors of Principal Component Analyses of Mobility and
Intermarriage Data

		MOBILITY			INTERMARRIAGE		
		1st P.C.[a]	2nd P.C.	3rd P.C.	1st P.C.	2nd P.C.	3rd P.C.
1	Self-employed professionals	1.522	1.175	0.022	1.212	0.370	0.233
2	Salaried professionals	1.430	-0.014	0.035	0.914	0.170	0.127
3	Salaried managers	1.317	0.074	-0.277	1.208	-0.072	-0.099
4	Self-employed proprietors	0.586	0.299	-0.262	0.901	0.100	-0.115
5	Sales workers	1.122	0.125	-0.050	0.504	0.000	0.312
6	Clerical workers	1.001	-0.638	0.440	0.285	-0.010	0.098
7	Craftspeople	-0.234	-0.587	-0.169	-0.117	-0.266	-0.123
8	Operatives	-0.753	-0.535	-0.202	-0.540	-0.460	-0.299
9	Service workers	-0.418	-0.797	0.154	-0.100	-0.360	-0.040
10	Laborers	-1.333	-0.683	-0.008	-1.252	-0.360	0.054
11	Farmers	-1.563	0.811	0.682	-0.852	0.648	-0.582
12	Farm laborers	-2.675	0.770	-0.366	-2.162	0.320	0.445
	EIGENVALUES						
	Raw	20.869	4.881	1.035	12.192	1.195	0.845
	Percent of total	73.525	17.196	3.646	81.891	8.080	5.673
	Cumulative percent	73.525	90.722	94.368	81.891	89.990	95.592

[a] Principal component

distances among positions defined on the basis of structural equivalence do not differ much from those defined in terms of direct links.

In order to identify structural dimensions that can explain the observed parallels in processes of status attainment and marriage selection, a special form of principal-component analysis (Schwartz, 1977) is performed using the covariance matrixes corresponding to the data in Tables 3.5 and 3.6. The results are in Table 3.7, which crosstabulates the twelve occupational categories and the first three principal components extracted from the separate analyses of mobility and intermarriage, showing the *eigenvectors* (equivalent to factor loadings from a factor analysis) in the cells. As can be seen in the bottom row, the first two principal components account for 91% of the total variance of the modified mobility LORs and 90% for intermarriage. Thus two dimensions can largely explain the social differences among occupational groups that find expression in (low) intergenerational mobility and intermarriage. Using the first two compo-

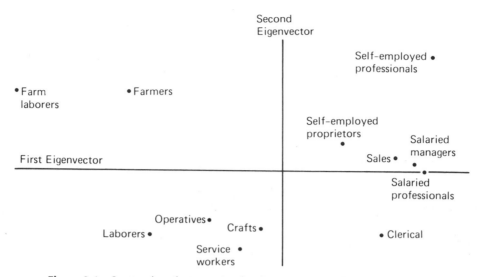

Figure 3.1   Scatterplot of occupation loadings on two mobility eigenvectors.

nents of the mobility and intermarriage analyses, two-dimensional plots of the social positions of the twelve occupational categories are shown in Figures 3.1 and 3.2. The first (horizontal) dimension of each, which is by far the most important (accounting alone for about three-quarters of the variance in modified LORs), primarily reflects socioeconomic status. There is a conspicuous gap between manual and nonmanual workers, and clerks, despite their low salaries and routine work, are unquestionably classified with other white-collar workers on this dimension. There is another large difference between farm laborers and all other occupations in socioeconomic status. Service workers, whose average socioeconomic index is slightly lower than that of operatives, have a higher position than operatives in terms of the distance measures used here, perhaps because service workers' opportunities to meet members of higher strata enable them to help their children's careers and to intermarry more than their education and income lead one to expect.

The meaning of the vertical dimension is not so clear. It cannot refer to self-employment, although the two self-employed occupations have the highest positions, because the position of farm laborers is superior to that of proprietors. It may refer to freedom from supervision and bureaucratic constraints.[17] Manual workers and clerks, who often are employed in large organizations, have the lowest positions on this dimension. Other white-collar workers have intermediate

[17]Laumann (1973:73–82), using different procedures in his analysis of friendship choices classified by occupational group, obtains a quite similar two-dimensional solution. The first is clearly social status. He calls the second *bureaucratic* organization, which suggested our only slightly different idea of freedom from bureaucratic constraints.

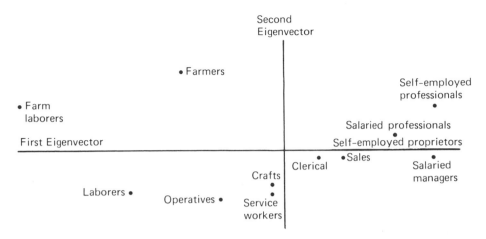

Figure 3.2 Scatterplot of occupation loadings on two intermarriage eigenvectors.

positions, and so have proprietors. Although self-employed, most proprietors are owners of small shops and often strictly controlled by their suppliers. Owners of gas stations and independent cleaners are examples. In any case, proprietors have a somewhat higher position on this dimension than most employees, though not as high a position as self-employed professionals, farmers, and, surprisingly, farm laborers. Perhaps farm laborers are not so different from sharecroppers, who are classified as farmers. Working outdoors may give both of them more freedom than the many subordinate employees in large factories or offices have.

Comparing the locations of each occupation in the two figures shows that the patterns of mobility and intermarriage are least similar for proprietors and clerks. A quantitative indication of the overall similarity of the figures is obtained by correlating occupations' positions on the horizontal axes of the two figures (loadings on both first eigenvectors in Table 3.7) and again correlating their positions on the corresponding vertical axes (second eigenvectors). These two correlations are .96 and .90, respectively. In summary, the main conclusion revealed by the data and figures is that the same underlying social dimensions govern occupational mobility and intermarriage.

Conclusions

Social mobility and intergroup associations are two social processes that link different positions, groups, and classes in a social structure. These links are attenuated by social barriers that inhibit the chances for mobility and for intimate relations between members of different groups and classes. Such conditions weaken the integration of a community or society. Mobility and intergroup relations exert reciprocal influences. Extensive mobility increases the rate of intergroup relations (T-4) because it implies that many members of any one group are simultaneously members of another group (the one where they originated), and they are likely to have associates in both groups. Some of these associates may be introduced to each other by them, and these thereafter may become associates themselves. At the same time, intergroup relations foster mobility (T-6) because having friends in another group or stratum makes it easier to move there. The former theorem rests on the assumption that persons in the same or proximate positions become associates in disproportionate numbers (A-1), and the latter theorem, on the newly introduced assumption that associates in other groups or strata facilitate mobility there (A-3). If mobility between two groups is predominantly in one direction, it alters their relative size, with the result that the rates of intergroup association are based on different denominators, which changes the rates for any given number of associations. The theorem implied (by T-1 and T-4) is that net outmobility raises rates of intergroup relations more than net inmobility (T-5).

Theorems can be derived from the joint implications of two others, as just illustrated, though care must be exercised to avoid long chains of deductions consisting of probability propositions because the other influences implicit in the probability statement or embodied in ceteris paribus are likely to overshadow the influence of the first on the last term in a long deductive chain, and thus to produce a wrong conclusion. But this danger is slight for deductions from only two theorems, provided the probability stipulated by each is substantial. Two of the theorems deduced in the preceding chapter imply, jointly with T-6, new theorems. If heterogeneity promotes intergroup relations (T-2) and intergroup relations promote social mobility (T-6), it follows that heterogeneity promotes social mobility (T-7). If inequality promotes status-distant relations (T-3) and status-distant relations promote mobility across status distances (T-6), it follows that inequality promotes mobility across relatively great status distances (T-8).

Social mobility precipitates structural change and mediates most of the influences of exogenous conditions on changes in the population structure. Thus, new technological or economic or political conditions typically lead to changes in population structures by stimulating intragenerational or intergenerational mobility of people from one social position to another, whether the movements are between firms, neighborhoods, occupations, cities, or social classes. (Only the consequences of mobility for people's distribution in a single dimension are discussed in this chapter; its implications for the relationships between several dimensions of differentiation are discussed in the next chapter.) For any nominal dimension, mobility from larger to smaller groups increases heterogeneity (T-9). For any status continuum, mobility to the upper-lower boundary in the hierarchy reduces inequality (T-10). The upper-lower boundary is the line at which the difference in the percentages of the population below and above it equals the Gini coefficient. The greater the inequality, the higher in the hierarchy is that boundary. Hence, the theorem implies that the upward mobility of upper-middle strata reduces inequality if there is much of it but increases inequality if it is not great already.

The principle underlying the two basic theorems in this chapter (T-4 and T-6) is that intergroup relations and social mobility are closely related. Since no data on social mobility are available for the 125 SMSAs, this principle and the other theorems cannot be directly tested by comparison of the 125 populations. However, the underlying principle can be indirectly tested with data from a published source on occupational mobility and intermarriage for a sample of American men. For this purpose, matrixes of log odds ratios for occupational mobility and intermarriage are generated, and the combined matrixes are then subjected to a principal-component analysis. The findings provide indirect evidence for the claim that mobility and intergroup relations are substantially related because the pattern of intergenerational mobility among 12 occupational groups and the pattern of intermarriage between spouses with the same 12 occupational origins are very similar. Two dimensions account for most of the differences in both mobility and intermarriage among occupations. The major dimension is socioeconomic status. A second dimension is most readily interpreted as freedom from bureaucratic constraints at work, which contrasts both farm workers and self-employed professionals, who are at opposite extremes on the status dimension but similar on the second dimension, with the majority of manual and clerical workers in larger factories and offices.

CHAPTER 4

Crosscutting Circles

The distinctive characteristic of the complex structures of modern societies and their large metropolitan centers is that they are delineated by many lines of social differentiation. Even the structure of simple tribes entails several social distinctions that influence social life. In virtually all tribes examined, Murdock (1949:314–321) found intimate relations to be influenced by age, sex, kin group, ethnic affiliation, social class, and political subdivision. In contemporary societies, social differentiation is not only much more pronounced, as illustrated by the division of labor, but there are also many more lines of differentiation—in religion, political position, industrial sector, place of employment, and formal education, to name just a few.

Simmel's concept of *crosscutting circles* centers attention on these numerous lines of differentiation and their implications. His microsociological focus is on the significance of crosscutting circles for individuals, whereas our macrosociological focus is on their significance for the patterns of social relations in large populations. Of course, crosscutting is not a dichotomy. It varies by degree. Indeed, two variations in degree are implicit in the concept: how little or much lines of differentiation are related to one another, and how many lines of differentiation are crosscutting. The strength of the relationship of two or more social differences can vary from complete independence to perfect association. Strongly related dimensions consolidate social positions and differences, thus reinforcing the barriers to social intercourse. The intersecting social differences resulting from weak relationships of the population distributions along various lines make group boundaries more permeable, status distinctions more easily bridged, and intergroup relations more frequent. Consolidated social differences and positions solidify ingroups and intensify group pressures. Crosscutting social differences put individuals at the intersection of a web of group affiliations that exert diverse and often counteracting pressures, weakening the hold any one group has on its members, widening the options of individuals, and increasing their freedom. More prevalent intergroup relations are an important manifestation of the weaker ingroup pressures owing to crosscutting circles. Intersection and consolidation are opposite poles of the continuum represented by the strength of association of several forms of differentiation, and the use of distinct terms for them is merely designed to emphasize the basic difference in social structure they reveal.

The relationships between various social positions and affiliations of individuals are the prototypical subject matter of sociological analysis. But our concern with these relationships is somewhat different from the usual one. Normally, the interest is in the ways some social attributes of individuals influence their attitudes or achievements, that is, other attributes or positions of theirs. Research on status attainment is a good example, which traces the influences of various background characteristics of individuals on their educational attainments, occupational achievements, and incomes (Featherman and Hauser, 1978). Macrosociological analysis, in contrast, is not generally concerned with attributes of individuals at all but with global characteristics of society, such as the influence of the economic organization on the political system, of religious institutions on the economy, or of the division of labor on social solidarity. While our approach is macrosociological, we *are* concerned with the relationships of people's social affiliations and positions (and analyze processes of status attainment in the next chapter). However, our prime interest in the relationships of various characteristics of individuals within a metropolis is to use them as measures of the degree of structural intersection or consolidation in order to analyze implications of variations in these features of metropolitan structures. This is the topic of the present chapter.

Intersection and Consolidation

Many crosscutting social circles generate *multiform heterogeneity* (the simultaneous differentiation of a population in many dimensions). They produce a complex web of group affiliations, and individuals find themselves at the intersection of numerous groups. This creates cross pressures, which are stressful, but which also weaken the power of a given group to enforce restrictions on individuals, thereby expanding freedom of choice. In the study of small-group networks, the links are the relations between individuals, but in macrosociological studies, the location of persons at the intersection of several groups makes these persons the links that connect the groups (Breiger, 1974). If all kinds of differences among individuals are taken into consideration, there are probably hardly any people, if any, who have the same combination of social attributes, even in a population of millions. Practically, of course, one can only examine a limited number of factors, so that many people are observed at the same intersection of social affiliations. If the crosscutting differences among nominal groups are further intersected by status differences—in education, income, and authority, for instance—and particularly if these status differences are also weakly related to one another, the multiform heterogeneity is still more pronounced. (Generally, various forms of achieved status based on different resources are more closely related than most ascribed group affiliations, but there are exceptions, the most important one in our society being race.)

The complexity of a social structure depends in part on the extent of heterogeneity and diversity—its division of labor, industrial diversity, ethnic heterogeneity, diversity in socioeconomic status—but it depends, in even greater part, on the degree to which various dimensions of differentiation are related. Take two polar extremes (both of which are not really possible): all dimensions of social differentiation among people coincide, and all dimensions of differentiation among them are completely unrelated. In the first case, there is in effect only one dimension of social differentiation and one set of social positions, with the differences and boundaries strongly reinforced by multiple distinctions—in race, income, power, prestige, and so forth. In the second case, there would be a multitude of social positions or roles differing in some way or other, many more than there are people even in the largest societies. The actually observed variations in intersection and consolidation produce similar though less extreme differences. If the dispersion among distinct social positions is the criterion of structural complexity, consolidation decreases and intersection increases it.

Although consolidation of both nominal and graduated social differences reduces structural complexity, its effects on multiform heterogeneity and inequality are in the opposite direction.[1] Crosscutting group differences engender multiform heterogeneity as noted, and consolidated ones, by the same token, diminish overall heterogeneity because many people who share one kind of group membership also share several other kinds; for instance, they have the same national background, religion, and class position. In contrast, the consolidation of several dimensions of status or resources increases, not decreases, overall inequality because people who differ in both education and income are further apart than those who only differ in one of them. Why does the consolidation of several lines of differentiation have opposite consequences for two kinds of differentiation—heterogeneity and inequality? The reason is that heterogeneity refers to unordered categories whereas inequality refers to ordered ones among which a population is distributed. Several dimensions of unordered nominal categories cannot be combined in any meaningful way (how could one combine occupation and place of birth?), but the resources underlying the or-

---

[1]Maximum heterogeneity and status diversity in one dimension entail maximum complexity, but maximum inequality does not because the concentration of resources reduces the extent to which many positions differ, whereas the first two forms of differentiation increase distinctions in positions.

dered categories of several graduated dimensions provide a common standard for meaningfully combining the dimensions into an indication of overall status. Total inequality is greater when people exhibit parallel differences in many resources than when the people who have much of one resource are not the same as those who have much of others. If we assume that all forms of inequality refer to somewhat comparable resources, we can justifiably infer that consolidated inequalities enhance total inequality whereas consolidated heterogeneities diminish total heterogeneity. However, both forms of consolidation strengthen ingroup ties and discourage relations with outsiders.[2]

Multiple intersection exerts compelling constraints to establish and maintain intergroup relations, because many crosscutting social differences imply that most ingroup associates on any given dimension are intergroup associates on some other dimensions. Of course, we can select our friends among those with whom we have several social affiliations in common, but the more we do so, the more we restrict the pool of persons who are similar in still other respects and thereby limit our ability to be selective along these lines. Moreover, social affiliations are not the only factors considered in choosing intimate associates. There are subtle psychological attributes that find expression in falling in love, such as enjoying the same music or sexual compatibility, and while these are affected by social affiliations, they come to exert influences in their own right that further restrain the choices of associates on the basis of shared group or class membership. These limits on opportunities to make ingroup choices do not exist for the majority or, at least, are much less severe if various social differences are strongly interrelated because such multiple consolidation implies that people who have some ingroup in common also have several other social positions in common.

Ingroup prejudice and discrimination may prevent individuals from having any intergroup relations in certain respects, but they cannot prevent intergroup relations in other respects when many intersecting dimensions of social differentiation create structural conditions that make most forms of intergroup relations (though not necessarily all forms) inevitable. No assumption is made that some people have outgroup preferences, although some undoubtedly do, but such an assumption is not needed to explain the existence of many intergroup relations under certain structural conditions. As a matter of fact, the opposite assumption is made, namely, that all people have ingroup biases. Of course, people's in-

---

[2]Correlated differences in two kinds of resources enhance the overall inequality, as is noted in the text, but the conventional measures of inequality fail to take this into account. If the possession of land and the possession of liquid assets are positively correlated, overall inequality of resources is apparently greater than if they are uncorrelated or negatively correlated. However, the Gini index of inequality based on the combination of two resources cannot be greater than the index based on only the more unequal of the two, and it can be that great only if the two are perfectly correlated. This is a limitation of the measure that it shares with most other measures of inequality.

group bias is not equally strong for every group to which they belong, and it is most unlikely that many thousands or millions of people have exactly the same preference ranking for the various kinds of ingroups to which they belong. For some people, religion may be most important, for others education is more significant, and for still others ethnic background is essential. Individuals are entirely free to choose friends and spouses in accordance with their (mutual) preferences. However, multiple intersection implies that their choices in terms of those ingroups that are most important to them tend to involve them in intergroup relations in terms of other dimensions, and unless everyone's first ingroup preference is the same,[3] intergroup relations will be observable in all dimensions if many dimensions intersect much.

Consolidated social differences, in contrast, discourage intergroup relations, even for dimensions for which there is no ingroup bias. The assumption that people do have ingroup preferences (A-1) is not intended to imply that each person is strongly biased in favor of every one of his ingroups. People may have no ingroup feelings for some of their groups, or their slight preference for these ingroups may be so low in their ranking that it is usually overridden by more important ingroup choices. For the sake of an illustration, let us again look at a polar case: everybody has an ingroup preference in only one respect and is completely indifferent to all other social affiliations, but the various lines of social differentiation are perfectly correlated. In this case, all people would have only ingroup relations in all dimensions, even though all of them have no ingroup bias in any but one dimension.[4] Although such an extreme case is empirically impossible, the tendencies it reveals are observable. Given the educational interests and preferences of academics and the substantial relationship between socioeconomic origins and education, especially between extremes, very few academics have friends whose parents were migrant workers, owing not so much to the origin difference as to the educational difference correlated with it. In short, ingroup bias in one dimension contributes to intergroup relations in others (by reducing the sheer number of ingroup members) when many social differences intersect, and lack of ingroup bias furthers intergroup relations little when such differences are strongly consolidated. Independent of individuals' freedom of choice of associates, the social structure governs the patterns of social relations, not only by limiting the opportunities of choice available, as shown in Chapter 2, but also by determining the implications of choices in one dimension for intergroup relations in others.

---

[3]Since one of two parties can prevent an association, it would suffice if the members of the dominant group all have the same ingroup preferences. Thus, if race were the most important dimension for all whites in a society, there would be no interracial associations, although even then there would be intergroup relations in other respects.

[4]In this case it makes no difference whether all have the same ingroup bias or different ones.

The foregoing analysis implies that close relations between people whose social affiliations differ tend to be the result of their having other social affiliations in common. Persons who share professional interests and positions have a basis for friendships that often overrides differences in socioeconomic origins, religion, and ethnic affiliation. Ethnic intermarriage has been explained in terms of the shared religion of spouses (Kennedy, 1944), and increases in it as the result of cultural assimilation after two or three generations in this country (Gordon, 1964). Bumpass (1970) attributes the growth of religious intermarriage to the decrease in socioeconomic differences of religious groups. Another implication of the analysis is that people living in communities with many intersecting social differences have complex *role sets* (R. Coser, 1975), which means that they have many friends outside their own groups. Four dimensions of complexity of role sets can be distinguished: (1) many friends outside one's ingroup in one dimension; for example, the Catholic with many Protestant friends; (2) many friends outside one's ingroups in several dimensions; the Catholic tailor with friends in other religions and other occupations; (3) many friends outside one's group who themselves belong to different groups; the Catholic with both Protestant and Jewish friends; (4) many friends outside one's ingroups in several dimensions who themselves belong to different groups; the Catholic tailor whose friends belong to several different religions and have a variety of occupations. Coser analyzes the tolerance, intellectual stimulation, and flexibility of individuals with complex role sets.

If intersection increases and consolidation decreases intergroup relations, the two should also have opposite significance for the group pressures that discourage intimate relations with outsiders. As mentioned in Chapter 3, the larger the proportion of group members who themselves are closely involved in intergroup relations, the more widespread is the apparent social acceptance in the group of social ties with outsiders. The lesser ingroup pressures to refrain from close relations with outsiders would be expected to further increase intergroup relations. Consolidation, since it reduces intergroup relations, makes such relations more deviant a social practice and thereby strengthens ingroup pressures to abstain from them, which would be expected to have an additional influence diminishing intergroup relations. The inference is that intersection has a multiplicative effect on intergroup relations, increasing them directly and also indirectly by weakening group pressures opposing them. If this is the case, and if the group pressures are reflected in explicit norms, it would indicate how purely structural conditions inherent in population distributions can influence cultural values and norms.

The original formulation of the theorems stipulated that intersection promotes and consolidation impedes intergroup relations (the wording has been simplified; see Blau, 1977: 83–87, 107–109). Empirical tests of the implications of these theorems for intermarriage indicate that they are false and must be revised.

Actually, the revision required is implicit in the analysis leading up to them (in the original as well as here), yet the fact remains that the propositions as formulated are falsified by research findings.

Multiple Intersection and Intermarriage: Empirical Tests[5]

The first test of the theorems is based on the implication of bivariate consolidation or intersection for intermarriage. The bivariate consolidation in an SMSA is indicated by a measure of association between two population distributions. Cramer's V is used for two nominal variables; eta (the square root of the correlation ratio), for a nominal and an interval variable; and the Pearsonian correlation, for two interval variables.[6] Intersection is the reverse or complement of consolidation (one minus the consolidation score). For every SMSA, 10 Cramer's Vs were computed for all pairs of five nominal variables (race dichotomy, national origin, birth region, major industry, major occupation); six Pearsonian correlations, for all pairs of the four interval variables (education, SEI, income, and earnings); 19 etas, for all but one (the exception is occupation and SEI because both are based on occupations) of the relationships between the five nominal and the four interval variables; and four etas, for the relationships of ethnic background (which is a combination of race and national origin) with the four interval variables.

The original theorem implies that consolidated social differences impede intermarriage. The prediction for bivariate consolidation is that it is negatively related to each of the two forms of intermarriage that correspond to the two variables in the consolidation measure. For instance, the strength of the consolidation (eta) between race and the socioeconomic index in an SMSA is expected to be negatively related to both interracial marriage and SEI intermarriage (marriages of spouses with great differences in occupational status). The tests were performed using WLS correlations. The two predictions in this illustration are confirmed; an SMSA's consolidation of race and SEI is negatively related to interracial marriage $(-.27)$ and to SEI intermarriage $(-.32)$. However, the empirical results do not consistently support the expectations. To confine the investigation to independent measures, those involving earnings, which is highly correlated with

[5]The research in this section was carried out in collaboration with Carolyn Beeker and Kevin M. Fitzpatrick. The results are reported, in different form, in Blau et al. (forthcoming).

[6]We also used lambda for two nominal variables and the correlation ratio (eta^2) for a nominal and an interval variable, but the results were so similar to those using the other measures that only those based on the latter are presented.

income, and those involving ethnic background, which is highly correlated with national origin, are eliminated. If the remaining WLS correlations are transformed into z-scores, a test for the combined scores reveals no consistent relationship.[7]

These empirical results fail to confirm the theorem as formulated. But with hindsight it becomes apparent that the formulation erred in simplifying the preceding theoretical analysis. Following Simmel, this analysis stressed that the intersection of *many* social circles is what promotes intergroup relations. Whether two social attributes are closely related or not should make little difference for friendship or marriage because in either case it would not be very difficult to find a person with whom one shares both in a large metropolis with many thousands of people. The theorem must accordingly be revised and retested in its revised form.

The multiple intersection of independent dimensions of social differentiation promotes intergroup relations (T-11). The theorem can be deduced from the assumption that associations are more prevalent for persons in proximate positions (A-1) and from another, which is now introduced as the fourth assumption being postulated: *The influence of every dimension of social differentiation is partly independent of that of any other dimension in a large population* (A-4). Note that it is not assumed that several dimensions cannot have combined or interaction effects on social relations. Nor is it even assumed that individuals never make their choices of others completely contingent on sharing with them a certain combination of several positions—only white Anglo-Saxon Protestants will do. What is postulated is that these combinations vary sufficiently among the members of a large population so that every social difference exerts an independent influence on enough social relations to make it empirically discernible. Although all people may only associate with others with whom they share, say, seven social affiliations, as long as those are not the same seven for everybody, each of the seven is likely to exert an independent influence on social life.

If people associate disproportionately with others in proximate positions (A-1) and if every dimension of positions exerts some independent influence on social relations in a large population (A-4), it follows that many intersecting dimensions of differentiation promote intergroup relations (T-11) because the ingroup tendencies in one dimension produce intergroup relations in others. This is the formal deduction of the theorem. It applies to graduated as well as nominal social differences. Hence, a corollary is that the weaker the concomitant variations of several aspects of status, the more prevalent are relations between status-distant persons. Concomitant variations are indicative of little intersection, which is the opposite of consolidation and thus exerts opposite influences. Another corollary is that the concomitant variations of many nominal and graduated parameters,

---

[7]The Mantel–Haenszel test for the combined z's (based on the formula $\Sigma z / \sqrt{N}$) is .10, which indicates essentially no relationship.

which consolidate social positions, group boundaries, and status distinctions, depress tendencies to maintain intergroup or status-distant relations.

To test the theorem that multiple intersection promotes intergroup (or status-distant) relations (T-11), it is necessary to construct measures of multiple intersection. Such measures should refer to the extent to which a given dimension of social differences in an SMSA intersects with several others there, for example, the degree to which ethnic background intersects with various other group or status differences. All ten variables for which we have bivariate measures of consolidation are used. For each of the ten, the mean for all its bivariate measures of consolidation is computed as a rough indication of multiple consolidation. The indicator is somewhat refined by examining the scale's reliability and deleting any item (bivariate measure) if its deletion improves Cronbach's (1951) alpha by .05. The resulting score, which can vary between zero and one, is subtracted from one to yield an index of multiple intersection. These indexes, the bivariate measures on which they are based, and Cronbach's alpha are presented in Appendix C.[8]

The prediction is that multiple intersection in an SMSA increases its rate of intermarriage. But heterogeneity and inequality also tend to raise intermarriage rates, as the empirical findings in Chapter 2 indicate. To control these other influences, regression analyses of intermarriage rates on multiple intersection and heterogeneity or inequality are performed. Constrained intermarriage rates are used, except in the case of race (for which unconstrained ones are used for reasons explained in Note 17 of Chapter 1). The same substantive factor (such as race or occupation) is used for the three variables—multiple intersection, heterogeneity, and intermarriage—in all regressions but one. The reason for the exception is that we unfortunately failed to construct any measures of the extent to which mother tongue is associated with other attributes, but mother tongue turns out to be a more sensitive indicator of the significance of national descent than whether one parent is foreign-born, the criterion of national origin. As an admittedly second-best alternative, national-origin multiple intersection is used as a proxy for mother-tongue multiple intersection in the regression analysis of mother-tongue intermarriage on mother-tongue heterogeneity and national-origin intersection.

The results of the ten WLS regression analyses are shown in Table 4.1.[9] These

[8]If the variances of Cramer's V were higher than those for eta and r, the mean of the three might produce misleading results, but the variances are actually comparable (see Note 16).

[9]The weight used in this chapter is the number of couples in an SMSA on which the marriage rates are based (e.g., the number both of whom are in the labor force for occupational and SEI intermarriage) because the dependent variables involve several different measures of intermarriage, depending on the variable under investigation (e.g., income differences between spouses adjusted for sex differences in income). In Chapter 2, where *all* intermarriage measures are based on a dichotomy (percentage not inmarried), a more refined weight is used (see Note 19 in Chapter 1). The differences in weights account for minor differences in the coefficients for the same relationships.

TABLE 4.1
Weighted-Least-Squares Regressions of Intermarriage on Multiple Intersection and Differentiation

	b	β	R^2
1 RACE			
Racial intersection	.11	.71	
Racial heterogeneity	.05	.45	.20
2 MOTHER TONGUE			
National-origin intersection	.52	.25	
Mother-tongue heterogeneity	.62	.95	.61
3 ETHNIC GROUP			
Ethnic intersection	.53	.32	
Ethnic heterogeneity	.47	.91	.71
4 BIRTH REGION			
Birth-region intersection	.68	.10	
Birth-region heterogeneity	.76	.94	.86
5 INDUSTRY			
Industry intersection	.83	.19	
Industry heterogeneity	1.79	.38	.20
6 OCCUPATION			
Occupation intersection	1.41	.21	
Occupation heterogeneity	.90*	.07	.05
7 EDUCATION			
Education intersection	.07*	.11	
Education inequality	.83	.70	.43
8 INCOME			
Income intersection	1.06	.25	
Income inequality	1.18	.20	.08
9 EARNINGS			
Earnings intersection	1.05	.22	
Earnings inequality	1.54	.28	.10
10 SEI			
SEI intersection	.76	.42	
SEI inequality	1.24	.32	.31

Note: In all 10 panels, the dependent variable is the indicated form of intermarriage (unconstrained for race and constrained for all others; see Note 17 in Chapter 1), and the two independent variables are multiple intersection and differentiation (heterogeneity or inequality), with respect to the same social attribute. $N=125$, except for race, where it is 124 (excluding Honolulu). The WLS weight is the number of couples on which the SMSA's intermarriage rate is based.

* Not significant at the .025 level (one-tailed); all other coefficients are.

constitute eight independent tests of the predictions because two pairs of dependent variables are so closely related that they cannot be considered independent tests—mother tongue and ethnic background (WLS correlation for constrained intermarriage, .69), and income and earnings (.91).[10] Nine of the 10 indexes of multiple intersection are positively related to intermarriage, and the 10th is also when one other condition is controlled.

Infrequent as interracial marriage is, it is less rare in SMSAs where racial boundaries are intersected by differences in industry, occupation, and other respects, giving many members of different races some similar affiliations, which provide common meeting grounds that increase opportunities for intimate relations to develop. Although the multicollinearity resulting from the high correlation between the two independent variables ($-.79$) shakes our confidence in the finding, it should be noted that the F-test indicates that both regression coefficients are significant far beyond the .005 level. Besides, the simple correlation between racial multiple intersection and intermarriage is .35, whereas that for racial heterogeneity and intermarriage is insignificant (as Table 2.3 shows). This indicates that the multiple intersection of race with other social positions does raise the rate of interracial marriages, owing to the diminished differences between nonwhites and whites entailed by such intersection. The finding that socioeconomic differences between races also lessen the likelihood of racial intermarriage (Table 2.4) lends additional support to the conclusion that racial intersection and intermarriage are positively related, as the theorem predicts.

The second panel of Table 4.1 shows that multiple intersection in national origin (used as proxy for mother tongue) and mother-tongue heterogeneity in an SMSA are both independently related to high rates of intermarriage between persons with different language background. Heterogeneity exerts the dominant influence on intermarriage, but that of multiple intersection is not trivial. While there is some multicollinearity (correlation for the two independent variables is $-.74$), the simple correlation between intersection and intermarriage is substantial (.45). However, the multicollinearity combined with the fact that a substitute for mother-tongue intersection had to be used raises some doubts about the finding. For this reason, the analysis of ethnic background in panel three is especially important. Although its results are not independent of those on mother tongue, as noted, they are free from their limitations. All three variables are based on the same ethnic classification (15 categories, including 3 racial and 12 national-origin ones), and there is no multicollinearity ($r = -.39$). The results indicate that those in panel two are not misleading. Multiple intersection in an SMSA of people's ethnic affiliation with other social attributes increases rates of

[10]In contrast, only one of the 28 correlations for the 8 other dependent variables exceeds .30 (that between birth region and income intermarriage).

ethnic intermarriage considerably, controlling for the strong influence of ethnic heterogeneity on these rates.[11]

The heterogeneity of an SMSA's population with respect to birth region, which is positively correlated with net-immigration (.51), exerts a very strong influence on intermarriage. Since it accounts for 85% of the variance in it, there is not much variance left for which other influences can account. Nevertheless, multiple intersection influences birth-region intermarriage, and while its effect is small, it is significant at the .005 level (one-tailed; $F = 8.5$).

The four factors considered so far refer to ascribed positions that do not change during a person's lifetime, whereas the other six refer to achieved positions that may change. This poses a methodological problem for the measures of intermarriage because the positions of spouses in the early years of marriage, on which these measures are based, are not necessarily the same as the ones they had when they decided to marry, which is the information of interest. The problem is minimal for education, which includes only individuals who have completed their education, and most probably had completed it before marriage or at least knew how much they would complete when they got married. Industry, occupation, and SEI (which is based on occupational status) pose more of a problem because young people often change jobs; nevertheless they usually remain in the same industry and occupation for a few years, and even when they do not, they can usually anticipate rather accurately their own and their prospective spouse's industry and occupation a few years ahead. Income and earnings in 1970 are the least reliable indicators of those at the time of marriage. They are subject to rapid change for young people, and though marital decisions may be more influenced, consciously or unconsciously, by expected future rather than by premarital economic standing, the expectations may turn out to be inaccurate. Moreover, the very wage or salary of one spouse may have a negative influence on that of the other; for example, a wife's higher income or earnings reduce the need for the husband's, and his lower earnings increase the need for hers.

In the average metropolis, four-fifths of the young couples who both work are employed in different major industries, and more than four-fifths belong to different major occupational groups (see Table 2.3, column 2).[12] Multiple intersection of an employee's industry with other social affiliations further increases intermarriage between spouses in different industries, as shown in panel 5 of Table 4.1. Similarly, multiple intersection of differences in major occupational

[11]There is no appreciable multicollinearity in the remaining six regression analyses in Table 4.1 either. The correlation for the two independent variables is $-.55$ for education and less than .30 for all other pairs.

[12]Nevertheless, disproportionate numbers of young married couples—more than chance expectation—are in the same industry and have the same occupation, as we saw in Chapter 2, in accordance with the assumption that ingroup relations are prevalent (A-1).

group with other forms of social differentiation in an SMSA increases the already high proportion of young couples who do not have the same occupation. Although not strong, the coefficients for both kinds of intersection are significant beyond the .025 level (one-tailed).

However, the multiple intersection of educational attainment with other social positions, though in the predicted direction, just fails ($t = 1.62$) to exert a significant influence on educational intermarriage. On the other hand, the three remaining cases in Table 4.1 more clearly support the theorem. The multiple intersection of socioeconomic status with various social affiliations is significantly related to intermarriage. Whether income, earnings, or the socioeconomic index is the measure, the more the socioeconomic differences among an SMSA's population cut across other differences in the population, the greater is the tendency for people whose socioeconomic positions differ considerably to marry. The influence of multiple intersection on intermarriage is most pronounced for the index of socioeconomic status, SEI. Despite the caveat we entered about the questionable reliability of the economic measures, the findings based on them conform to the implications of the revised theorem (T-11) that multiple intersection promotes intermarriage.

Nine of 10 findings, representing 7 of 8 independent tests, corroborate T-11. What accounts for the negative case, the insignificant influence of educational intersection on intermarriage? One possible reason for this finding may be the interfering influence of patronage and nepotism and other personal connections that help some people to get ahead. Multiple intersection of education implies that such positions as occupation, income, and SEI depend only little on education, which suggests that the intersection index reflects the weak influence of merit on advancement. In exploring this conjecture, it is discovered that the correlation ratio between occupation and earnings, possibly resulting from such extraneous influences on advancement (though this is sheer speculation), acts as a suppressor of the influence of educational intersection on intermarriage. Table 4.2 shows that when this factor as well as educational inequality is controlled, multiple intersection has the predicted influence on education intermarriage. With one minor adjustment in research procedure, all empirical tests corroborate the theorem that multiple intersection promotes intermarriage by increasing opportunities for intergroup contacts and, undoubtedly, also by increasing tolerance.

This conclusion assumes that the variations in metropolitan structures observed in 1970 were similar to those in the preceding years when most of the marital choices predicted to be influenced by these structural conditions were made. An attempt to test this assumption with 1960 data from published sources was made, but methodological problems limit the significance of the results. Seven bivariate measures of consolidation could be obtained, and these yielded

TABLE 4.2
Weighted-Least-Squares Regression Analysis of Educational Intermarriage[*]

	b	β	R^2
Educational intersection	.11	.16	
Educational inequality	.87	.74	.44
Eta of occupation and earnings	.11	.12	

[*] All coefficients are significant at the .05 level (one-tailed).

four indexes of multiple intersection.[13] The four measures—for multiple inter-section of race, industry, occupation, and earnings—are presented in the lower part of Appendix C. As can be seen, two of the measures—those for industry and occupation—consist of only two items each after one item was eliminated because doing so improved Cronbach's alpha by .05, and even after these improvements, their alphas are considerably below conventional standards of acceptability. These two are neither reliable indexes nor indexes of *multiple* intersection because each refers only to the intersection of one factor with two others. Despite these misgivings, we present the results of the regression analyses of these two as well as the other two indexes of intersection in Table 4.3.

The more racial differences in 1960 intersect with differences in various achieved positions, which implies that the racial differences in the chances to achieve these positions were comparatively small,[14] the more prevalent racial intermarriage appears to be during the next decade, as indicated in the table's first panel. Similarly, the last panel shows that the intersection of differences in earnings with other social differences in 1960, which implies that other social differences did not restrict earning chances as much as in other SMSAs, increased the tendency of persons with different earnings to marry in the later

[13]The 1960–1970 correlation for the four bivariate measures of consolidation of race with another factor is high (race with industry, .80; with occupation, .96; with education, .95; and with earnings, .95); the two referring to the consolidation of industry with another factor are substantial (with occupation, .55; with earnings, .49); but the 1960–1970 correlation of the consolidation of occupation and earnings is only .18. These are OLS correlations because the large (full-sample) case base in even the smallest SMSAs keeps the standard errors minimal.

[14]Heterogeneity is a necessary, though not a sufficient, condition for consolidation because an attribute of people cannot be related to another in an SMSA unless there is some variance in both. Hence, racial intersection may be indicative of low racial heterogeneity in a place or of a lack of racial differences in other social attributes. The assumption here that it implies the latter is justified, inasmuch as racial heterogeneity is controlled in the regression analysis.

TABLE 4.3
Weighted-Least-Squares Regression of 1970 Intermarriage on 1960 Intersection and
1960 Differentiation

	b	β	R^2
1 RACE			
Racial intersection	.06	.44	
Racial heterogeneity	.01*	.05	.16
2 INDUSTRY			
Industry intersection	.01*	.01	
Industry heterogeneity	1.28	.36	.13
3 OCCUPATION			
Occupation intersection	-.09*	-.07	
Occupation heterogeneity	20.86	.19	.04
4 EARNINGS			
Earnings intersection	.75	.42	
Earnings inequality	.80	.28	.10

Note: See note in Table 4.1.

* Not significant at the .05 level (one-tailed test); all other coefficients are.

1960s. These findings parallel those obtained with the corresponding 1970 structural measures (Table 4.1) and support the causal assumption that the direction is from structural conditions to intermarriage. The indexes for 1960 industrial and occupational intersection reveal no significant relationship with intermarriage in Table 4.3, thus failing to support the assumption about causal sequence, but the reasons may well be methodological. The low reliability of these two indexes is one reason, and another is that each refers only to one factor's intersection with two others, which is not very different from bivariate intersection (or consolidation), and we already know that bivariate measures are not consistently related to intermarriage. Even if the two negative findings for 1960 can be dismissed on methodological grounds, however, the two positive ones can be questioned on such grounds because there is very serious multicollinearity in the racial analysis ($r = -.87$) and some in the analysis on earnings ($-.66$). But two pieces of information lessen the doubts raised by multicollinearity and increase confidence in the findings. Both regression coefficients are significant beyond the .005 level (one-tailed), and the simple correlation of multiple intersection with intermarriage, which is in either case larger than that of the control variable, is substantial for race (.40) and respectable for earnings (.24).

Although the 1960 data give only limited support to the causal assumption implicit in the theorem that multiple intersection promotes intermarriage (T-11), other considerations warrant the assumption that this is the correct direction of causal influence. The 1970 empirical results strongly confirm T-11's implication that there is a positive relationship between multiple intersection and intermarriage when controlling for heterogeneity or inequality, both of which also influence intermarriage. It is virtually impossible to explain these relationships except in terms of structural influences on the marriage of young persons because it is not plausible that the marriage choices of a small fraction of the population could affect the structure of the entire metropolitan population, and neither is it likely that some other factors affect both and produce spurious correlations between them. The only plausible alternative is to assume that the observed empirical relationships are the result of the influences of the larger population structure in a metropolis on the marriage opportunities and probabilities of the young people living there, as implied by the theory.

The empirical results in Table 4.1 and 4.3 also have bearing on another implication of the theory. According to T-3, inequality promotes intermarriage. The empirical investigation in Chapter 2 finds considerable support for the prediction that inequality and status-distant marriage are positively related, but it fails to find such a positive relationship for 1970 income inequality and intermarriage and for 1960 inequality in earnings and intermarriage. The reason is that the influence of multiple intersection in these cases suppresses those of inequality. When multiple intersection is controlled, 1970 income inequality is seen to have the predicted positive relationship with intermarriage (Table 4.1, panel 8), and so is 1960 earnings inequality (Table 4.3, last row).[15]

Multiple intersection has implications for mobility as well as intergroup relations, which can be formulated as the twelfth theorem. If the multiple intersection of lines of social differentiation promotes intergroup relations (T-11) and if intergroup relations foster social mobility along nonascribed dimensions (T-6), it follows that *multiple intersection tends to increase social mobility* (T-12). Since the premises are not deterministic theorems but each stipulates one—presumably strong—influence while recognizing that there are others (though the required ceteris paribus is left implicit), the theorem deduced from it represents a lesser likelihood than the two premises, which the more tentative wording is designed to indicate. But intersection does influence social mobility, which has important implications for structural change.

[15]Three of seven tests of the inequality theorem did not reveal the theoretically predicted positive association with status-distant marriage in Chapter 2. Two of them do so, as we just noted, when multiple intersection is controlled. The same control cannot be performed for the third test that failed to confirm the prediction—the one based on the 1960 socioeconomic index—because no measure of multiple intersection for SEI in 1960 is available.

Structural Change

Social structure has been defined in terms of a population's distributions in various dimensions or the variations among people in these dimensions. The two ways of viewing social differences in a structure are equivalent. Three general forms of structural parameters that have been distinguished refer to three types of variation in a population. Heterogeneity is the variation of people among nominal categories; inequality is the variation among people in terms of a status gradation (or possession of resources); consolidation is the concomitant variation of several kinds of social differences among people, and intersection is its reverse, that is, how closely variations in several respects approximate being orthogonal. Changes in the population among nominal groups, in the distribution of resources or status among the population, and in the degree of intersection of several social differences constitute structural change; developments that do not find expression in any of these three forms are not considered structural change.

How responsive a social structure is to new external conditions and how readily it changes to adjust to these conditions depends in good part on whether closely related social differences consolidate social positions and vested interests or whether intersecting forms of differentiation create countervailing forces that may reduce stability but also enhance flexibility. If numerous differences among people are closely related, it consolidates group boundaries and intensifies class differences. The consolidation of social positions reduces the number and enhances the importance of social distinctions. Intersecting social differences, in contrast, foster conflicting allegiances and contradictory tendencies. They engender a multiplicity of diverse group pressures that diminish the impact of any of them and leave individuals more freedom. No group can command complete loyalty and submission when individuals are at the intersection of many social circles with diverse memberships and with interests that are not identical.

Structural mobility, which involves a change in a population distribution, is often distinguished from *exchange mobility,* which involves circulation within an unchanging distribution. When increasing numbers of the American population remain in school longer and raise their educational attainment, the intergenerational educational mobility alters the educational distribution of the population, which exemplifies structural mobility. On the other hand, if some people increase their wealth while others lose theirs without any change in the overall distribution of wealth, it illustrates exchange mobility, which is sometimes held not to involve structural changes. But in our terms, it does. Once one looks not merely at a single dimension but at many dimensions of population distributions, it becomes obvious that mobility never involves simultaneous changes of all people on all dimensions. Hence, even exchange mobility alters the relationships between various dimensions of social differentiation. The circulation of the elite is a pure case of exchange mobility in terms of power, but it changes the relationships of power to social origins, education, often ethnic background, and various other factors. In short, even when exchange mobility does not alter the distribution in any given dimension, it usually changes the degree to which various dimensions are interrelated or intersect, which is a most important form of structural change.

Accordingly, social mobility leads to structural change of one kind or another, although not all structural change depends on social mobility, as the illustration of the changes produced by differential fertility in Chapter 3 indicates. It is not entirely clear how one should conceptualize the causal nexus between mobility and change. One perspective is that a change in available positions produces mobility. For instance, the decline in available farm jobs led to mobility to urban jobs. An alternative perspective is that mobility changes the distribution of people among positions. In this view, the mobility from farms to factories created the altered occupational distribution of the labor force. In a sense, these are merely two ways of looking at the same phenomena. Yet it is advantageous to conceptualize the sequence of influences unambiguously, and at the same time, to distinguish causal influences from processes that not so much cause but entail a change in structure. In these terms, one can think of a change in labor demand, which in turn results from exogeneous technological and economic developments, as the stimulus that produces mobility; and the resulting social mobility entails structural change, whether it redistributes people among positions or alters the intersection of various distributions or does both. A 13th theorem is implicit in these considerations.

Intersecting lines of differentiation further structural change (T-13). The theorem is deducible from T-12 and the foregoing conception of mobility. If intersection promotes social mobility (T-12) and if social mobility entails structural change, it follows that intersection furthers structural change (T-13). Although the first premise is already the second link in a deductive chain, the second is an analytic proposition essentially defining a concept and thus deterministic, which compensates for the weaker other link. Intersection is viewed not as the ultimate cause of change but as its catalyst that makes the social structure more adaptable to new exogenous conditions by fostering mobility that adjusts the structure to these conditions and implements change in it. A corollary of T-13 is that consolidation engenders rigidities and resistance to change in the social structure.

Social mobility increases the consolidation of various lines of differentiation (T-14). This surprising theorem that seems to conflict with T-13 and especially T-12 and that certainly counteracts the influences they specify is logically implied by the first and third assumption. If people predominantly associate with others in proximate positions (A-1) and if associates in other groups or strata facilitate mobility there (A-3), people are most likely to move in one dimension to social positions where they have many ingroup members in other dimensions. If German Jews have to move to a new location, they are likely to look for a suburb or neighborhood where many German Jews live. Persons born and raised in the South are more likely to find jobs in firms where other Southerners work than in other firms. The chances of upward mobility into executive positions in major corporations are improved by going to an ivy league college, at least in part because many executive positions in large corporations are occupied by persons who are also alumni of these colleges. The many Irish on the police force in numerous large cities make careers as police officers especially attractive to large numbers of Irish.

All these moves involve going from combinations of positions that are rarer to combinations that are more frequent, thereby reducing intersection and increasing consolidation. These processes of mobility are reinforced by others that rest on the convertibility of resources. Resources of one kind can often be used to acquire resources of another kind, so that one aspect of status influences another status dimension. The best educated children in the working class are most likely to achieve a socioeconomic status superior to that of their parents. Those officials in positions of high political authority who command little wealth are most likely to lose their exalted political position. These moves, if occurring in sufficient numbers, also make people more alike on several dimensions than they were before and thus strengthen consolidation. Since intersection and consolidation are complementary, a corollary of T-14 is that social mobility reduces the degree of intersection in the social structure.

This result, implying a counteracting feedback loop, was not anticipated but arrived at by tracing the implications of the assumptions initially postulated. Intersecting lines of differentiation make the structure more responsive to new external conditions and further social mobility and structural change, but the most likely social mobility seems to diminish intersection and thus make the social structure more resistant to further change. To be sure, social mobility necessarily involves changing to an unfamiliar environment, and it is often stimulated by an interest in escaping one's old surroundings. Thus, mobility often entails deliberate efforts to change one's old group or class, and it not infrequently involves trying to change several social positions. Yet moving to new surroundings is easier if people there have some social affiliation in common with the prospective mover, and adjustment to the new situation after having moved typically involves finding associates with whom one shares some social attributes. It is this reasoning that underlies the assumption that associates in other groups facilitate mobility there (A-3) and the implication derived from it that people's mobility is more likely to increase than to decrease the consistency of their social positions (implicit in T-14).

In today's interdependent world, many external conditions and dynamic developments impinge on social structures and demand internal adjustments. But it appears that social structures have self-regulating mechanisms that not only restore equilibrium but also channel the changes that occur in the course of adjustment in directions that make the structures more resistant to further change. These stabilizing mechanisms are, of course, a conservative force that protects the status quo. Rarely do pressures build up so much that they erupt in revolutions to counteract these conservative tendencies.

Roots of Consolidated Metropolitan Structures

The importance of consolidated lines of differentiation for resistance to social change makes it desirable to try to discover whether there is an underlying dimension of overall consolidation that accounts for many of the specific forms of consolidated differences and to find what conditions in a metropolis govern consolidation. For this purpose, we analyzed 46 bivariate measures of association within SMSAs (listed in Table 4.4). Fifteen of these are Cramer's V's, referring to the association between two nominal variables in an SMSA; 26 are etas, referring to the association between a nominal and an interval variable; and five are Pearsonian correlations, referring to two interval variables.[16]

The basic substantive question arises as to whether our focus should be on identifying those attributes that have the highest level of consolidation or on those attributes whose consolidation varies extensively across SMSAs. The distinction between these two approaches can be readily seen by comparing the first two columns of Table 4.4. The first column shows the average level of each form of bivariate consolidation. Clearly, consolidation is greatest, though far from perfect, for the central stratification variables of education and occupation (both SEI and major occupational category). It is also very high for the consolidation of sex with both industry and occupation, indicating substantial sex segregation in the job market despite negligible sex differences in SEI. These same attributes are substantially consolidated with earnings and total personal income. At the other extreme, the consolidation of several pairs of ascribed characteristics—such as race and sex—is very low, as one would expect.

The pairs of attributes that exhibit the highest average levels of consolidation do not necessarily exhibit the most variability across SMSAs. The second column of Table 4.4 shows the standard deviation of each form of bivariate consolidation for the 125 SMSAs. In fact, there is little variation in the consolidation of achieved characteristics: the high levels of consolidation are relatively invariant

---

[16]The present analysis is based on three different types of scales—Cramer's V, eta, and r. There is little doubt that eta and r are comparable. In exploring whether Cramer's V, despite varying between zero (for two independent variables) and one (for perfectly associated variables), might have inherently higher (or lower) values or variance than eta and r, we found that it seems to have the same or slightly higher values and the same or somewhat less intrinsic variance. This implies that the conclusions we are about to report are, if anything, conservative. (See Addendum to Chapter 5 for further discussion of the comparability of Cramer's V to r and eta.)

TABLE 4.4

Means, Standard Deviations, and Factor Loadings of Measures of Bivariate Consolidation

Measure of consolidation

Attribute	with Attribute	Mean	Standard deviation	Factor loading
Sex	Race dichotomy	.032	.013	.04
Sex	National origin	.045	.016	-.17
Sex	Birth region	.045	.021	.35
Sex	Industry	.410	.056	1.57
Sex	Occupation	.519	.031	1.14
Race dichotomy	National origin	.200	.118	-4.60
Race dichotomy	Birth region	.250	.114	-1.18
Race dichotomy	Industry	.094	.075	6.89
Race dichotomy	Occupation	.249	.128	12.35
National origin	Birth region	.106	.031	1.26
National origin	Industry	.094	.030	-.09
National origin	Occupation	.099	.031	-.11
Birth region	Industry	.098	.028	.25
Birth region	Occupation	.102	.021	.44
Industry	Occupation	.404	.024	.13
Sex	Education	.036	.024	-.28
Sex	SEI	.042	.035	.57
Sex	Personal income	.346	.043	-1.72
Race dichotomy	Education	.136	.105	9.50
Race dichotomy	SEI	.178	.119	11.58
Race dichotomy	Earnings	.102	.060	5.76
Race dichotomy	Personal income	.097	.059	5.69
National origin	Education	.186	.081	-4.02
National origin	SEI	.146	.057	-.95
National origin	Earnings	.124	.044	-.33
National origin	Personal income	.099	.040	.41
Birth region	Education	.203	.060	2.20
Birth region	SEI	.176	.048	2.03
Birth region	Earnings	.108	.031	.58
Birth region	Personal income	.099	.032	1.07
Ethnicity	Education	.262	.079	3.50
Ethnicity	SEI	.251	.094	8.15
Ethnicity	Earnings	.167	.052	3.65
Ethnicity	Personal income	.146	.055	4.34
Industry	Education	.390	.040	.46
Industry	SEI	.437	.048	1.22
Industry	Earnings	.247	.053	-.11
Industry	Personal income	.236	.049	.19
Occupation	Education	.602	.029	.17
Occupation	Earnings	.419	.032	.10
Occupation	Personal income	.415	.030	.29
Education	SEI	.598	.033	.83
Education	Earnings	.302	.046	1.63
Education	Personal income	.339	.037	1.00
SEI	Earnings	.339	.035	1.06
SEI	Personal income	.339	.034	1.18

across SMSAs. Similarly, most forms of consolidation of sex with another attribute are relatively invariant. The greatest variation among SMSAs involves the consolidation of race with other attributes, both achieved and ascribed (except sex). The consolidation of ethnicity, which is a combination of race and nativity, with the achieved characteristics also varies considerably among cities.

For purposes of descriptive analysis, one might well focus on the level of consolidation in SMSAs. In principle, this might lead one to conduct a separate factor analysis of the 10 or 11 attributes for each of the 125 SMSAs in order to identify underlying dimensions of consolidation. The degree to which a small number of factors could account for most of the variances of the attributes would be indicative of the extent of consolidation in a particular SMSA. The ratio of common variance to total variance would be an alternative indicator. A practical problem of this approach involves the use of nominal attributes with three or more categories in a factor analysis because etas and especially Cramer's V's are not Pearsonian correlations (the usual input to a factor analysis). Yet, even ignoring this practical problem, the information in the first column of Table 4.4 enables us to confidently anticipate that the primary dimension of consolidation is centered around the traditional stratification variables of education, occupation, and income; sex would either be part of this same cluster or would be at the center of a second dimension of consolidation. Given the high levels of these forms of consolidation and the relative lack of variability among SMSAs, we would expect this pattern to be repeated in virtually every SMSA in the country. While this is certainly of interest as a phenomenon of American society, it is not the most appropriate focus for a comparative analysis of SMSAs.

Comparative macrosociological analysis must concentrate on those SMSA characteristics that vary most. In the extreme, multivariate analysis cannot assist in the elaboration of either antecedents or consequences that do not vary: invariant structural characteristics cannot account for differences in intermarriage rates. Conversely, those forms of consolidation that vary most are likely to be most successful in accounting for differences in intermarriage rates. Accordingly, our primary goal is to identify underlying dimensions that might account for variability among SMSAs in consolidation. From this *explanatory* perspective, the high levels of consolidation among the achieved stratification variables are likely to appear less consequential than the more variable forms of race consolidation (see Column 2 of Table 4.4.). Although metropolitan structures vary much more in some respects than others, they nonetheless differ substantially in most conditions, as the next chapter shows.

These considerations led to the decision to perform a factor analysis based on the 125 SMSAs, with each item measuring the consolidation between two social attributes of individuals within an SMSA. But does this procedure not ignore the extent to which various social differences among people within each SMSA are interrelated, because it only examines differences among SMSAs? One's first reaction is to give an affirmative answer to this question, but on second thought one realizes that the problem is not so simple. The items are, after all, measures of association between two social attributes of individuals in SMSAs. If a factor analysis of these items (each referring to the nexus between two variables within an SMSA) would show that items that load highly on an important factor have one variable in common, it would indicate that this variable—say, people's eye color—distinguishes SMSAs where it is strongly related to other attributes of individuals from those SMSAs where it is weakly correlated to them. Of course, we must not commit the ecological fallacy and infer from these loadings that most people with similar eye color necessarily have all these other attributes also in common. The only thing the high loadings would demonstrate is that eye color is much more highly related in some SMSAs than in others to a variety of social attributes of individuals, though it may not be the same individuals for whom it is strongly related to occupation or to education or to income. But this suffices for macrosociological analysis, which is interested in the extent to which certain social attributes are consolidated with (related to) a variety of others in a popula-tion, regardless of whether (to return to the illustration) the same individuals' eye color is related to various social characteristics of theirs or whether the multiple consolidation results from the strong relationships of some individuals' eye color with their education, other persons' eye color with their occupation, and still others' with their income. The latter as well as the former is indicative of a consolidated structure.

A maximum likelihood factor analysis of the 46 items (within-SMSA bivariate consolidation measures) was performed, using the covariance rather than the correlation matrix. Basing the analysis on a covariance matrix has the advantage that the factors take the variance of items into account: that is, they are most influenced by those consolidation measures that differ substantially among SMSAs. (This, of course, requires that the items be measured on comparable scales—see Note 16.)

The factor analysis reveals one dominant factor. (Its factor loadings are shown in the last column of Table 4.4.) We started by using 11 factors, then reduced them to six, and then to two. The first factor remained essentially the same (whereas some of the others changed), and it always explained more than two-fifths of the total variance. The second factor accounted for only one-tenth of the total variance even in the two-factor model, and its loadings did not convey a clear idea of the substantive dimension it represents. It was, therefore, decided to restrict the analysis to the first factor,[17] the meaning of which is unequivocal. It represents the significance of race for various achieved positions, and it accounts for 44% of the total variance in 46 forms of bivariate consolidation among

[17]The analysis is based on the single-factor model, though this actually makes no difference because this single factor is correlated 1.00 with the first factor in the two-factor model.

TABLE 4.5
Regression Analysis of Consolidation Factor[*]

	b	β	R^2
Percentage nonwhite	48.02	.62	
South	5.10	.36	.90
Percentage foreign stock	-5.98	-.10	

Note: The analysis is based on 124 SMSAs, excluding the outlier, Honolulu.

[*] All coefficients are significant at the .005 level (one-tailed).

SMSAs. Six of the seven highest loadings involve measures of association of race with each of the achieved positions (industry, occupation, education, income, earnings, and SEI), and the seventh is the eta for ethnic group (which is a combination of race and national origin) and SEI.[18] Since most consolidation measures with high loadings on the dominant factor have one variable (race) in common, the factor can be considered to refer to multiple consolidation of race within SMSAs. Specifically, the factor indicates the variations among SMSAs in the extent to which racial differences are consolidated by various socioeconomic differences within a metropolis. This constitutes the major underlying dimension of consolidation that distinguishes SMSAs. Whether the same blacks or different ones experience the various disadvantages, which we cannot tell from the data, does not affect the conclusion that the strength of the influences of race on various achieved positions is the source of most variation in structural consolidation among large metropolitan areas in the United States.

What conditions in a metropolis are at the roots of the consolidation and rigidity of its social structure? To answer this question, a regression analysis of the estimated factor scores on several demographic characteristics of the 125 SMSAs was carried out (based on OLS; see Note 13). The results are in Table 4.5. It shows that three metropolitan conditions influence overall consolidation and account for 90% of the variance in the factor scores (and thus for about two-fifths of the total variance [.44 × .9]). Since the factor refers largely to racial

[18]The importance of race for consolidation emerges from the analysis and does not result from race being more often than other variables represented in the consolidation measures that constituted the input of the factor analysis. It is a conclusion (not an artifact) that racial consolidation is most important for explaining the variation in consolidation among SMSAs. If we were to compare various forms of consolidation within SMSAs, the results would not be the same. For instance, sex is generally more highly consolidated with income than race is, but the degree of sex-income consolidation varies little among SMSAs.

consolidation, it is hardly surprising that an SMSA's racial composition exerts most influence. The percentage who are nonwhite in an SMSA accounts for most of the variation in consolidation. This is not the result of the larger proportions of nonwhites in Southern SMSAs and the more consolidated structures of these SMSAs because location in the South is controlled in the analysis.[19]

As the proportion of a racial minority in a metropolis increases,[20] their chances for achieving social positions that are comparable with those of the white majority group decrease in the North as well as in the South. A number of previous empirical studies observed parallel relationships between the relative size of racial minorities and the discrepancy between their and the white majority's occupational positions and incomes (Turner, 1951; Blalock, 1956; Brown and Fuguitt, 1972; Frisbie and Neidert, 1977). These results have usually been interpreted in terms of discrimination, which increases as the growing proportion of minority members infringes more and more on the socioeconomic opportunities of the majority. Blalock (1967) suggests two reasons for the greater discrimination in places with larger racial minorities. There is more economic competition if the minority constitutes a growing portion of the population, and their larger number poses an increasing power threat to the majority. These are plausible theoretical interpretations, although Blalock (1967:154–173) notes that it is difficult to obtain evidence that can distinguish between them. Our data indicate that the size of the nonwhite minority in an SMSA not only adversely effects their opportunities to achieve comparable positions with whites but also, as a result, increases the extent to which various dimensions of social position are interrelated, which consolidates and rigidifies the metropolitan structure. The presence of many nonwhites raises the consolidation of racial differences with various other social differences, which in turn increases the consolidation of some of the other differences with one another. An indication of this is that several bivariate measures of consolidation that do not include race (such as the etas for education and birth region, and SEI and birth region) have high loadings on the consolidation factor which is largely grounded in racial differences.

The racial composition of a metropolis exerts a dominant influence on its social structure. To the degree that SMSAs vary in consolidation, race largely determines whether differences among people are strongly related, consolidating social distinctions and positions, inhibiting intergroup relations and mobility, and diminishing the flexibility of the social structure and its ability to adjust to

[19]Though the Southern SMSAs and the percentage of nonwhites are substantially correlated (.66), we are still able to determine that each has an independent effect.

[20]Nonwhites are in the minority in 124 of the 125 SMSAs, the exception being Honolulu (which is excluded from this analysis and all others involving race because it is an outlier). The strong correlation of percentage nonwhite and the consolidation factor implies that racial heterogeneity is also strongly correlated with it. Indeed, the correlation of this factor with detailed-race heterogeneity is .71 and that with the race-dichotomy heterogeneity is .73.

new conditions. Whatever may have happened since 1970, at that time there was little evidence of any declining significance of race in our society.[21] But the racial composition of a metropolis is not the only condition that affects the consolidation of its structure. Independent of its racial composition, a metropolis' location in the South also exerts a substantial influence on its consolidation, as Table 4.5 shows. There is undoubtedly more discrimination against blacks in the South than in other regions, but the finding may also reflect the stronger conservativism and resistance to change in Southern places.

The final variable in Table 4.5 shows that the proportion of persons of foreign stock in an SMSA lessens its consolidation.[22] Although the influence of this factor is not strong (it adds only one percent to R^2), it is unquestionably significant, and it helps to explain other influences. White ethnic minorities are much less discriminated against than racial minorities. To be sure, immigrants tend to be a disadvantaged group who often occupy low socioeconomic positions, but "their children—the second generation—enjoy somewhat greater economic success than men born to native parents" (Featherman and Hauser, 1978:438). The proportion of white ethnic (foreign stock) minorities and that of racial (nonwhite) minorities are inversely correlated ($-.39$). One might say that a metropolitan economy needs only one or the other disadvantaged group to fill its menial jobs. A possible reason that SMSAs with small racial minorities have less consolidated structures than others is that their predominant minorities are white ethnics who are not so strongly discriminated against. The proportion of the population of foreign stock in Southern SMSAs is small ($r = -.51$), which partly explains the high consolidation in Southern SMSAs, not only because the second-generation has relatively high rates of mobility but also because many persons of foreign stock create a diverse cosmopolitan situation. Controlling foreign stock reduces the influence of Southern location on consolidation without by any means suppressing it completely.

The theory, specifically T-11, implies that structural consolidation that is primarily rooted in the significance of racial differences for other social differences should inhibit racial intermarriage. The empirical data confirm this prediction. The simple WLS correlation between the consolidation factor and racial intermarriage is $-.42$, and controlling racial heterogeneity raises the regression coefficient further, as Table 4.6 shows.[23] Since the factor is assumed to represent the major form of metropolitan consolidation, it would be expected to

[21]Reference is, of course, to the title of Wilson's book (1978).

[22]Foreign stock includes foreign-born and second-generation, even if only one of the two parents is foreign-born.

[23]The WLS regression analysis uses the racial dichotomy, the unconstrained intermarriage measure, and 124 SMSAs (excluding Honolulu). There is some multicollinearity but it is not excessive (the correlation of the two independent variables is .73). The regression coefficient for the consolidation factor is significant far beyond the .0001 level ($F = 34.5$), the simple correlation is pronounced, and it is substantially higher than that of the other independent variable, racial heterogeneity.

TABLE 4.6
Weighted-Least-Squares Regression of Intermarriage on Consolidation Factor and Differentiation[*]

	b	β	R^2
1 RACE DICHOTOMY[a]			
Consolidation factor	-.0015	-.67	.23
Racial heterogeneity	.0449	.35	
2 ETHNIC GROUP			
Consolidation factor	-.0056	-.39	.77
Ethnic heterogeneity	.3945	.77	
3 INCOME			
Consolidation factor	-.0043	-.30	.10
Income inequality	1.351	.23	
4 EARNINGS			
Consolidation factor	-.0046	-.26	.12
Earnings inequality	1.598	.29	
5 SEI			
Consolidation factor	-.0034	-.30	.22
SEI inequality	1.494	.39	

[*] All coefficients are significant at the .01 level (one-tailed).

[a] Based on 124 SMSAs (excluding Honolulu) and using unconstrained measures of intermarriage.

influence other forms of intermarriage, not only racial intermarriage. Indeed, this is the case, as the regressions in Table 4.6 (Panels 2–5) indicate. When differentiation is controlled (as well as when it is not), structural consolidation is negatively related to ethnic intermarriage and to status distance between spouses with respect to income, earnings, and socioeconomic status (SEI). To be sure, the consolidation factor is not significantly related to all forms of intermarriage, nor should it be because numerous bivariate consolidation measures do not have high factor loadings. It primarily refers to the consolidation of racial differences with various achieved positions, and it accordingly has the strongest negative influence on racial intermarriage.

Conclusions

Simmel's concept of crosscutting social circles refers to the fact that people in modern societies belong to numerous groups that have, at least partly, different memberships; hence, individuals are at the intersection of a complex web of group affiliations. The basic principle—which can be applied to status gradations, such as income, as well as nominal groups, such as race—refers to the extent to which various kinds of social differences are independent of one another. We have distinguished two opposite extremes: complete intersection, when two or more dimensions of social positions are orthogonal, and complete consolidation, when two or more exhibit perfectly concomitant variations. Actually, the strength of the relationships of various social differences is a matter of degree between these polar extremes, and intersection and consolidation are merely different perspectives for looking at the same phenomenon, which is the extent to which several factors are interrelated. As intersection increases, consolidation simultaneously decreases, and vice versa. The empirical indicator of bivariate consolidation is a correlation or other measure of association, while the complement of a measure of association indicates intersection. Multiple consolidation and intersection are estimated by averaging several bivariate measures.

A series of empirical tests of the hypothesis that bivariate intersection encourages intermarriage did not find evidence supporting it. A revised theorem was formulated that had already been implicit in the theoretical discussion. It specifies that multiple intersection is the factor that promotes intermarriage. Eight independent empirical tests of this theorem corroborate it. The data also show that inequality leads to status-distant marriages, a theoretical prediction that was not consistently observed in Chapter 2 because this influence of inequality is sometimes concealed by intersection (or lack of it) and becomes apparent only when intersection is controlled. There are good rational grounds for accepting the assumption about causal direction implicit in the intersection theorem, but the 1960 data from published sources used in an attempt to test this assumption turned out to be too weak to supply convincing support for it.

Social mobility entails structural change, and multiple intersection, by promoting mobility, tends to foster structural change. However, the social mobility involved in structural change appears to have a feedback effect that reduces intersection. If these inferences are correct, they suggest that social structures have self-regulating feedback mechanisms that limit the effects of new exogenous conditions and the reciprocal influences of internal conditions, thereby maintaining a slow pace of structural change by directing the changes that do occur—in the distribution of resources among people or of people among social positions—in ways that tend to strengthen structural consolidation and limit the rate of change.

The last question raised in the chapter is whether there exists an overall dimension of structural consolidation that distinguishes American SMSAs. Factor analysis of all available bivariate measures of consolidation yields one dominant factor that refers to such a dimension. It reflects primarily the extent to which racial differences are related to differences in various kinds of achieved positions, such as occupation, socioeconomic status, and income. The most important condition in a metropolitan area influencing this consolidation dimension is its racial composition. The larger the proportion of nonwhites, the higher is the degree of such consolidation in all regions of the country. Racial consolidation, in turn, exerts a pronounced negative influence on the likelihood of interracial marriage. In sum, the significance of race for achievement is the major factor that differentiates more consolidated and rigid metropolitan structures from more flexible ones with intersecting lines of social distinctions.

CHAPTER 5

Process and Structure

The macrosociological theory and the empirical tests of its major theorems presented in the preceding chapters analyze how the structural conditions existing in a metropolis, a society, or any other large collectivity generally influence intermarriage and intergroup relations. Implicit in this analysis is the assumption that there are variations in social structure, even among the communities in the same society; for unless structural features vary, they cannot account for differences in intergroup relations. So far we have taken these variations in structural features among metropolitan areas as given and not asked what produces them; for example, what produces the degree of income inequality or the consolidation of education and earnings in a community. The structural parameters of a metropolis—the various forms of heterogeneity, inequality, and consolidation–intersection—have been treated as given exogenous conditions whose consequences for social relations are analyzed but whose antecedents and interrelations are not further investigated. However, social conditions taken as the givens—the exogenous variables—on one level of structural analysis can become the phenomena to be explained on another level.

Social structures constitute nested series of more and more encompassing scope. Small groups have social structures, as do entire societies, as do collectivities with intermediate scope, for example organizations or SMSAs. Social structures have emergent properties, the criterion of *emergent* being that the individual elements cannot be characterized by that property. Since an emergent property refers to the composition of, or relations among, individual elements, it characterizes the social structure and not the individuals within it. Thus, ethnic heterogeneity necessarily describes an entire population and cannot characterize an individual or a particular ethnic group. The same, mutatis mutandis, is true for other forms of heterogeneity and for various forms of inequality and consolidation–intersection. These emergent properties, which are our structural parameters, are the result of social processes within the structures. For instance, the occupational distribution in a metropolis and the degree to which occupational status intersects with background characteristics can be dissected by analyzing the internal processes of status attainment in the SMSA.

This chapter addresses the issue of how internal processes in SMSAs influence the structural parameters which have been, up to now, taken as given and treated as exogenous conditions. How do background characteristics affect occupational achievement and earnings? How much of their influence is direct and how much is indirect, mediated by education? These processes of status attainment and social mobility not only account in part for the occupational and earnings distributions (only in part, because economic and industrial conditions in the metropolis strongly influence these distributions) but simultaneously determine the degree and kind of consolidation—for example, how much education is consolidated with occupational and economic achievements. The dissection of the internal processes will also help explain the interrelations of structural parameters, for example, the high correlation between racial heterogeneity and race-earnings consolidation (.87) or the substantial correlation between educational and occupational-status inequality (.23). In short, the analysis is now extended to explore both the social processes within SMSAs that influence their structural features and the variation in social process that exists among SMSAs.

The Process of Status Attainment

The main endeavor in this book is to start with a previously developed, strictly deductive (or axiomatic) macrosociological theory of social structure and to test implications of this theory for the influence of metropolitan structure on intermarriage. At this point, we extend the analysis backwards and examine what conditions in a metropolis influence various aspects of its social structure. But we have not developed a systematic deductive theory about the conditions that influence the structure of social positions, nor do we know of such a deductive theory in the literature. There is, however, an inductive theoretical model that stipulates the social processes through which antecedent conditions and attributes of people affect their distribution in status hierarchies, for example, their occupational or economic status. This is the status-attainment model of social stratification, on which much research has been done in recent decades (Blau and Duncan, 1967; Duncan *et al.*, 1972; Featherman and Hauser, 1978; Jencks *et al.*, 1979). The stratification system or class structure is of course a central, if not the central, part of a social structure.

Both the status-attainment model and the macrostructural theory here under consideration focus on the distributions of a population along various lines, that is, on the degrees of various forms of differentiation in a social structure. Differences in people's achieved status—in an entire society or in a community— are the explicanda that the status-attainment model seeks to account for on the basis of differences in background characteristics and their direct and indirect influences on people's achievements. On the other hand, the differences in status and group membership in a population—its inequalities and heterogeneities—are the explicans of the macrostructural theory and are treated as given (exogenous) conditions whose influences on social relations are analyzed. In other words, the macrostructural theory centers attention on the consequences of population distributions for social relations, whereas the status-attainment model directs attention to the antecedents affecting some of these distributions. Since the status distributions that the macrostructural theory employs as exogenous variables are the macro-level effects of differences in individuals' attainments that the status-attainment model seeks to explain in terms of background attributes and social processes influencing these attainments, the model can help answer the question of what antecedent factors and processes influence the parameters of social structure. However, the two approaches use different units of analysis, which must be explicitly taken into account lest examining the connections between the two confounds the analysis instead of clarifying it.

A crucial difference is that the unit of analysis of status-attainment studies is the individual, whereas the unit of analysis of the present macrostructural theory is an entire population, be it that of a community, a society, or another collectivity. The variables of status-attainment research are attributes of individuals. For example, investigations in this tradition report how individuals' education or occupational status is affected by ascribed characteristics, such as parental status, race, and sex. This, in turn, has macro-level implications for how much of an SMSA's variation in education or occupational status is attributable to variation in ascribed characteristics. The variables in macrostructural theory are not properties of individuals but emergent properties of populations—heterogeneity, inequality, or consolidation–intersection. Status-attainment studies are usually based on samples of individuals from an entire society, though they can also be based on samples from a city, SMSA, or state. From the macrosociological perspective, such an investigation is merely a case study because, regardless of the large number of persons sampled, it deals with distributions of individual attributes in only a single population. It thus provides emergent structural properties—racial heterogeneity, income inequality, etc.—for only one case. Macrostructural analysis is inherently comparative, with a population being the unit of analysis—in our case this is an SMSA but it can in principle be a state or a nation—and quantitative investigation requires data on many populations. The product of status-attainment studies is the starting point for macrostructural studies.

Another difference is that the associations between characteristics of individuals in a population play a different role in the two approaches. For the macrostructural approach, these correlations are exogenous variables, indicating the extent of consolidation or intersection in one population. In the status-attainment approach, however, these correlations are dissected to discover the causal links or paths and thus the social processes that produce a given status distribution; for instance, how background characteristics, directly and indirectly, affect occupational status. Moreover, the causal paths discerned in status-attainment analysis also explain various forms of consolidation or intersection, such as what direct and indirect influences produce the consolidation of race with occupational and economic achievements. By revealing the underlying causal processes producing a given kind of consolidation—which, in turn, affects the rate of intergroup relations—status-attainment investigations nicely complement macrostructural analysis.

Both approaches use the term *structural parameter* to refer to the fundamental characteristics of social structure, but they use it in somewhat different ways and they employ somewhat different, though not unrelated, operational measures even when referring to essentially the same concept. Table 5.1 presents the concepts and operational measures each model employs to describe and analyze social structure. The fundamental structural parameters of the status-attainment model[1] are the variances of ascribed attributes, the covariances of pairs of ascribed attributes (for achieved characteristics, variances and covariances are not basic parameters but derived from them), regression coefficients reflecting direct effects, and the variances of the (unexplained) residuals. The macrosociological theory being advanced and tested conceptualizes the basic parameters of social structure as the different kinds of variation in a single dimension among the members of a population that are indicative of heterogeneity and inequality and the concomitant variations of two or more attributes in the population that are indicative of (bivariate or multivariate) consolidation-intersection. These parameters of social structure are actually the exogenous social conditions or independent variables in terms of which the macrosociological theory explains differences in intergroup relations among populations. Parameters of social structure in this sense must be distinguished from the parameters of a theoretical model in the mathematical sense, in which parameters refer to the constants in the equation(s) representing the model.[2]

---

[1]It is important to note, as in Table 5.1, that discussions of status-attainment models often refer to both the fundamental parameters of the model *and* other characteristics of the social structure (that are sometimes called *endogenous parameters* because they are functions of the model's fundamental parameters). The judgment that specific parameters are more fundamental than others is implicit in the method of structural equation models (see Duncan, 1975; Goldberger and Duncan, 1973; and Note 5, below).

[2]The structural parameters of the status-attainment model are parameters in this latter sense. However, as is often true of regression models, in contrast to structural equation models, we have not placed any emphasis on the parameters of the macrostructural *model* in this sense. Indeed the macrostructural scheme has not yet been developed to the point where we could specify a structural equation model indicating how each rate of intergroup relations is simultaneously determined by the various parameters of social structure. Instead, we have begun by examining and presenting the direction and degree of association (correlations and their statistical significance) between the independent and dependent variables of the model.

TABLE 5.1
Comparison of Macrostructural and Status Attainment Models' Parameters of Structure

Macrostructural model's parameters of social structure		Status attainment model's structural parameters	
Concept	Operationalization	Concept	Operationalization
Heterogeneity Inequality	Gibbs-Martin index Gini coefficient	Differentiation	Variance[a]
Bivariate consolidation	Pearson's r Eta Cramer's V	Bivariate association	Pearson's r[b] Covariance
Multivariate consolidation	Average of several correlations	"Explained" variance	R^2[c]
No comparable parameters		Direct effects	Standardized/ unstandardized regression coefficients
No comparable parameters		"Unexplained" variance	Variance of residuals $(1-R^2)$
No comparable parameters		Indirect and total effects	(Nonlinear) functions of direct effects[c]

[a] Only the variances of ascribed characteristics are basic parameters. The variances of achieved characteristics, like the indirect and total effects, are functions of the basic parameters.
[b] The bivariate associations between ascribed characteristics are basic parameters, but all others are functions of the basic parameters.
[c] These are not basic parameters of the status attainment model, but are functions of the basic parameters.

Let us examine the relationships of the concepts and measures of the two approaches. Differentiation in a nominal dimension, heterogeneity, is usually measured in the macrosociological approach by the Gibbs-Martin index, which is closely related to the status-attainment measure of differentiation, variance. In order to fully operationalize an exogenous nominal variable in a regression analysis or structural-equation model, the standard procedure is to create a set of dichotomous (dummy) variables that collectively indicate to which nominal category any particular individual belongs. In the addendum (at the end of this chapter) we show that the Gibbs–Martin index for a nominal variable is equivalent to the total variance of this corresponding set of dummy variables and thus the status-attainment and macrostructural operationalizations of differentiation are directly comparable.

For graduated dimensions, the macrostructural and status-attainment measures of differentiation are also quite closely related. The Gini coefficient, like almost all measures of inequality, is a scale-invariant measure of variation in the distribution of a ratio variable. Although their most common formulae are quite different, Kendall and Stuart (1969:47) show that the numerator of the Gini coefficient and the standard deviation (or variance) used in status-attainment studies belong to the same family of measures. (See addendum for details.) Neither of these measures is scale invariant, but each becomes so when it is divided by the mean. This division yields, respectively, the Gini coefficient and the coefficient of variation (CV), another well-known measure of inequality. Because of the squaring of deviations, the coefficient of variation will be more sensitive to extremes of the distribution, especially if it is skewed. Nevertheless, the Gini and CV are closely related both mathematically and empirically. Across the 125 SMSAs, the correlation between them is .851 for earnings inequality, .991 for SES inequality, and .999 for educational inequality.

The third type of parameter of social structure is consolidation, which refers to the extent to which two or more attributes of people are associated in a population. For attributes that are graduated, bivariate association is measured by the Pearson correlation coefficient r. In status-attainment research, bivariate association between two interval-level variables is also measured by Pearson's r. If one or both variables are nominal, bivariate consolidation (association) is measured by eta or Cramer's V, but since these are not used in the present chapter, a discussion of their relationship to Pearson's r is confined to the addendum. Multiple consolidation, which the last chapter shows to be more important for social relations than bivariate consolidation, can be operationally defined as the average correlation of one attribute with several others; for instance, the average correlation of race (dichotomized) with education, occupational status, earnings, and other factors. Accordingly, multiple consolidation is a function of several forms of bivariate consolidation. Perhaps the closest analogue of multiple consolidation in the status-attainment model is the R^2 of the structural equation because it indicates how strongly the dependent variable is associated with the various independent ones. (However, if only one of several simple correlations is high, R^2 will be high but the mean correlation will not be. Hence, the mean correlation is a better measure than R^2 of the degree to which one variable is simultaneously correlated with several others.)

The status-attainment model, in effect, dissects the observed multivariate distribution of individuals' attributes into the factors and social processes that produce it. These are indicated by additional parameters and measures (as shown in Table 5.1) that have no direct parallels in macrostructural analysis. The most important of them is the standardized or unstandardized regression (path) coefficient, which reveals the (direct) effect of an independent variable on a dependent variable, controlling for other variables that are causally prior to the dependent variable. These parameters are more fundamental to the attainment models than the level of overall bivariate association and are described presently. Unstandardized models also use an unstandardized measure of overall association rather than a standardized one. This unstandardized measure, the covariance, is related to the correlation coefficient and standard deviations: $S_{xy} = r_{xy}s_x s_y$. Finally, measures of the *total (causal) effect* of one variable on another are often derived and discussed. Though substantively interesting, they are not basic parameters of the model but functions of the direct effects.

Having discussed the basic concepts and operational measures of the two approaches, we turn to the ways they complement each other by examining the implications of either for the other. As already noted, the macrostructural approach treats its three parameters of social structure as exogenous; the relationships among them—among the various indicators of heterogeneity, inequality, and consolidation-intersection—are not an issue that either the theory or empirical analysis addresses. Instead, the effects of differentiation (Chapter 2) and intersection (Chapter 4) on the patterns of social relations are studied. When the effects of several indicators of the same type—various forms of inequality or various forms of heterogeneity—are empirically investigated (one at a time), the results are interpreted as independent replications or tests of the theory's implications (though only if the absence of appreciable correlations of the dependent variables—the intermarriage rates—supplies evidence supporting the assumption that the tests are independent).

The status-attainment researchers might well object to our neglecting to analyze the interdependence of various parameters, particularly since the concept of consolidation clearly implies that population distributions are often related and that their relationships have important consequences for social life. The causal model of status attainment helps elucidate these connections by dissecting the social processes (within a given structure) that produce the associations between various dimensions of differentiation. From the perspective of status attainment, our structural parameters could be reorganized to reflect three basic phenomena. First, in any population there are ascribed characteristics that differentiate people, and these characteristics may be consolidated, to varying degrees, with each other. Second, these ascribed characteristics can affect achievement along various status dimensions, implying that achieved characteristics are, to some degree, consolidated with ascribed characteristics. For example, race and sex discrimination in the labor market create such consolidation. Of course achievement along one dimension also influences achievement along other dimensions, resulting in consolidation among achieved characteristics. Third, the consolidation of one particular characteristic (call it Y) with all causally prior characteristics plus the differentiation of unknown other determinants of Y (summarized in the residuals) *determine* the amount of differentiation in Y.[3] Thus from the status-

---

[3]In practice, the largest component of the variance of an endogenous variable is usually the variance of the residuals which, although conceptually rather amorphous, can be interpreted as the aggregate of all components that are independent of those causally prior attributes specifically incorporated into the model.

attainment perspective, the differentiation of achieved characteristics is not an independent parameter of social structure but is, itself, the result of causally prior differentiation and consolidation.[4]

It is worthwhile to reiterate that we must not let the distinctive uses of the term parameter by the two approaches confuse us. The parameters of the status-attainment model and the parameters of social structure that constitute the independent variables of the macrostructural model are related but systematically different. Using causal-model terminology, the variances of the exogenous ascribed attributes of individuals and the covariances of these attributes are structural parameters of both theoretical approaches. From the macrostructural perspective, the differentiation of achieved attributes and the consolidation of these variables with other attributes of individuals (whether ascribed or achieved) are also structural parameters. From the status-attainment perspective, however, the latter are not parameters but results of status-attainment processes determined by two, more fundamental,[5] sets of parameters: (1) path coefficients indicating the direct effect of one attribute of individuals on another, which Duncan (1975:53) also calls *structural coefficients;* and (2) the distributions of ascribed attributes, their correlations, and the residuals of the endogenous variables.[6]

At the same time, the comparative nature of the macrosociological approach makes a contribution to the status-attainment model by empirically testing an implicit assumption of this model. Duncan (1975:56) clearly suggests that for a structural-equation model to explain anything about status attainment, some of its parameters must be invariant: "there would not be much purpose in devising a model to use in interpreting data if we did not have some hope that at least some features of our model would be invariant with respect to some changes in the circumstances under which it is applied." It is clear from the discussion that although Duncan thinks that the distributional parameters for the exogenous variables and residuals may vary from one population or subpopulation to another, the structural (path) coefficients should generally remain invariant if the model is to be an explanatory model rather than a descriptive one. A change (or

---

[4]If chronological time is specifically incorporated into the model, then social and geographic mobility (or change) is a fourth phenomenon affecting the differentiation and consolidation of socially relevant attributes within each community.

[5]It should be noted that the method of structural equation models uses all of the variances and correlations / covariances to estimate the model's parameters. The former can be directly estimated from the data (without any causal model) but are nevertheless theoretically conceived as a consequence of the latter.

[6]In standardized models, the residuals are *scaled* to have a variance of one, and a path coefficient from the residuals to the dependent variable is introduced. For recursive models, the square of this path coefficient equals $1 - R^2$ and indicates the proportion of variance of the dependent variable that is accounted for by the residuals. This squared path is directly comparable to the variance-of-residuals parameter of the corresponding unstandardized model.

difference) in the structural coefficients must be considered a structural change.[7]

Since most analyses of the status-attainment process involve only a single population at one point in time, it is not possible to test this assumption of invariance. Hence, this approach attempts the impossible, namely to generalize from a case study (of one population) to principles about the structure of most populations. But this question of invariance raises yet another issue: when, for example, we examine a status-attainment model for the U.S. adult male population and learn that the structural coefficient for the effect of education on SES is, say, 4.5 points of SES per year of education, we usually recognize that this is a summary figure and is not meant to apply precisely to every individual. Nevertheless, there tends to be an implicit and largely untested assumption that this estimate is also applicable within various subunits—such as regions, states, or cities—of the whole population.[8] That is, we tend to assume that the parameters of the status-attainment process estimated for the full population are invariant across subunits of this population. Without this assumption, the structural coefficients might not describe the attainment process anywhere, but rather would be estimates of the *average* of several different processes that operate in different localities.[9]

By estimating the parameters of social structure separately for each SMSA, we are in a position to examine both the variability of the distributional parameters of the ascribed and residual variables in the status-attainment model and the degree of invariance of the structural coefficients. In this manner, we will assess the invariance of the status-attainment process across urban subunits of the U.S. population. This is particularly interesting since the Census Bureau defines the boundaries of SMSAs so as to encompass geographically distinct, economically integrated urban areas.[10] We briefly discuss research procedures before reporting the results of the empirical analysis.

[7]It is at this juncture that the aims of the two theoretical approaches are most divergent. Explanation for the status-attainment model requires that most of the macrolevel parameters be relatively invariant. In contrast, the macrostructural approach requires that there be substantial variations among the social structures of the communities being investigated: if there is no variation in the parameters of social structure, then differences in structure cannot explain (account for) differences in rates of intergroup interaction.

[8]Some analyses partially examine this assumption by controlling, usually in a statistical manner, for region of residence and whether respondents live in an urban, suburban, or rural environment. However only a very few status-attainment models ever explore whether the structural coefficients linking other variables (e.g. education and SES) vary or remain invariant across these different environments. Featherman and Hauser (1978: Chapter 7) compare two regions—South and non-south—and conclude that there are substantial differences between their corresponding structural coefficients.

[9]This would make our usual interpretation of structural coefficients analogous to the statement, "the typical worker in Company X is 65% male, 25% black, 72% married, and has 2.3 children."

[10]One caveat that should be kept in mind is that individuals and families are more or less free to migrate from one area to another. Assuming that people seek to attain status in one or more of its

Path Models for 125 SMSAs

It would be a massive undertaking to return to the 1,223,000 cases and estimate separate regression equations for each SMSA. However, it is possible to use the univariate and bivariate distributional information in our aggregate-level data file to recreate an approximate correlation matrix (implicitly using pairwise deletion) that can be used with the means and standard deviations to estimate a limited path model of the status-attainment process for each SMSA. This aggregate (macro-level) file contains correlations among graduated dimensions and correlations of these dimensions with the dichotomous nominal dimensions. It is not possible to include nondichotomous nominal attributes such as birth region or national origin since this would require correlations of *sets* of dummy variables with each other and the graduated attributes, which are not available in the aggregate file.

Our path analyses therefore portray the causal relationships among six variables, three ascribed and three achieved characteristics. The ascribed characteristics are sex (1 = male), race (1 = white), and age (which is not empirically distinguishable from cohort). Unfortunately, the Census does not contain background information on the status of one's family of origin. The achieved characteristics, listed according to their presumed causal ordering, are years of education, occupational status (Duncan SEI), and earnings. For comparability, we have estimated the just-identified recursive model for every SMSA and thus have made no zero-path assumptions. However, the usual regression (recursive model) assumptions are being made: specifically, that the relationships between the variables are linear and that the residuals of each endogenous (achieved) variable are uncorrelated with all causally prior variables.

There are both theoretical and methodological weaknesses in the analysis that we have conducted. At the theoretical level, several variables that are known to influence individuals' status attainment are either not available in the census data or could not be incorporated into the analysis for practical reasons. These include parental status, number of siblings, region of birth, and intelligence. The exclusion of these variables almost surely biases estimates of the structural coefficients (of those variables that are available), perhaps altering the degree to which they vary or do not vary across SMSAs. Their exclusion also increases the variances

---

various forms, they may migrate from a region where it is relatively difficult to acquire status to another where things are easier. The economic principles of supply and demand that are hypothesized to govern the competition for status and scarce resources would lead one to predict that differences in SMSAs will steadily be reduced through a process of homogenization. This process is further hypothesized to eventually result in an equilibrium where there are no longer economic incentives to migrate. In short, this is one of several possible arguments supporting the assumption that the attainment process should be invariant: if it were not, people would migrate until it was. (A second rationale is the *national organization* of higher education and the job search process that follows completion of a higher degree.)

of the residuals because the residual terms incorporate the effects of all excluded variables that cannot be predicted from the causally prior variables.

At a methodological level, we do not have the sample mean and standard deviation of age for the *adult* population, and these were therefore treated as constant (mean = 43, standard deviation = 11) across all SMSAs.[11] Second, we do not have correlations of age with either sex or race, which therefore have been uniformly set equal to zero in every SMSA.[12] Finally, though we have the magnitude of the correlation of race with sex (since Cramer's *V* equals the absolute value of the Pearson correlation for two dichotomous variables) we do not know its sign. Rather than assume they were all positive (or negative), we have used published data to reestimate the race-sex correlation for each SMSA.

One might well wonder whether there is any value in estimating an incomplete path model, because we can be fairly sure that many of the parameter estimates will be biased. The question becomes even more salient when one observes that the macrostructural approach's parameters of social structure—heterogeneity, inequality, and consolidation–intersection—are not biased by the exclusion of variables. Though debatable, our answer is unequivocal. First, if we are going to try to understand the process that generates the macrostructural parameters, it is better to estimate a version of the model that is incomplete than not to estimate any model. To do otherwise is to implicitly ignore the underlying process. Of course, the reader must maintain an appropriately critical perspective when interpreting the results. Second, the analysis presented in this chapter is viewed primarily as illustrative of the type of comparative analysis that can be done. Though the broad conclusions are probably correct, the analysis' obvious weaknesses—especially the problem of omitted variables—are too severe for us to place much confidence in the specific findings.

To review, the data for the analyses are the means, standard deviations, and correlations that were previously computed for each SMSA from micro-level data. These are used to compute three regression equations for each SMSA. The result is a set of estimates of the parameters of our simple structural equation model. These analyses will allow us to make preliminary comparisons among SMSAs with respect to the effect of ascription on three dimensions of achievement as well as the effect of causally prior forms of achievement on later ones.

---

[11]This affects the unstandardized and relative (described below) coefficients of age, but has absolutely no impact on any other parameter estimates of the model.

[12]In actuality, age tends to be slightly correlated with being white and being female. The correlations among these three ascribed characteristics are, in some sense, theoretically zero. Any deviations from zero, apart from sampling variation, must be due to demographic factors such as differential fertility, mortality, or migration rates. We know of no evidence of differential sex ratios at birth for whites and nonwhites, although the difference between male and female mortality rates may be greater for nonwhites than for whites. It is true that nonwhite males cause the Census Bureau the greatest difficulty in terms of nonresponse.

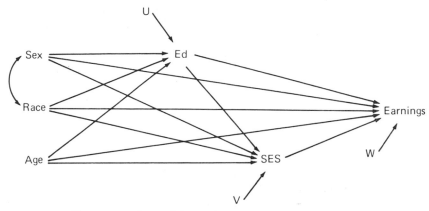

Figure 5.1   General form of path model to be estimated.

Since the Census has no data on parental status, we are unable to study mobility. The basic path model that we have estimated separately for each SMSA is presented in Figure 5.1.

The three structural equations of this model are clear:[13]

$$\mathrm{Ed}_{ij} = a_{\mathrm{E}j} + b_{\mathrm{ES}j}\mathrm{Sex}_{ij} + b_{\mathrm{ER}j}\mathrm{Race}_{ij} + b_{\mathrm{EA}j}\mathrm{Age}_{ij} + u_{ij}$$

$$\mathrm{SES}_{ij} = a_{\mathrm{O}j} + b_{\mathrm{OS}j}\mathrm{Sex}_{ij} + b_{\mathrm{OR}j}\mathrm{Race}_{ij} + b_{\mathrm{OA}j}\mathrm{Age}_{ij} + b_{\mathrm{OE}j}\mathrm{Ed}_{ij} + v_{ij}$$

$$\mathrm{Inc}_{ij} = a_{\mathrm{I}j} + b_{\mathrm{IS}j}\mathrm{Sex}_{ij} + b_{\mathrm{IR}j}\mathrm{Race}_{ij} + b_{\mathrm{IA}j}\mathrm{Age}_{ij} + b_{\mathrm{IE}j}\mathrm{Ed}_{ij} + b_{\mathrm{IO}j}\mathrm{SES}_{ij}$$
$$+ w_{ij}.$$

However, depending on how the variables are scaled, there are *three* plausible sets of regression coefficients that will result. The first two sets—unstandardized and standardized—are familiar. Nevertheless, to be explicit, if the variables are left in their usual scales—for instance, education coded in years and SES coded by the Duncan index—then the unstandardized $b_{\mathrm{OE}j}$ estimates the expected (average) difference on the Duncan SEI between two persons in the jth SMSA who differ by one year of education but have the same sex, race, and age. If each of the variables is standardized (i.e., transformed into z scores using each SMSA's mean and standard deviation), then the estimation of the above structural equations results in standardized coefficients where, for example, $b_{\mathrm{OE}j}$ estimates by what proportion of the standard deviation of SES in SMSA j two persons from that SMSA will, on average, differ if they are of the same sex, race, and age but they differ by one standard deviation in education. Of these two sets, the former is substantively more meaningful because one standard deviation

[13]The lowercase subscripts index individual i in SMSA j whereas the uppercase subscripts refer to the first letter of a variable (using O for occupational SES).

is a different amount in each SMSA, and it is usually recommended (Tukey, 1954) when coefficients are being compared across populations (SMSAs). However, the latter is commonly used to indicate the relative strengths of the effects of several independent variables on a dependent variable. Although standardized coefficients are more closely associated with the percentage of explained variance (but see Cain and Watts, 1970, and Hope, 1971, for discussions of possible pitfalls in such interpretations), Duncan (1975:51) argues, and we would agree, that standardized coefficients tend "to obscure the distinction between the [true] structural coefficients of the model [which are expected to be applicable across populations] and the several variances and covariances that describe the joint distribution of the variables in a certain population."

In addition to the commonly used standardized and unstandardized coefficients, there is a third type, which, to our knowledge, has not been used before. The argument in favor of using measures of inequality that are scale invariant implies that the absolute difference between individuals on some graduated dimension (such as income) is only indirectly of consequence. Rather, it is their difference *relative to the average income* that is socially relevant. From this perspective, it makes sense to divide all the graduated dimensions by their mean so that, for example, someone's value on the income variable indicates the ratio of that person's income to the average income in the SMSA. It turns out that if each graduated dimension is divided by its mean, then its standard deviation equals the coefficient of variation (CV) and its variance, of course, equals the square of the CV (an obvious alternative measure of inequality). This makes *explaining variance* virtually equivalent to *explaining inequality*. If the above structural equations are estimated using these variables, then we will call the resulting estimates *relative coefficients*. The relative coefficient b_{IEj} estimates by what proportion of the mean earnings (I) of SMSA j two persons will on the average differ if they are of the same sex, race, age, and occupational status but differ in education by an amount equal to the average education (E) in their SMSA. Analogous to the standardized coefficients, one must bear in mind that the averages of achieved characteristics vary across SMSAs. For this type of analysis, we have not transformed the dichotomous independent variables and so, for example, b_{ESj} estimates by what proportion of the overall mean years of education in SMSA j men and women differ, on the average, holding race and age constant.

It should be understood that from one perspective, these three sets of coefficients that will be estimated for each SMSA simply represent translations from one version of our model into another *algebraically equivalent* one. Because of this, any one set of coefficients can be easily computed from another: for example,

$$b_{IEj(\text{unstd})} = b_{IEj(\text{std})} \, (s_{Ij}/s_{Ej}) = b_{IEj(\text{Rel})} \, (\overline{X}_{Ij}/\overline{X}_{Ej}).$$

Another indication of their equivalence is that the R^2 for a structural equation does not change when the variables are transformed into z-scores or relative scores.

On the other hand, when it comes to comparing coefficients across SMSAs and examining their invariance, the three sets of coefficients could yield different results. This is because the standard deviations and the means are not constant across SMSAs. Thus it is entirely possible for an unstandardized coefficient to be higher in SMSA 1 than in SMSA 2, the standardized coefficient to be lower in SMSA 1 than in SMSA 2, and the relative coefficients to be the same in both SMSAs. Therefore, if there is a structural equation model whose coefficients are invariant across populations, their invariance can only be detected if the variables are in the proper form. Duncan urges us to ask the question: which form of the model (which set of coefficients and, implicitly, variables) corresponds to the "real" structural model? "The answer," he says, "is that invariance is where you find it—in the world or in your theory—and no analysis of a model's formal properties can determine whether its coefficients are invariant" (1975:154). That is, the theoretical generalizations should be formulated so that they are represented by those coefficients that reveal invariance. We do not have any a priori theoretical basis for predicting which version of the coefficients will exhibit the greatest invariance.[14] Our bias favors the unstandardized or relative coefficients over the standardized ones, but the invariance of all three types will be empirically examined.

Averages for the SMSAs

Figures 5.2a–c and Tables 5.2a–c present the unweighted averages of the parameter estimates for the 125 separate SMSA path models: the unstandardized (5.2a), standardized (5.2b), and relative (5.2c) versions of the model. The tables also contain information about the estimates of the distributional parameters of the model that are not shown in the path diagrams. In addition to the mean, across SMSAs, of the estimates of each parameter, the tables present three other indicators of the distribution of these estimates: their standard deviation plus the 10th and 90th percentiles. These are relevant for the next section's analysis of variation of estimates among SMSAs.

As suggested in the above discussion of the three sets of regression coefficients, the unstandardized are the simplest to interpret. Figure 5.2a (and Table 5.2a, second panel) indicates that in the average SMSA there is a very small

---

[14]This is closely related to our not having solid theoretical grounds for preferring raw scores, z scores, or relative scores when comparing individuals who live in different SMSAs. (Within an SMSA, the three types of scores are equivalent interval-level scales.)

TABLE 5.2a
Summary Statistics for the Distribution of Parameters for the 125 <u>Unstandardized</u> Models

Distributional Parameter Estimates for Exogenous Variables

| | Heterogeneity | | | | Consolidation |
	S_{sex}	S^2_{sex}	S_{race}	S^2_{race}	$Covar_{sex,race}$
10th percentile	.4992	.2492	.1549	.0240	-.000654
mean	.4996	.2496	.2918	.0959	.000969
90th percentile	.4999	.2499	.4380	.1919	.003336
standard deviation	.0003	.0003	.1040	.0617	.002243

Estimates of structural coefficients and variances of residuals

Education equation

| | Structural coefficients | | | Variances of residuals | |
	B_{sex}	B_{race}	B_{age}	S_{res}	S^2_{res}
10th percentile	-.0640	.3335	-.1143	2.7774	7.7138
mean	.1703	1.3125	-.0931	3.0886	9.6033
90th percentile	.4553	2.4732	-.0648	3.4030	11.5807
standard deviation	.2131	.9600	.0170	.2540	1.6144

SES equation

	B_{sex}	B_{race}	B_{age}	B_{ed}	S_{res}	S^2_{res}
10th percentile	-4.8236	.4383	.3585	3.9000	16.2701	264.72
mean	-2.4363	6.3120	.4813	4.5058	16.9999	289.31
90th percentile	.0452	11.9813	.6112	5.1134	17.7804	316.14
standard deviation	1.8704	5.2971	.0997	.4832	.5637	19.25

Earnings ($1000) equation

	B_{sex}	B_{race}	B_{age}	B_{ed}	B_{SES}	S_{res}	S^2_{res}
10th percentile	3.3813	-.2868	.1436	.3883	.0241	4.1966	17.61
mean	4.2844	.4607	.1833	.5618	.0433	5.0712	26.23
90th percentile	5.0684	1.0135	.2275	.7522	.0595	6.0139	36.17
standard deviation	.7114	.6569	.0358	.1384	.0138	.7154	7.40

difference between men and women in average educational attainment (.17 years), controlling for race and age. The comparable difference between whites and nonwhites, 1.31 years of education, is almost eight times as much. The cohort (age) effect is very substantial, with each successive 10-year cohort acquiring an average of almost one year (.93) more schooling than the previous cohort.[15] Thus, the extremes of the age distribution differ much more in educational attainment than either the two race groups or sexes. The standardized and relative coefficients for the education equation, shown in Figures 5.2b and 5.2c and Tables 5.2b and 5.2c, imply very similar conclusions.[16]

Turning to the estimates of the SES structural equation (third panels in Tables 5.2a–c), we first observe a strange consequence of occupational segregation by sex, which others (England, 1979; Messner and Yuchtman-Yaar, 1979; Cranor et al., 1981) have noted: the average SES (Duncan's SEI) of men is slightly lower than the average of women. Working women are very heavily concentrated in a few lower and middle white-collar occupations that have relatively few male incumbents. These occupations include secretaries (who make up 9.4% of the female labor force, and of whom 99.1% are women), bookkeepers (4.5, 88.3), elementary school teachers (3.4, 84.5), retail salesclerks (4.8, 69.0), and registered nurses (2.5, 97.8) (Reagan, 1979).[17] Since almost all white collar jobs have higher SES than blue collar jobs, the effect of this occupational distribution is that the average SES of women in a typical SMSA is 2.44 points greater on the Duncan SEI than that of men, holding race, age, and educational attainment constant.[18] The difference in average SES between whites and nonwhites is substantial (6.31 points) even after controlling for their differences in educational

[15]The unstandardized (and relative) age coefficients must be interpreted very tentatively because they directly depend on the assumption that the standard deviation of age is 11 (and that the mean is 43) in each SMSA. The standardized age coefficients are not affected by this assumption, and they also now show (see Figure 5.2b) that the effect of age on education is greater than that of race or that of sex.

[16]Of these three coefficients, only the race coefficient can be compared to Featherman and Hauser's (1978:235) OCG-II results. Our coefficient is about twice as large as theirs due, we believe, to the correlation of race with other background characteristics that substantially affect education. Our inability to control for these should upwardly bias our race coefficient. However, the race coefficients in the SES and earnings equations should not be as strongly biased because the omitted background characteristics tend to have weak *direct* effects on later forms of achievement.

[17]Although women tend not to be engaged in primary or secondary sector production, they do dominate a few manufacturing occupations such as garment sewers and stitchers. Occupational segregation by sex is equivalent to consolidation of sex and occupation, the large extent of which was noted in Chapter 4 (Table 4.4).

[18]Cranor et al. (1981) and Karasek et al. (1982) show that the degree of job discretion or autonomy is substantially lower for women (and female dominated jobs) than it is for men. Although there is evidence (Bose, 1973) showing that the rank ordering of the status of occupations is very similar for men and women, others (England, 1979; and Messner and Yuchtman-Yaar, 1979) question the usefulness of directly comparing SES scores of men and women.

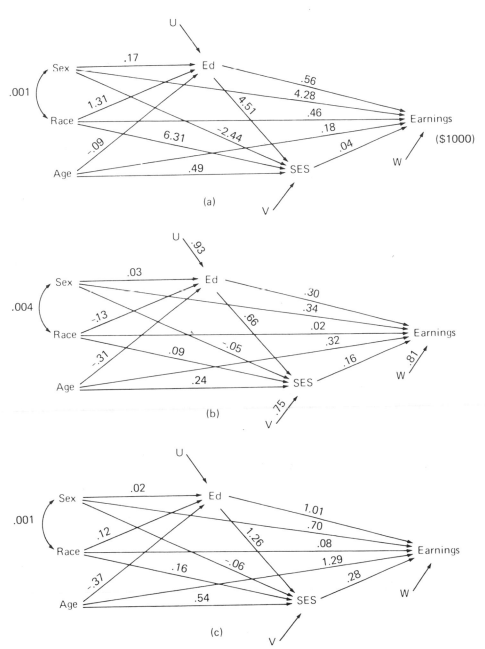

Figure 5.2 (a) *Unstandardized* path model (averages of 125 independently estimated models). (b) Average of 125 *standardized* path models. (c) Average of 125 *relative* path models.

TABLE 5.2b
Summary Statistics for the Distribution of Parameters for the 125 <u>Standardized</u> Models

Distributional parameter estimates for exogenous variables

	Heterogeneity				Consolidation
	S_{sex}	S^2_{sex}	S_{race}	S^2_{race}	$Cor_{sex,race}$
10th percentile	These equal 1.0,				-.0064
mean	by assumption,				.0044
90th percentile	for every SMSA				.0153
standard deviation					.0116

Estimates of structural coefficients and variances of residuals

Education equation

	Structural coefficients					Variances of residuals	
	B_{sex}	B_{race}	B_{age}			S_{res}	S^2_{res}
10th percentile	-.0094	.0168	-.3768			.8995	.8091
mean	.0255	.1318	-.3102			.9320	.8694
90th percentile	.0692	.2882	-.2212			.9635	.9283
standard deviation	.0316	.1095	.0576			.0287	.0523

SES equation

	B_{sex}	B_{race}	B_{age}	B_{ed}		S_{res}	S^2_{res}
10th percentile	-.1071	.0045	.1777	.5921		.7211	.5200
mean	-.0540	.0916	.2397	.6580		.7539	.5690
90th percentile	.0011	.1960	.3056	.7096		.7856	.6172
standard deviation	.0415	.0703	.0491	.0453		.0264	.0398

Earnings equation

	B_{sex}	B_{race}	B_{age}	B_{ed}	B_{SES}	S_{res}	S^2_{res}
10th percentile	.2887	-.0090	.2657	.2066	.0944	.7706	.5938
mean	.3427	.0219	.3229	.2977	.1556	.8082	.6539
90th percentile	.3921	.0521	.3858	.3882	.2068	.8424	.7098
standard deviation	.0477	.0294	.0534	.0677	.0455	.0266	.0428

attainment as well as age and sex. This is very similar to Featherman and Hauser's (1978:256) estimate of 7.12. After controlling for the three other variables, age still has a positive effect on SES that we usually associate with seniority and acquired job experience. A 10-year difference in age is associated with an almost 5-point difference in SES. It is immediately apparent that educational attainment is a major determinant of occupational attainment. Holding the three exogenous variables constant, we see that individuals who differ by one year of education will, on the average, differ by 4.51 points on the SEI. Extrapolating, the expected difference between someone with a college degree and a comparable individual with only a high school diploma is about 18 points. This is also the expected difference between persons with a high school diploma and those with only an eighth-grade education.[19]

It is only when we examine the earnings equation (in the bottom panel) that we observe a major difference between women and men in their status attainment: in our terms, a substantial degree of consolidation of sex with an achieved characteristic. After controlling for the (rather small) sex differences in race, age, educational attainment, and SES, male and female average earnings in the typical SMSA differ by a staggering $4284 (in 1969 when the average earnings of all workers in the typical SMSA were $6114). An unmeasurable portion of this difference is certainly due to the greater tendency for women to work part-time. However, the remainder is due to wage-rate differentials between comparably educated men and women in comparable jobs.[20] The earnings differential between whites and nonwhites, controlling for the other variables in the earnings equation, is a relatively small $461. As we describe below, this direct effect is not larger because most of the overall earnings difference between the races is due to the indirect effects of nonwhites' lower education and occupational status. Again holding the other variables constant, age is strongly related to earnings; a 10-year age difference is associated with a $1833 earnings differential. Finally, as everyone knows, one form of status attainment tends to be rewarded with other forms (even controlling for various third forms), and so 1 year of educational attainment is associated with an expected $562 increase in earnings whereas a 10-point difference in SES is associated with a $433 difference in earnings.

---

[19]The equivalence of these two estimated differences is built into the model. Our simple structural equations do not allow for differences between the effect of a year of grade school and a year of college. Such differences are reported in Featherman and Hauser (1978) and Jencks *et al.* (1979). Our estimate of the effect on SES of one year of education is almost exactly equal to the average of Featherman and Hauser's effects for one year of grade school (2.22) and of college (6.73).

[20]Sometimes these differences are between women and men in the same occupation, but often the difference is between men and women in different occupations that have the same SEI. Although it probably only accounts for a small portion of the earnings-differentials, there is evidence that comparably educated women and men have often studied different subjects (Grant and Eiden, 1982:117–121) or learned different skills that are, possibly unfairly, differentially remunerated in the labor market (U.S. Bureau of the Census, 1980:192–199).

The education coefficient in the earnings equation is fairly similar to Featherman and Hauser's (1978:293) estimate, but their race and SES coefficients are 50 to 100% larger than ours. (Exact comparisons are difficult, given differences in the average earnings and the inclusion of different control variables in the equation.) It is almost certain that some, perhaps most, of the difference is due to the inclusion of women in our analysis: if we could estimate earnings equations separately for men and women (or include sex-interaction terms in the present equation), we would expect that most of the male coefficients would be larger than the corresponding female coefficients.

Although it is certainly not obvious how (or if) one should compare the size of one unstandardized regression coefficient with another (except, perhaps, when the independent variables are measured on the same scale or are both di-chotomous variables), we believe that most readers will in fact have acquired a reasonably accurate sense of their relative strengths from the interpretive remarks of the preceding paragraphs. Whereas at least one of the present authors would disagree, many researchers feel that they can only compare standardized (path) coefficients. Overall, the substantive conclusions that would be drawn from the standardized coefficients (in Table and Figure 5.2b) are very similar to the above. Perhaps the main difference is that the path coefficients of race seem relatively lower. From one perspective, this is an example of what Duncan refers to as the confounding of the structural coefficients with the exogenous distribu-tional parameters. More specifically, if whites and nonwhites differed by the same amount as males and females (on any achieved characteristic), the effect of one standard deviation in race would be less than the effect of one standard deviation difference in sex because racial heterogeneity is substantially lower than sex heterogeneity. In other words, the variation in race will tend to account for less of the variation in some dependent variable than will the variation in sex, even if the effects of race and sex are equal, simply because there is less variation in race. Bearing this in mind, we might nevertheless note that the standardized coefficient of education in the SES equation is quite large, as are, to a lesser degree, the coefficients of sex and age in the earnings equation.

Apart from their connection to R^2, the tendency to compare standardized coefficients evolves from one approach to dealing with the problem that different variables are usually measured on different scales—years of age, years of educa-tion, dollars, or the Duncan scale—and we do not have any obvious method of making the units of these scales comparable. Standardization finesses this inher-ently substantive problem by arbitrarily equating a one standard deviation dif-ference on each scale. While the goal of making scales (and, therefore, estimates of their effects on other variables) comparable is indeed desirable, there is little substantive justification for accepting this particular solution (unless one is a complete relativist who believes that the degree of differentiation in a distribution is of no social consequence).

Another approach that may or may not be equally arbitrary is to equate (for ratio variables) the means of the different variables. This is implicitly what all the scale-invariant measures of inequality do. Measures like the Gini coefficient and coefficient of variation are fundamentally based on the differences between individuals *relative to the overall mean*. Thus, educational inequality is judged to be much lower (average CV across 125 SMSAs is .30) than SES (.57) or earnings (1.03) inequality because the differences in education are smaller relative to the mean education.[21] This assumed equivalence of means is implicit in any direct comparison of one relative coefficient (Figure and Table 5.2c) with another.[22] Without wishing to defend this assumption too vigorously, we note that this would lead one to emphasize the importance of age in every structural equation. To be more explicit, a difference between individuals of one mean in birth cohort or age (43 years, by assumption) is associated with 37% less education than the SMSA mean, an improvement in SES of more than one-half of the SES mean in the SMSA, and an increase in earnings that is 129% of the average in the SMSA, controlling for the other independent variables in the respective structural equations.

These relative coefficients are analogous to, though different from, standardized coefficients in a second way. Just as the algebraic decomposition of the (standardized) normal equation for the variance of a dependent variable includes the squared path coefficients that are sometimes used as measures of *unique variance explained*,[23] so the squared relative coefficient indicates the rate at which inequality in the independent variable (squared CV) is translated into inequality in the dependent variable (controlling for other variables). For example, the process by which educational qualifications are converted into SES substantially magnifies (by 58%) the inequality of the education distribution: squaring the average of the education coefficients (in the 125 SES equations; see

---

[21]Computationally, this equating can be achieved by dividing each variable by its mean. This leaves the zero-point of the ratio scale unchanged and transforms the remaining values so that each variable will have a mean of one. As mentioned earlier, the standard deviation of the transformed variable equals the CV of the original variable.

[22]We have not transformed the race and sex variables, because they are dichotomous and not ratio variables, and so their coefficients, which are comparable to each other, are not directly comparable to the coefficients of graduated variables.

[23]For example, the decomposition of the variance of SES is

$$\sigma_{OO} = b_{OS}\,\sigma_{SO} + b_{OR}\,\sigma_{RO} + b_{OA}\,\sigma_{AO} + b_{OE}\,\sigma_{EO} + \sigma_{vv}$$
$$= (b^2_{OS} + 2b_{OS}b_{OE}b_{ES})\,\sigma_{SS} + 2(b_{OS}b_{OR} + b_{OS}b_{OE}b_{ER} + b_{OR}b_{OE}b_{ES})\,\sigma_{SR}$$
$$+ (b^2_{OR} + 2b_{OR}b_{OE}b_{ER})\,\sigma_{RR} + 2(b_{OS}b_{OA} + b_{OS}b_{OE}b_{EA} + b_{OA}b_{OE}b_{ES})\,\sigma_{SA}$$
$$+ 2(b_{OR}b_{OA} + b_{OR}b_{OE}b_{EA} + b_{OA}b_{OE}b_{ER})\,\sigma_{RA} + (b^2_{OA} + 2b_{OA}b_{OE}b_{EA})\,\sigma_{AA}$$
$$+ b^2_{OE}\,\sigma_{EE} + \sigma_{vv}.$$

For a standardized model, all of the variances on the right side of this normal equation *disappear* because they equal 1.0.

TABLE 5.2c
Summary Statistics for the Distribution of Parameters for the 125 <u>Relative</u> Models

Distributional parameter estimates for exogenous variables

	Heterogeneity				Consolidation
	S_{sex}	S^2_{sex}	S_{race}	S^2_{race}	Covar$_{sex,race}$
10th percentile	.4992	.2492	.1549	.0240	-.000654
mean	.4996	.2496	.2918	.0959	.000969
90th percentile	.4999	.2499	.4380	.1919	.003336
standard deviation	.0003	.0003	.1040	.0617	.002243

Estimates of structural coefficients and variances of residuals

| | Structural coefficients | | | | | Variances of Residuals | |

Education equation

	B_{sex}	B_{race}	B_{age}			S_{res}	S^2_{res}
10th percentile	-.0060	.0298	-.4462			.2459	.0605
mean	.0151	.1201	-.3664			.2817	.0802
90th percentile	.0396	.2284	-.2465			.3184	.1014
standard deviation	.0191	.0888	.0758			.0294	.0174

SES equation

	B_{sex}	B_{race}	B_{age}	B_{ed}		S_{res}	S^2_{res}
10th percentile	-.1229	.0102	.3886	1.0264		.3952	.1562
mean	-.0617	.1590	.5369	1.2579		.4314	.1871
90th percentile	.0014	.3043	.6882	1.4882		.4764	.2289
standard deviation	.0498	.1383	.1190	.1712		.0311	.0271

Earnings equation

	B_{sex}	B_{race}	B_{age}	B_{ed}	B_{SES}	S_{res}	S^2_{res}
10th percentile	.6038	-.0467	1.0424	.6902	.1518	.7262	.5274
mean	.6982	.0752	1.2889	1.0125	.2809	.8310	.6994
90th percentile	.7752	.1749	1.5426	1.3640	.3935	.9579	.9176
standard deviation	.0730	.1105	.2117	.2387	.0909	.0944	.1576

Table 5.2c, third panel) yields 1.258^2 or 1.583. Thus, the process of status attainment in our society does not merely preserve relative educational differentials in the distribution of socioeconomic status but substantially magnifies them so that the average relative variation in years of schooling in an SMSA is transformed into more than 1½ times the average relative variation in SES.[24] It seems possible that state minimum-education laws reduce the relative variance (inequality) of educational attainment. But state laws probably cannot greatly influence the inequality of the SES distribution. Minimum-wage laws may reduce the inequality of earnings (and perhaps simultaneously increase unemployment).[25]

The averages of the relative-age coefficients in both the education and SES equations ($-.37$ and .54, respectively) indicate that only a fraction of the inequality of the age distribution is transmitted to the distributions of education and SES. However, on the average, the inequality in age is more than reproduced in the earnings distribution: The part of the squared CV of earnings which is due directly to age equals 1.29^2 (Table 5.2c, panel four) or 166% of the squared CV for age. Turning to the averages of the other relative coefficients of the earnings equation, the education relative coefficient suggests (since it is near unity) that the direct effect of education alone leads to about the same relative differences among individuals in earnings as exist in education. (Of course the other causes of earnings further increase the inequality of its distribution.) Parallel to the standardized and unstandardized coefficients, the average value of the relative coefficient of SES (in the earnings equation) is a rather small .28. This indicates

[24]With an appropriate dataset that includes family background variables, one could use relative coefficients to address the question raised by neo-Marxists as to whether the American education system primarily preserves status differentials from one generation to the next or acts to equalize the effect of differences in background (e.g., Bowles and Gintis, 1976). It should be remembered that the utility of the relative coefficients, as well as scale-invariant measures of inequality (Allison, 1978), depends on the assumption that the variables are measured on a ratio scale.

[25]Standardized regression coefficients cannot convey as much information as relative coefficients about the transmission of inequality from one status dimension to another. The square of the average standardized education coefficient in the SES equation (.658) indicates that 43% ($.658^2$) of the variance of SES is *uniquely attributable* to education. However, because all variables are scaled to have unit variance for the standardized model, differences in the inequality of the education and SES distributions are ignored. Using the relative model, however, we can begin by observing that the average variances (squared coefficients of variation) of the relative education and SES variables are, respectively, .092 (not reported in any table) and .329 (shown in the last column of Table 5.3c, upper panel). The penultimate term ($b^2_{OE} \sigma_{EE}$) of the decomposition of SES variance (Note 23) is due directly to education and equals 1.582 (.092) or .146. As stated in the text, this component of the relative variance of SES is 58% larger than the total relative variance of education. Although this conclusion can only be reached from the perspective of the relative model, we can of course also compute what percentage .146 is of the total SES relative variance: $.146/.329 = 44\%$. (For a single SMSA, this percentage exactly equals the squared standardized regression coefficient; the present deviation—43 versus 44%—is due entirely to our use of averages of 125 separate path models.)

that by controlling for the other variables in the equation, the expected difference in earnings (relative to the average earnings in the SMSA) between two persons who differ in SES by an amount equal to the average SES is only .28. Thus, a given relative difference between individuals in SES only generates about one-fourth as large a relative difference in earnings.

Throughout the above discussion of the three sets of coefficients, we have been reporting average estimates of the effect of one variable on a second, controlling for several other variables. In causal-modeling terminology these are refered to as *direct effects* and are, as we saw in Table 5.1, basic parameters of the structural-equation model. However, one of the most important contributions of causal modeling is the conceptualization and operationalization of *indirect* and *total* effects. These are *not* basic parameters of the model but (nonlinear) functions of the direct effects. It is intuitively clear that if nonwhites have less education than whites and differences in educational attainment contribute to differences in SES, the differences in SES between whites and nonwhites (*not* controlling for education) will be larger than the direct effect of race on SES. The average unstandardized indirect effect (see Table 5.2a) of race on SES mediated by education is approximately[26] the product of 4.51 (SES points per year of education) and 1.31 (years of education difference between races), that is, 5.91 SES points difference between whites and nonwhites. The total effect of one variable on a second equals the sum of its direct effect and any indirect effects operating through causally intervening variables. Thus, the unstandardized total effect of race on SES is 6.31 + 5.68 (see note 26) or 11.99. Obviously, the total effect is a more comprehensive measure of the causal relationship between two variables than is the direct effect.

The distributions of the unstandardized, standardized, and relative estimates of total effects for the 125 SMSAs are presented in Tables 5.3a–c. The relationship between total effects and direct effects is necessarily the same across the three types of estimates and so can be quickly summarized. We have just seen that the average total effect of race on SES is almost twice as large as the average direct effect. Its average total effect on earnings is close to four times as great as the average direct effect. Thus, at each step in the status-attainment process, the indirect effects cumulate on top of new direct effects until the average difference in earnings between whites and nonwhites, controlling for sex and age, reaches $1723.[27] The total effects of sex on achieved characteristics are not substantially different from the direct effects. This is a consequence of sex having a large

[26]This is only approximate because the actual average of the SMSA indirect effects is the average of the analogous product of two direct effects for each SMSA that generally is not the same as the product of the averages of the two direct effects. The actual average unstandardized indirect effect is 5.68.

[27]Although the following verbal summary applies equally well to the three sets of coefficients, the numerical values refer to the unstandardized model (Table and Figure 5.3a).

TABLE 5.3a
Summary Statistics for the Distribution of Total Effects for the 125 <u>Unstandardized</u>
Models

Total effects for education structural equation

These equal direct effects (Table 5.2a) since
there are no intervening variables

Total effects for SES structural equation

	c_{sex}	c_{race}	c_{age}	c_{ed}^a	s_{total}	s_{total}^2
10th percentile	-4.3422	3.7895	-.0504	3.9000	21.59	466.17
mean	-1.6551	11.9907	.0715	4.5058	22.56	509.42
90th percentile	.6218	20.9569	.2006	5.1134	23.36	545.62
standrad deviation	2.0602	7.5236	.0949	.4832	.65	29.38

Total effects for earnings structural equation

	c_{sex}	c_{race}	c_{age}	c_{ed}	c_{SES}^a	s_{total}	s_{total}^2
10th percentile	3.3620	.5841	.0971	.5937	.0241	5.2052	27.09
mean	4.3135	1.7229	.1331	.7545	.0433	6.2688	39.98
90th percentile	5.0635	2.9010	.1727	.8976	.0595	7.3524	54.06
standard deviation	.7627	1.0575	.0276	.1270	.0138	.8263	10.73

[a] Equals the corresponding direct effect (Table 5.2a), since there are no intervening variables.

direct effect only on the last achieved characteristic in the model, earnings. The negative direct effect of age cohort on education (average, from Table 5.2.1, equals $-.093$) causes the total effects of age on earnings ($133 per year) and especially SES (.072 points of SES per year) to be substantially less than the corresponding direct effects ($183 and .49 points of SES, respectively, per year). Finally, the average total effect of education on earnings of $754, which includes an indirect effect through SES, is about one-third greater than the average direct effect of $562.

So far, we have only discussed, albeit from several perspectives, the average effect of one variable on another. The existence of these causal connections among ascribed and achieved characteristics implies that there is consolidation. We conclude the summary of the average of 125 path models by briefly examining the estimates of the distributional parameters of the model (Table 5.2a). The average variances of sex and race simply confirm that the heterogeneity of sex is

TABLE 5.3b
Summary Statistics for the Distribution of Total Effects for the 125 <u>Standardized</u> Models

Total effects for education structural equation

These equal direct effects (Table 5.2b) since
there are no intervening variables

Total effects for SES structural equation

	C_{sex}	C_{race}	C_{age}	C_{ed}^a	S_{total}	S_{total}^2
10th percentile	-.0957	.0301	-.0257	.5921	equals 1.0	
mean	-.0369	.1760	.0345	.6580	by	
90th percentile	.0140	.3924	.0961	.7096	assumption	
standard deviation	.0458	.1242	.0459	.0453		

Total effects for earnings structural equation

	C_{sex}	C_{race}	C_{age}	C_{ed}	C_{SES}^a	S_{total}	S_{total}^2
10th percentile	.2906	.0180	.1805	.3254	.0944	equals 1.0	
mean	.3442	.0896	.2343	.3990	.1556	by	
90th percentile	.3994	.1878	.2955	.4667	.2068	assumption	
standard deviation	.0461	.0628	.0422	.0515	.0455		

[a] Equals the corresponding direct effect (Table 5.2b), since there are no intervening variables.

almost at the maximum possible value and is substantially greater than that of race. The variance (inequality) of age is set by assumption, for lack of appropriate data, and, therefore, is not a result that merits comment. The covariance of race and sex is small and of almost no consequence. The variances of the residuals for the unstandardized model equal that portion of the variances of the dependent variables that cannot be accounted for by the independent variables, but their numerical values are not very readily interpretable. The residual variances (see Note 6) of the standardized model (Table 5.2b) equal the percentage of unexplained variance $(1-R^2)$ and indicate that a much higher percentage of the variances of SES and earnings than of education is "explained" by the included variables. (If parental-status variables were available, much more of the variance of education could be accounted for.) However perhaps more substantively important, the residual variances of the relative model (Table 5.2c) indicate that in terms of total amount of unexplained inequality, earnings has by far the most,

TABLE 5.3c
Summary Statistics for the Distribution of Total Effects for the 125 <u>Relative</u> Models

Total effects for education structural equation

These equal direct effects (Table 5.2c) since
there are no intervening variables

Total effects for SES structural equation

	c_{sex}	c_{race}	c_{age}	c_{ed}^{a}	s_{total}	s_{total}^{2}
10th percentile	-.1137	.1042	-.0577	1.0264	.5340	.2851
mean	-.0429	.3027	.0772	1.2579	.5722	.3287
90th percentile	.0158	.5219	.2202	1.4882	.6216	.3864
standard deviation	.0555	.1939	.1024	.1712	.0353	.0410

Total effects for earnings structural equation

	c_{sex}	c_{race}	c_{age}	c_{ed}	c_{SES}^{a}	s_{total}	s_{total}^{2}
10th percentile	.6156	.0929	.7469	1.1316	.1518	.9197	.8458
mean	.7019	.2841	.9362	1.3586	.2809	1.0285	1.0626
90th percentile	.7742	.4886	1.1967	1.6403	.3935	1.1462	1.3137
standard deviation	.0752	.1777	.1721	.1976	.0909	.0950	.1940

[a] Equals the corresponding direct effect (Table 5.2c), since there are no intervening variables.

followed distantly by SES and then education. Part of the reason that the model explains such a small percentage of the inequality of educational attainment is probably that there is not very much inequality of education, compared to SES and, especially, earnings.

Variation among SMSAs

In the previous section, the results of estimating a separate path model for each of the 125 SMSAs were summarized. This was done by reporting and interpreting the average of the 125 estimates of each parameter of the model. In this section the issue of variation among the SMSAs is addressed: Does the process of status attainment vary from one SMSA to another?

We begin by examining the distributional parameters (panel one of Table 5.2a) because, as indicated earlier, the logic of structural equation modeling implies that most of the variation among SMSAs in the model estimates should be concentrated in the distributional parameters rather than the structural coefficients. Despite this methodologically based a priori expectation, there are virtually no differences among SMSAs in sex heterogeneity: the variance of sex only varies from 0.249 to 0.250. Even with the very large sample sizes being used, Bartlett's test (Snedecor and Cochran, 1967:296) of the null hypothesis that all 125 variances are equal cannot be rejected. As stated previously, we do not have the univariate-distribution statistics which would be necessary to perform the analogous between-SMSA comparisons of the variance of age. Although we have assumed no differences, assigning a variance of 121 to each SMSA, actually some differences undoubtedly exist.

There is, however, substantial variation among SMSAs in racial heterogeneity. Some SMSAs, such as Binghamton (NY), Johnstown (PA), and Duluth-Superior (MN/WI) have very few nonwhites and, therefore, very little racial heterogeneity while several others, such as Honolulu (HA), Memphis (TN), and Jackson (MS), are more than 30% nonwhite. As a result, there is an eightfold increase in race heterogeneity between the 10th percentile ($s^2 = .024$) and the 90th percentile ($s^2 = .192$) of the 125 SMSAs. These differences are so large as to leave little cause for applying a formal significance test for differences of variances or heterogeneity. Hence, other measures that are related to heterogeneity will exhibit more between-SMSA variation if they involve race than if they involve sex. In particular, this implies that there is likely to be much more *variation across SMSAs* in racial consolidation (as measured by the correlation or covariance of race with other attributes) than there is variation in sex consolidation. This is true even when the average level of sex consolidation is much higher than the average level of race consolidation (as is the case for earnings). Stated differently, regardless of the degree of sex consolidation, it is relatively constant across SMSAs whereas race consolidation is much more variable across SMSAs, owing to the greater variability of racial heterogeneity. This is exactly what we found in Chapter 4.

Table 5.4 illustrates this distinction between average level of consolidation and among-SMSA variability in consolidation. Column 3 of the top panel is a repetition from Table 5.2a, first panel, indicating that race heterogeneity varies much more across SMSAs than sex heterogeneity. Columns 4, 5, and 6 present average levels of consolidation of sex and race with the three achieved characteristics as well as the variation among SMSAs in level of consolidation. They show that of these six forms of consolidation, sex and earnings consolidation is the greatest, averaging .35 across the SMSAs. The other two types of sex consolidation are lower, on the average, than the three types of race consolidation. However, examination of the variation among SMSAs indicates that all three types of race consolidation vary more than each type of sex consolidation. (Even the difference in the standard deviations of sex-earnings consolidation [.045] and

TABLE 5.4

Relationship Between Heterogeneity of Ascribed Characteristics and Consolidation of Ascribed with Achieved Characteristics

Univariate Statistics

Ascribed characteristic (1)	Distribution across SMSAs (2)	Heterogeneity of (1) (3)	Consolidation[a] of (1) with		
			Educ (4)	SES (5)	Earn (6)
Sex	average	.2496	.0355	.0420	.3470
	standard deviation	.0003	.0235	.0354	.0451
Race	average	.0959	.1325	.1747	.1003
	standard deviation	.0617	.1092	.1241	.0620

Correlations of Sex and Race Heterogeneity with their
Consolidation with Achieved Characteristics

Heterogeneity of (1)	Consolidation of (1) with		
	Educ (2)	SES (3)	Earn (4)
Sex	.1765*	-.0069	.1114
Race	.8460**	.8853**	.8711**

* p < .05
** p < .001

[a] Consolidation, for each SMSA, is measured by the Pearson correlation of the ascribed characteristic with an achieved characteristic.

race-earnings consolidation [.062] is significant beyond the .01 level.) The lower panel of Table 5.4 shows that the degree of race consolidation with achieved characteristics is very closely related ($r > .80$) to the degree of race heterogeneity. This is not true for sex, precisely because the differences in sex heterogeneity are so small that they can, at most, be only weakly related to anything.[28]

The residual variances (shown in Tables 5.2a–c) also vary significantly among SMSAs. Without going into detail, we can observe that for each achieved char-

[28]Whereas this observed relationship between heterogeneity and consolidation is reflecting a real phenomenon, some readers might reasonably suggest that such a relationship is, in some sense, not surprising and therefore not very interesting; that given our operationalization of differentiation and consolidation, it would only be surprising if a positive relationship did *not* exist. We return to this issue shortly.

acteristic, the absolute amount of variance (unstandardized model, Table 5.2a), the percentage of total variance (standardized model, Table 5.2b), and the amount of (squared) inequality (relative model, Table 5.2c) that cannot be accounted for by the independent variables of the corresponding structural equation vary from one SMSA to another (as indicated by the standard deviations of s_{res}^2).

The direct effects of every independent on every dependent variable in our structural equations are shown in Tables 5.2, and the corresponding total effects are in Tables 5.3. For both direct and total effects, the tables indicate the mean coefficient for the 125 SMSAs and the variation in coefficients among them (by presenting the standard deviation and two extreme percentiles, the 10th and the 90th). Since these coefficients are sample estimates, we would not expect any coefficient to be identical for every SMSA, even if there were no variation in the corresponding population parameters. This raises the question of whether the observed variation across SMSAs of a direct effect might be entirely attributable to sampling variation or whether it is also due to real differences in the influences reflected by the B's. Using the estimated B's and their sample standard errors it is possible to perform an ANOVA-like F test of the null hypothesis that the 125 unobserved SMSA-population parameters are equal to some common value. We are, thus, testing what is usually an implicit and untested assumption of structural equation models: that the structural parameters are invariant across populations. The F statistics in Table 5.5 summarize the results of applying this test to each of the 12 structural parameters of our three path models.[29] For all 36 tests, the null hypothesis of invariance across populations is unequivocally ($p < .0001$) rejected. It appears that one of the insights our comparative approach offers is that the conceptual distinction between exogenous-distributional parameters that can vary across populations and structural parameters that remain generally valid beyond any particular population is, at least, questionable.[30]

Whereas all the F statistics are clearly significant, they vary substantially in size. From the same analyses which produced these F statistics, it is possible to estimate what percentage of the observed variation in each structural coefficient

[29]It should be noted that although our populations are independent of each other, the different B's within our model are *not* independent of each other and therefore these 12 tests are not completely independent. Nevertheless, under the null hypothesis that all 12 parameters are constant across the 125 SMSAs, each F test is valid. More specifically, each test implicitly assumes that the other 11 parameters are constant across SMSAs, and if we reject the null hypothesis, we can conclude that either the parameter in question is not constant *or* at least one of the other parameters is not constant. In either case, we are led to reject the assumption of global invariance of structural parameters.

[30]It could be validly argued that one reason for the observed lack of invariance of structural parameters is that relevant correlated variables are missing from the path models. Assuming that their population specific parameters differed across SMSAs, this would introduce varying amounts of bias into the above B's for the 125 SMSAs. While we would be the first to admit that our path models are incomplete, we doubt that this would account for all or even most of the great variation in B's among SMSAs.

TABLE 5.5
Analysis of Invariance of Structural Coefficients: F Statistic and Estimated
Ratio of True Variance of Coefficients to Observed Variance (alpha)

Coefficient		Unstandardized model	Standardized model	Relative model
$B_{ed,sex}$	F^a	5.141	4.922	4.840
	alpha	.805	.797	.793
$B_{ed,race}$	F	26.776	41.686	27.652
	alpha	.963	.976	.964
$B_{ed,age}$	F	13.580	14.011	18.700
	alpha	.926	.929	.947
$B_{SES,sex}$	F	7.091	7.197	6.926
	alpha	.859	.861	.856
$B_{SES,race}$	F	10.341	20.414	10.687
	alpha	.903	.951	.906
$B_{SES,age}$	F	12.560	12.269	14.686
	alpha	.920	.918	.932
$B_{SES,ed}$	F	15.776	5.776	26.574
	alpha	.937	.827	.962
$B_{earn,sex}$	F	15.508	10.409	6.703
	alpha	.936	.904	.851
$B_{earn,race}$	F	3.779	3.982	3.512
	alpha	.735	.749	.715
$B_{earn,age}$	F	16.855	13.033	10.754
	alpha	.941	.923	.907
$B_{earn,ed}$	F	10.045	8.185	8.267
	alpha	.900	.878	.879
$B_{earn,SES}$	F	6.103	4.346	6.091
	alpha	.836	.770	.836

[a] These F statistics each have 124 degrees of freedom in both the numerator and denominator and are significant beyond the .0001 level.

is real, that is, not due to sampling error. We call this ratio *alpha,* borrowing the name of the analogous statistic in reliability analysis, and report it for each coefficient in Table 5.5. For most of the coefficients, more than 80% of the observed between-SMSA variation is real. There is no coefficient for which the sampling variation accounts for more than 30% of the observed variance.

In the introductory remarks about path analysis, we suggested that there were two reasons for estimating and presenting three sets of structural coefficients. First, although they are algebraically related to each other, their magnitudes must be interpreted somewhat differently and this, of course, affects comparisons of one parameter with another. Second, we suggested that there are few or no theoretical grounds for assuming a priori which set of coefficients is the "true" set of structural coefficients and therefore should remain most invariant across populations.

For the majority of the coefficients, the differences among the three alphas of corresponding unstandardized, standardized, and relative parameters are less than 3%. In these cases, the differences in degree of invariance are small. Furthermore, none of the three types of coefficients is systematically more likely to be the most or least invariant. For those remaining coefficients—$b_{\text{SES,race}}$, $b_{\text{earn,race}}$, $b_{\text{earn,sex}}$, $b_{\text{earn,SES}}$, and $b_{\text{SES,ed}}$—there are clear differences (on the order of 5%) in the degree of invariance of the three types of parameters. Here, the most obvious pattern is that when race is an independent variable, the standardized coefficient is likely to confound the structural coefficient with the variance (heterogeneity) of race. The substantial variation among SMSAs in race heterogeneity increases the variation in the standardized race coefficient. A second pattern involves only the coefficients of the earnings structural equation: because there are cost-of-living differences among SMSAs, a dollar does not mean the same thing in every SMSA. Both the standardized and relative coefficients adjust for this, albeit in somewhat different ways. Thus, the unstandardized coefficients of the earnings equations should be most sensitive to differences in the cost of living, and this almost surely raises their variance (relative to the corresponding standardized and relative coefficients). Last, we note that the standardized $b_{\text{SES,ed}}$ varies less among SMSAs than the corresponding unstandardized and relative coefficients. This is consistent with the notion of the returns to education being strongly dependent on the supply of and demand for individuals with various amounts of training: in such a situation, rewards to education would depend on one's relative position (e.g., percentile rank) in the distribution and not the absolute difference or the difference relative to the mean.

For the final step of our analysis of the 125 SMSA path models, we examine the relationship between each structural coefficient and some characteristics of the SMSAs for which we have data. The purpose of this analysis is to determine whether the variance among SMSAs of each structural coefficient is associated with some specific demographic features of the SMSAs. The five characteristics are South (whether or not the SMSA is located in the south); the size (population) of the SMSA; the percentage of families in the SMSA living below the poverty line (a nationally defined poverty level that is adjusted for family size and structure); the percentage increase in per capita income from 1960 to 1970; and a measure of the SMSAs age (the number of years since the central city of the SMSA attained a population of 50,000 persons).

We regress the structural coefficients (weighting SMSAs by the inverse of the estimated variance of the coefficient) on these five SMSA characteristics. In total, 36 regression equations are estimated—one for each of the 12 coefficients of the three types of models—using a stepwise regression procedure. The results are summarized in Table 5.6, where only the direction and significance of the effect of each demographic characteristic that entered an equation are indicated. The first observation that one can make about Table 5.6 is that the three equations for the unstandardized, standardized, and relative versions of a coefficient tend, in general, to be quite similar: most of the time a demographic SMSA characteristic is either in all three equations or not in any of them. Even the significance levels for the effect of an SMSA characteristic, as indicated by the number of pluses or minuses, are usually similar for each of the three equations in a set.[31]

Several of the coefficients vary according to whether or not the SMSA is located in the South. Table 5.6 clearly shows that the race structural coefficients for all versions of the education, SES, and earnings equations are larger in the Southern SMSAs. This indicates that the differences in average levels of achievement between blacks and whites (controlling for the other variables) are consistently larger in the South. This is in accordance with Featherman and Hauser's (1978: Chapter 7) findings of regional differences[32] in the differential attainment of blacks and nonblacks (see especially p. 403 for education and p. 423 for earnings). We also find that the SES returns to education are lower in Southern than in other SMSAs and this, too, agrees with Featherman and Hauser (1978:410 and Tables 7.5 and 7.6). Both studies find no systematic difference between regions in the earnings returns to education, but do find that the earnings returns to SES ($b_{earn.SES}$) are higher in Southern SMSAs. The latter result appears to represent a change from the early 1960s when, according to Featherman and Hauser's analysis of the OCG-I data (see their Table 7.7), earnings

---

[31]The major exceptions to this pattern of similarity are the effects of SMSA size on the unstandardized structural coefficients $b_{earn.sex}$ and $b_{earn.age}$. These coefficients are significantly positive whereas the effect of size on both the standardized and relative coefficients are significantly negative. The positive effects of size on the unstandardized coefficients are due to variations in the cost of living, which are positively related to SMSA size. In additional analyses, not reported in Table 5.6, once we control for the average earnings of the SMSA (a common indicator of cost of living), the effects of size on the two unstandardized coefficients reverse, becoming very significantly negative.

[32]Featherman and Hauser only present and compare unstandardized coefficients.

TABLE 5.6
Weighted Regressions of Structural Coefficients on Demographic Characteristics of SMSAs*

| Coefficient | Model | Demographic Characteristics | | | | | R^2 |
		South	Size	% Poor	Economic growth	Age	
$B_{ed,sex}$	unstd		++++		-		.401
	std		++++		--		.400
	rel		++++		-		.407
$B_{ed,race}$	unstd	++++	--		+		.530
	std	++++					.416
	rel	++++	--	+	+		.573
$B_{ed,age}$	unstd		+++			----	.197
	std	+++	++++			----	.261
	rel		+++			----	.200
$B_{SES,sex}$	unstd	+	----	---	++		.356
	std	+	----	---	++		.353
	rel	+	----	---	++		.320
$B_{SES,race}$	unstd	++++	++				.482
	std	++++	++	++		+	.663
	rel	++++		+++			.470
$B_{SES,age}$	unstd	--	----	--			.457
	std	--	----	-		--	.504
	rel	----	----			--	.555
$B_{SES,ed}$	unstd	----	----	----			.681
	std	---	----	-		+++	.342
	rel	----	---	----	-		.747
$B_{earn,sex}$	unstd		++	----			.427
	std		----	----	--		.426
	rel		----	----			.281
$B_{earn,race}$	unstd	+++	++++		---		.284
	std	++++	++++		-		.304
	rel	++	++++		--		.217
$B_{earn,age}$	unstd		++++	----			.292
	std	--	----			++	.199
	rel		--				.097
$B_{earn,ed}$	unstd			----		++	.236
	std						0.000
	rel			--			.068
$B_{earn,SES}$	unstd	++	++++			---	.379
	std	+	++++			--	.203
	rel	++++	++++			-	.303

*
   + or - $p < .05$
 ++ or -- $p < .01$
 +++ or --- $p < .001$ two-tailed
++++ or ---- $p < .0001$

[a] South – 1 if SMSA located in south, 0 otherwise.
[b] Size – Population of SMSA (sometimes transformed to logarithm).
[c] Percentage Poor – Proportion of families living below the "low income level" (adjusted for family size and structure).
[d] Economic Growth – Percentage increase in per capita income from 1960 to 1970.
[e] Age – Number of years since central city attained a population of 50,000.

returns to SES were higher in the nonsouth. Thus, where comparisons are possible, all differences that we find between the process of stratification that operates in Southern SMSAs, compared to Northern SMSAs, agree with those reported by Featherman and Hauser (1978).[33]

The SMSAs population size is also strongly related to many of the structural coefficients of our status-attainment models, as Table 5.6 indicates. The larger an SMSA is, the more the average educational attainment of men tends to exceed that of women. We saw earlier (Tables 5.2) that women's average SES attainment, controlling for education, age, and race, tends to exceed that of men, resulting in a negative $b_{SES,sex}$ structural coefficient in most SMSAs. This coefficient tends to be *more* negative in larger SMSAs, indicating that like education, the difference between sexes is again largest in the more populated SMSAs (see Note 31). With respect to racial differences, we find that the differences between black and white averages of SES and earnings, controlling for the other variables in the equations, are greatest in the larger SMSAs. Thus, once we control for whether an SMSA is located in the South, we find that blacks fare worse economically, relative to other persons, in the big cities.

The differences in attainment between age cohorts are consistently smaller in larger SMSAs. In larger SMSAs, older cohorts are not so inferior in education and not so superior with respect to SES and earnings (see again Note 31) as in smaller SMSAs. Finally, we find that the SES returns to education are smaller in the large SMSAs whereas the rate at which differences in SES translate into differences in earnings increases with population size. In a large metropolis, there seem to be more alternative avenues to education for getting a good job, but such a job is more important for a high income than in a smaller SMSA.

The other three demographic characteristics tend to exhibit more sporadic and less significant relationships with the structural coefficients. Table 5.6 does, however, indicate that women do better, relative to men, with respect to SES and earnings, in those SMSAs with a higher percentage of poor families (where men are more inferior to women in SES and less superior to them in earnings). Women in such communities may, on the average, have relatively greater responsibility for the economic well-being of the household and, therefore, be more likely to work in the relatively higher-status occupations and better-paying full-time jobs. There is also some evidence that it is harder to convert educational attainment into increased SES and earnings in those communities that have a higher incidence of poverty. If the percentage of families living below the poverty line is an indicator of the status of an SMSAs economy, it may well be that the norm of ''get a good education in order to get a good job'' cannot operate

---

[33]Though no comparison to the Featherman and Hauser study is possible, we also find that the differences between birth cohorts in SES, as measured by $b_{SES,age}$, are substantially smaller in Southern SMSAs, whereas the SES differences between women and men ($b_{SES,sex}$) are somewhat larger.

effectively in these economically depressed communities. Poverty also increases racial differences in SES, probably because poor employment opportunities affect the underprivileged minority most.

Looking at the possible effect of economic growth on the status-attainment process, we see that those SMSAs whose per capita income increased the fastest during the 1960s have somewhat smaller differences between the sexes in all three types of attainment. It is also these same communities that tend to have a smaller earnings gap between the races. Though these effects are not large, they suggest that economic growth may facilitate the reduction of differences in attainment that are due to ascribed characteristics, such as sex and race. It appears that economic growth diminishes discrimination.

Older people seem to be more at a disadvantage, compared with younger ones, in older rather than newer metropolitan areas. The inferior education of older cohorts is more pronounced in older cities, and the superior socioeconomic status of older people is less pronounced there than in cities that have more recently become large metropolitan places. Perhaps the migrants responsible for recent population growth have particularly good educations and particularly high socioeconomic achievements, which could account for the observed findings, but we have no interpretation to explain the tendency for the financial returns to SES being somewhat smaller in older SMSAs.

Conclusions

Every collectivity—small or large—has a social structure. There are many levels on which social structure can be analyzed, ranging from the structure of small groups to the structure of entire societies. Social structure on any level has emergent properties that do not characterize its elements on lower levels because they refer to the composition of and relations among its various elements. Three types of such emergent structural elements are (1) the composition of different elements—various forms of heterogeneity and inequality; (2) the relationships of various dimensions of differentiation in the structure—the extent of consolidation or intersection; and (3) the social relations between people, particularly between different groups or strata—intergroup relations, such as intermarriage. The unit of analysis is the collectivity whose social structure is under investigation; social structures on higher levels constitute its social context whereas social structures on lower levels constitute its elements, the relations among which define its emergent properties. Thus, the metropolis is the unit of analysis of this inquiry, the region or society is its social context, and the groups and strata to which individuals belong are the elements whose relations define its properties.

The study of causal influences always takes some social conditions as given and examines their effects on other social conditions. In the study of social structure, such influences may be distinguished on three levels. First, its social context influences a structure's characteristics. For example, the nature of the society influences the metropolitan structures within it. To examine these influences requires comparison of different societies. Second, various antecedent conditions of the unit of analysis itself may influence its social structure, such as its economic growth during the past decade. Third, the internal social processes that connect its elements—for instance, processes of status attainment—influence the social structure. It is the latter influences that have been the focus of this chapter. The status-attainment model was employed to dissect how background characteristics affect, directly and indirectly, the achieved positions of individuals and, in the process, generate a structure of interrelated positions. Of course, ascribed positions are not the only factors that influence education, occupational status, and earnings. Economic and industrial conditions are the major factors that determine the opportunities to achieve these positions. (The other influences are reflected in the residuals of the path models.) Given these conditions, however, the extent to which ascribed and achieved positions intersect or are consolidated is largely governed by the process of status attainment.

Thus, the internal causal process of status attainment was analyzed in each of the 125 SMSAs. Naturally, the results were not discussed for every SMSA. Instead, we examined the averages for the 125 cases and the variations among them. In briefly reviewing the main findings, we start with the direct effects. Controlling other conditions, educational differences are very small for sex, substantial for race, and pronounced for age cohorts. For every decade difference in birth cohort, there has been an increase of nearly 1 year in average years of schooling. Education, in turn, exerts the dominant influence on occupational status. The strongest direct effects on earnings are those of education, sex (men, of course, earning much more than women), and age. The pronounced difference between whites and blacks in earnings is largely the result of indirect effects, mediated by the lower education and occupational status of blacks. In contrast, sex has little indirect influence on earnings, so that its total effect is hardly different from its direct effect. The total effect of age on earnings is less than its direct effect, owing to the counteracting influence via education (that is, the lower education of older cohorts).

A basic assumption of the status-attainment model is that the path coefficients—also called *structural coefficients*—are relatively constant. For unless one assumes that they are more or less invariant, one can only describe, but cannot generalize about, a status-attainment process. But this assumption of invariant path coefficients is rarely tested, because status-attainment research is nearly always based on only a single case of social structure (that of one society or of one city), which makes testing it impossible (for a partial exception, see Note 8). The comparative approach of our inquiry, which involves 125 cases of social structure, makes it possible to test this assumption. The analysis reveals

that the hypothesis of invariance across population structures must be unequivocally rejected for all 12 coefficients examined.

These results negate a fundamental implicit assumption of the status-attainment model and suggests that it might better be considered as a base-line model
for a general theory. At the same time, the findings justify the assumption of our
macrosociological approach that there is sufficient variation in consolidation-
intersection among social structures to make its implication for social relations of
great interest for structural inquiry. The question arises as to what conditions in
SMSAs can account for these variations in their parameters of social structure.
Merely the slightest exploration of this issue has been possible in this chapter. To
give a few illustrations: in the South, compared to other parts of the country, race
is more consolidated with various aspects of achieved status; occupational returns to education are lower; but earnings returns to occupational status are
higher. The larger an SMSA, the greater are the sex differences in education
(being higher for males) and in occupational status (being higher for females).
Economic differences between whites and blacks are also greater in big cities,
obviously in favor of whites. Poor economic conditions in an SMSA seem to
intensify racial differences in socioeconomic status, whereas good economic
conditions reduce racial differences in earnings.

The main conclusion of this chapter is that causal processes of status attainment within SMSAs exert substantial influences on their social structure. In
particular, these internal processes generate the degrees and kinds of intersection
or consolidation found in the social structure. This analysis tried to explain
important macrosociological features of metropolitan structures—intersection
and consolidation—in terms of the underying social processes within them. But
the passages before the Conclusion and the preceding paragraph had the opposite
focus and analyzed the influences of macrosociological conditions (such as
SMSA size and economic circumstances) and even contextual factors (such as
regional location) on the microsociological processes of status attainment.

Addendum to Chapter 5: Relations among
Distributional Parameters

Differentiation of a Nominal Attribute

If a nominal variable has K categories and one defines a complete set of dummy
variables in the conventional manner,[34] then it can easily be shown that the sum
of their variances equals the Gibbs–Martin index for the distribution of the
original nominal variable.

[34]Given a nominal variable, X, with K categories $(1, 2, 3, \ldots , K)$, the kth dummy variable is
defined for the ith individual as $D_{ik} = 0$ if $X_i \neq k$, $D_{ik} = 1$ if $X_i = k$.

Proof: If the dummy variables are defined as in Note 34, then the mean of D_k equals P_k, the proportion of people in the kth category of X. The variance of D_k equals $P_k(1 - P_k)$. Therefore, the sum of the variances is

$$\sum_k \sigma_{D_k}^2 = \sum_k P_k(1 - P_k) = \sum_k P_k - \sum_k P_k^2 = 1 - \sum P_k^2,$$

which is the computational formula for the Gibbs-Martin index.

For the special case of a dichotomous nominal variable, such as sex, the variances of the two dummy variables (D_1 and D_2) both equal the variance of the nominal variable (assuming standard $0/1$ or $1/2$ coding) and therefore the Gibbs–Martin index equals twice the variance of each.

Differentiation of a Ratio Attribute

As noted in Chapter 1, the numerator of the Gini coefficient equals the average (expected) absolute difference between all pairs of individuals. Using basic algebra, we now show that the standard deviation is a fixed proportion (70.7%) of the *square root* of the average *squared* (absolute) difference between all pairs:[35]

$$\frac{\sum_i (X_i - \bar{X})^2}{N} = \frac{\sum X_i^2 - N\bar{X}^2}{N}$$

$$= \frac{2N \sum X_i^2 - 2 \sum X_i \sum X_i}{2N^2}$$

$$= \frac{N \sum_i X_i^2 + N \sum_j X_j^2 - 2 \sum_i X_i \sum_j X_j}{2N^2}$$

$$= \frac{\sum_{ij} X_i^2 + \sum_{ij} X_j^2 - 2 \sum_{ij} X_i X_j}{2N^2}$$

$$= \frac{\sum_{ij}(X_i^2 - 2X_i X_j + X_j^2)}{2N^2}$$

$$= \frac{\sum_{ij}(X_i - X_j)^2}{2N^2}$$

$$= \frac{\sum_{ij}|X_i - X_j|^2}{2N^2}.$$

From this, it follows that

$$\text{Standard deviation } (\sigma) = \sqrt{(\sum_{ij}|X_i - X_j|^2)/2N^2} = \sqrt{E(|X_i - X_j|^2)/2}.$$

[35]Just as some statisticians refer to the concept of a *generalized mean*—$[(\sum X^p)/N]^{1/p}$—that yields the usual mean when $p = 1$, so the numerator of the Gini coefficient can be considered a special case of a *generalized standard deviation*, or vice versa. The standard deviation is, of course, the square root of the variance.

Since the coefficient of variation equals the standard deviation divided by the mean whereas the Gini coefficient equals the Gini-numerator divided by twice the mean, it follows that except for using a generalized mean in its numerator (in place of an ordinary mean), the equation for the coefficient of variation equals $\sqrt{2}$ times the equation for the Gini coefficient.

Measures of Consolidation

The correlation ratio (Eta), which the structural approach uses to measure the consolidation of a graduated and a nominal variable, is the one-way analysis-of-variance equivalent of the Pearson correlation. Eta equals the maximum possible correlation between the interval variable and any scaling of the nominal variable. Cramer's V, the measure of consolidation for two nominal variables, does not in general have an obvious correspondence to a Pearson correlation. However, it is true that for two dichotomous variables, Cramer's V, Eta, and r are all identical (except that V and Eta are not usually permitted to be negative and therefore equal the absolute value of r).

All three measures of consolidation have a maximum attainable absolute value of 1.0—indicating perfect consolidation—while zero indicates a complete absence of consolidation, corresponding to maximum intersection. They all are standardized (or relative) in the sense that they are invariant with respect to linear transformations of graduated attributes and any one-to-one invertible transformation of the nominal attributes.

CHAPTER 6

Concentric Circles

A complex system is one that comprises successive levels of subsystems, according to Simon (1962). He calls this criterion of complexity the hierarchical organization of systems because it involves interdependent elements repeatedly combining with others in a hierarchy of more and more encompassing systems and supersystems. Thus, interacting particles that in turn may consist of quarks constitute atoms; interrelated atoms compose molecules; and one can continue until one gets to planetary systems and entire galaxies. Simon applies this principle to a variety of phenomena, from solving difficult problems, which requires subdividing them into simpler elementary tasks, to biological evolution, because complex organisms consisting of millions of interdependent elements probably could not have developed had they not evolved step-by-step as simple subsystems recombined into increasingly complex systems. Social systems, like all complex ones, have this character.

The components of a complex social structure are themselves social structures. One can consider this the analytical distinction between macrosociological and microsociological inquiry. The latter analyzes the structures of interrelated individual roles, whereas the former analyzes social structures, the elements of which are also social structures. Nations have provinces or states; these consist of cities and villages, which comprise neighborhoods; and each of these subunits of society has a social structure. However, the structure of society is not merely the sum of the structures of its subunits, be they regions, districts, or communities. For society's structure entails variations and relations among, as well as within, its subunits. There are emergent properties on every level of social structure, and the combinations and interrelations of subunits are what produces these emergent properties. The analysis of society's structure must take the differentiation and the connections both among and within communities (or other subunits) into account.

From the perspective of individuals, the successive levels of more encompassing structure constitute concentric circles surrounding them, and membership in one bestows membership in the rest. Living in a neighborhood makes a person an inhabitant of a city, a resident of a state, a member of a region, and a citizen of a country. Such concentric circles exist not only in space but also in other dimensions, such as kinship, occupation, and religion. Society's differentiation can be decomposed into that within and that among its subunits. This is the case for any form of heterogeneity, any form of inequality, and any form of consolidated differences. Thus, a society may be ethnically heterogeneous either because most of its communities are heterogeneous or because its communities, though ethnically homogeneous, greatly differ in ethnic composition. Similarly, society's income inequality may be primarily a result of much inequality within most communities or of great differences in income among communities, with mostly rich people living in some places and mostly poor ones in others. Concomitant variations of several social differences, too, can be largely the result of such variations within or among communities. Moreover, all forms of differentiation can penetrate more or less deeply into successive levels of substructure. For example, ethnic heterogeneity may be found in cities as well as in the society at large but may not penetrate into the neighborhoods within cities. The present chapter addresses the question of how intergroup relations are affected by differentiation among subunits, differentiation within them, and the penetration of differentiation into successive subunits.

Decomposition of Differentiation

Any form of differentiation in a society—whether it involves heterogeneity, inequality, or consolidated differences—can be decomposed into two parts: the variations (or concomitant variations) within communities and the variation among communities. (When the subunits are SMSAs, the larger social structure is not the entire nation but only metropolitan America.) The initial analysis is confined to geographical subunits and to two levels—structure and substructure, such as society and community—although it will be later generalized to other than spatial dimensions and to more than two levels.

The problem under study now is not the significance of various forms of differentiation for social life in a society, nor is it their significance for social relations in communities. The theory presented in preceding chapters focused on these problems, inasmuch as it dealt with the implications of differentiation for intergroup relations in any collectivity, whether a society or community or some other large population. The research presented to test the theory centered attention on the influences of various forms of differentiation on intermarriage. The distinctive question raised at this point is what difference it makes for social life whether most of a social structure's differentiation is the result of differentiation within its various substructures or of the differences among its substructures. The reason that education, occupational status, and income are highly related in the United States could be mostly the result of the fact that they are highly related in every city. However, the correlations of the three in the country would also be observable if they were unrelated within cities but there existed parallel differences in all three respects among different communities, with some places being composed largely of educated managers and professionals with high salaries, others being inhabited primarily by poorly educated unskilled workers with low wages, and still other places having mostly residents in various intermediate class positions. Actually, of course, the total concomitant variations of the three variables are produced by a combination of both their within-group and their between-group correlations. What we want to know is how the relative proportion of the total variations within and among places affects intergroup relations.

The degree of heterogeneity within SMSAs varies much among SMSAs for some forms of heterogeneity and only little for other forms, and the same is true for the extent of inequality and the extent of consolidated social differences. For instance, the average internal racial heterogeneity is .19 for all 125 SMSAs, but it is substantially larger in Southern and smaller in Western SMSAs. The standard deviation of .13 indicates that there are considerable differences among SMSAs in racial heterogeneity. By contrast, although income inequality is pronounced, it is nearly the same in different places; the average Gini coefficient in the 125 SMSAs is .50, and the standard deviation is only .02. Racial heterogeneity for the entire country is .22; the reason that it is larger than the average for the 125 SMSAs is that this total heterogeneity in metropolitan America includes not only the internal heterogeneity in the 125 places but also the degree of racial heterogeneity among various places. There is more racial heterogeneity in some SMSAs than in the entire metropolitan population, but the (weighted) average of heterogeneity for all SMSAs cannot be larger than that for the entire population because the latter includes the between-SMSA in addition to the within-SMSA heterogeneity. This is the case for inequality, too, and it applies to any level of aggregation. The degree of differentiation in a social structure is always greater than the average degree of differentiation in its component substructures (unless all substructures are alike) because the differentiation in the large social structure includes that among as well as that within its substructures. (If the substructures differ in size, their averages must be weighted accordingly.)

The influences of differentiated social structures on social life can be studied on any level—entire societies, regions, communities, neighborhoods—although systematic analysis requires a sufficient number of these units of analysis for comparison. The decomposition of differentiation into that within and that among substructures, however, necessitates a more complex design with two levels of structure and a substantial number of cases within the substructures. One could use the data on many cities or metropolitan areas in the United States to decompose the country's differentiation of various forms into that within and that among these communities. But this would merely describe a single society and provide no comparative data for analyzing the influences of the decomposition. To find out what significance differentiation within and among subunits has for intergroup relations, it is necessary to have a substantial number of cases on three levels. First, we must have enough social structures—of societies, for example—for systematic comparison to dissect influences. Second, in each of these we need a sufficient number of substructures—such as communities—to distinguish the significance of differentiation within and among them. Third, there must be an adequate sample of cases within every substructure to estimate the various population distributions delineating the community structure, such as its ethnic heterogeneity, its income inequality, and how strongly race is related to other social positions.

This information is required to obtain empirical evidence on the effects of differentiation within and among substructures on social relations. However, the theory has implications that make it possible to formulate propositions that specify the relative influence of differentiation within and among substructures on social life, whether the substructures are states in a large nation or work groups in a small firm. In short, the theorems address the question of how intergroup relations are affected by the fact that proportionately much of the larger structure's differentiation is the result of differentiation within rather than among its substructures.

The more society's heterogeneity results from the heterogeneity within rather than that among its substructures, the more it promotes intergroup relations (T-15). *The more society's inequality results from the inequality within rather than among its substructures, the more it promotes status-distant relations* (T-16). These theorems are deducible from the assumptions that associations depend on social proximity (A-1) and on contact opportunities (A-2). The greater the proportion of the total difference among a population that occurs within rather than among dispersed places, the greater are the opportunities and constraints to associate with persons in different groups and strata (A-2), reducing the prevailing tendency to associate with others in one's own group or stratum (A-1). Alternatively, the theorem could be derived from T-11 that intersection promotes intergroup relations (which in turn follows from the first and fourth assumptions) because a large percentage of within-location differentiation implies that the differentiation under consideration—be it racial heterogeneity or income inequality—is little related and thus intersects substantially with place of residence (which is in this case treated simply as one type of social position that can be related to another).[1]

---

[1] One reason for deriving the two theorems (T-15, T-16) from A-2 and A-1 rather than T-11 is that T-11 refers to multiple intersection, whereas the decomposition theorems refer only to bivariate intersection (one differentiation dimension and the criterion of subdivision), and we saw in Chapter 4 that bivariate intersection has no consistent influence on intergroup relations, at least not on intermarriage.

These theorems are plausible enough. For example (T-15), if society's ethnic heterogeneity is the result of many different but internally homogeneous ethnic enclaves, there is less likelihood of interethnic relations than if the different ethnic groups do not live in separate ghettoes but together in the same neighborhoods. T-16 is also not unexpected. Economic inequality and the differences in life style accompanying it constitute less of a barrier to social intercourse if they are not further reinforced by the separation of different classes in different suburbs and urban locations.

The extent to which two (or more) social differences among people in a society are consolidated (correlated) can also be decomposed into the proportion of this concomitant variation occurring within communities and the proportion occurring among them, which together constitute the total concomitant variation. But this decomposition has paradoxical implications. Consolidated social differences impede intergroup relations, whereas intersecting ones promote them, as we saw in Chapter 4. Given the significance of contact opportunities, and hence of propinquity, for social associations (A-2), most associations occur between people who live in the same place and not between those in different cities. One would have thought, therefore, that the correlated social differences within the communities where most social associations take place would have a more inhibiting effect on them than do the ecological correlations of the mean differences among communities. But this inference is incorrect.

To be sure, consolidated social differences in a population inhibit social intercourse, according to T-11, because people who differ in several respects have little in common to attract each other. However, the question raised now is not how much consolidation there is in the entire society. On the contrary, this total consolidation is assumed to be given or statistically controlled,[2] and we now ask what proportion of that given consolidation is produced by *within-community* and what proportion by *between-community consolidation*. Thus, if education, occupational status, and income are strongly correlated, their consolidation discourages social relations among different classes. But it does not discourage these relations as much if the different classes live in the same towns and neighborhoods as it does if they live in different suburbs, which implies that much of society's consolidation results from between-community rather than within-community correlations. Hence, whatever the strength of the correlations of several social attributes, much between-community consolidation means that there is still more consolidation because these attributes are also correlated with yet another—place of residence—whereas predominant within-community consolidation does not indicate that the syndrome of correlated attributes is further

[2]Not only the degree of consolidation that is being decomposed but also the overall heterogeneity (or inequality) of the variables involved must be controlled to ascertain specific influences of the proportion within-subunits or the proportion between-subunits consolidation.

reinforced by this other factor—location. A decomposition theorem about consolidation can be formally derived. If group and status differences discourage social relations (A-1) and if the contact opportunities of people in the same community encourage social relations (A-2), it follows that *the more society's consolidated differences result from concomitant variations within rather than among substructures (communities), the less do the consolidated differences impede social relations* (T-17).[3]

As a matter of fact, disproportionately much variation within and disproportionately little of it among the communities in a society fosters social relations between members of different communities as well as between persons whose social attributes differ. This applies to heterogeneity, inequality, and consolidation. If people with the same attributes are dispersed among different places, which is implicit in the conception that most of society's differentiation occurs not among but within its communities, the assumed ingroup tendencies (A-1) provide incentives, particularly for members of small groups and small communities, to look for ingroup associates in other places. The greater the extent of religious heterogeneity resulting from such heterogeneity within communities, for instance, the greater is the pressure on Jews in small towns to go to other towns to associate with fellow Jews. Parallel considerations apply to within-community inequality and within-community consolidation.

Heterogeneity and inequality can only vary from zero to maximum differentiation (represented by unity), but consolidation can be negative as well as positive because it refers to associations of variables which can have either direction. Indeed, it is possible for a decomposition to reveal that the within-group and the between-group consolidation are in opposite directions. This is not merely a methodological issue but has interesting substantive implications. Studies have shown that people's choices are influenced by reference-group comparisons that modify initial preferences. For example, Davis (1966) found that college students with superior abilities are more likely to plan to pursue graduate work but that the average ability score in a college, holding constant individual's score, is negatively related to plans to go to graduate school. Students' evaluations of their chances of academic success are apparently influenced by comparisons with others in their social environment as well as by their own abilities. Similarly, people with higher incomes tend to report more psychological well-being than others, but the average income in a region and well-being are not positively related (Winship, 1976). People's economic circumstances compared with those of their neighbors influence their satisfaction, but as standards of living generally improve, the standards for judging satisfaction tend to rise. Thus, the social environment exerts sociopsychological influences on people's choices by gov-

---

[3]This theorem can also be deduced from T-11 that multiple consolidation of various social dimensions, including location, impedes intergroup relations.

erning reference-group comparisons, in addition to exerting structural influences on their choices by circumscribing opportunities, on which this book has centered attention.

Dimensions and Levels of Substructure

A society's geographical subunits, which often coincide with its political subdivisions (though not in the case of SMSAs), are not the only dimensions of substructure, and neither are societies the only units of analysis that can be divided into subunits for decomposing total differentiation in the larger population into within-group and between-group differences. Thus, one could compare major industries to determine how much of the division of labor in each occurs within rather than among its detailed industries and what effects this has on economic and social relations. Or one could compare major occupational groups to ascertain how much of society's differences in education, skills, and income result from variations within or variations among their detailed specialities.

Nominal parameters provide suitable subunits for decomposition; graduated ones do not. The interval scale on which a graduated population distribution is based does not demarcate distinct groups, which makes the categories one may use to divide an interval scale arbitrary. The exceptions are interval scales that entail natural breaks in the distributions. Years of schooling is an example that can be meaningfully divided into less than graduation from high school, high school graduation, some college, and college graduation or more education. Generally, however, nominal parameters are most appropriate as subunit criteria for decomposition.

Applying the decomposition procedure to other dimensions of society's subdivisions than its spatial subunits reveals the close connection of the decomposition theorems (T-15, T-16, T-17) with the intersection theorem (T-11). If people's differences in respect to Y are largely the result of differences *among* subgroups classified on the basis of X, it means that X and Y are closely related; knowing one makes it possible to predict the other, and the two social affiliations consolidate each other. However, if differences in Y are largely the result of *within*-group differences, group membership again being defined by X, the two are little related; one cannot be predicted from the other, and X and Y intersect. For example, between-sex differences in income indicate how strongly sex and income are related, whereas disproportionate within-sex income differences show that income and sex differences are little related and intersect. Thus, T-11 entails T-15, T-16, and T-17. But there are good grounds for formulating separate *decomposition theorems*. The community where people live has special significance for many of their social affiliations and is not usually considered merely one of many group memberships. A common place of residence provides contact opportunities that makes the three decomposition theorems deducible from the opportunity assumption (A-2), just as the principle of the influence of physical propinquity is deducible from this assumption. Hence, there is no reason to rely on indirect inferences and claim that the influence of physical propinquity is already implicit in the assumption of the influence of social proximity (A-1) or to claim that the influence of within-subgroup differences is already implicit in the theorem about the influence of intersection (T-11). Finally, as already noted, T-11 refers to multivariate whereas T-15 and T-16 refer to bivariate relationships.

If the extent to which society's differentiation results from within-community differentiation fosters intergroups relations (T-15, T-16, T-17) and if intergroup relations enhance the chances of social mobility (T-6), it follows that disproportionate differentiation within communities improves the chances of social mobility. Hence, the combination of one of the decomposition theorems and T-6 implies three further theorems. *The more society's heterogeneity is the product of within-community heterogeneity, the better are the chances of social mobility* (T-18). *The more society's inequality is the product of within-community inequality, the better are the chances of social mobility* (T-19). *The more society's consolidated differences are the product of concomitant variations within rather than among communities, the better are the chances of social mobility* (T-20).

When consolidated differences in important resources and social positions are further reinforced by spatial segregation of the different social classes, it greatly affects people's life chances as well as marital opportunities and social life generally. Status-attainment research has been criticized for conceptualizing stratification in terms of continua and ignoring the important difference between social classes, particularly between the dominant class, whose superior resources enable its members to exercise much power in society, and the working class, who lack such resources and who have little if any power (Wright and Perrone, 1977; Robinson and Kelley, 1979). The criticism often emphasizes that Marx centered attention on the distinction between owners of the means of production and workers who only own their labor power, whereas stratification research fails to take this crucial distinction between discrete social classes into account.

In today's corporate society, however, there is no such clear-cut boundary. Although people with great wealth and much power can easily be distinguished from the large majority of the population, a sharp line between them does not exist because there are gradations of wealth, authority, and power. But it really makes little difference, for Marx's theory or any other class theory, that there are many borderline cases whose classification in the ruling class or outside it is equivocal. The essential point is that there is a power elite whose vast resources and dominant positions clearly differ from the meager resources, lack of authority, and powerlessness of the large majority, and this important structural difference is not negated by the presence of intermediate cases, the persons with more resources and power than most but less than the members of the dominant elite. What tends to strengthen class differences, according to the theory advanced, is not so much neat class lines or even great inequality of one sort or another but the consolidation of dominant positions by superior resources and status in various respects. This is particularly relevant for the segregation of the upper class from others. Such spatial separation reinforces the import of consolidated class differences on people's life chances and social circles.

Morever, even if status is defined in terms of a continuum of important resources, such as wealth and power, there is a potential class line involving a fundamental conflict of interest. For any distribution on the basis of inequality has a dividing line, as noted in Chapter 3, below which people's improvement would reduce inequality and above which their further improvement would increase inequality. The greater the existing inequality is, the closer to the top is the line that divides those whose upward mobility from those whose downward mobility would reduce inequality. This implies that the upper–lower boundary, as the line is termed in Chapter 3, divides the population into a large group who are interested in reductions in the inequality of the distribution of resources and a smaller group who are interested in maintaining (if not increasing) existing levels of inequality. In short, there is a conflict of interest inherent in inequality that creates a potential class dichotomy, although other conditions must be favorable for this potential actually to be realized.

Multiple levels of successive subdivisions are of special interest. They are Simon's criterion of a complex structure. Not all differences in society involve successive subdivisions. Sex is an obvious example. There are men and women, but they cannot be further subdivided by the same criterion. In contrast, a country's spatial subdivisions can be subdivided repeatedly, as already mentioned, starting with broad regions and ending up with neighborhoods or even blocks. Similarly, American religions can be divided into Christianity, Judaism, and Islam; Christians are either Protestants or Catholics; the major religions are subdivided into specific denominations, such as Lutheranism or Greek Orthodox or Reform Judaism; and every denomination consists of specific congregations. The multiple subdivisions of conglomerates in the private sector and of government departments in the public sector are well-known cases of hierarchically organized bureaucracies. Occupations can be classified into major groups, such as the professions or detailed occupations, of which the Census recognizes more than 500 and the *Dictionary of Occupational Titles* many thousands (U.S. Employment Service, 1977). Even these narrower occupations can be further subdivided into specialties recognized only by experts in the field. Thus, high-energy theoretical physicists are divided into more than two dozen specialties. Another case is the kinship structure in traditional societies where most relatives outside the nuclear family are not lumped together as cousins but fine distinctions are made between closer relatives and more distant ones depending on how recently the ancestor lived from whom common descent is claimed.

Such successive levels of subdivision are concentric circles from the perspective of an individual. The social structure can be viewed by participants partly as concentric circles of ingroups with varying scopes—ranging from neighborhood to nation—and partly as crosscutting circles whose memberships differ and whose intersection defines their distinctive position—such as a single white male clerk of Irish descent who graduated from high school. Both kinds of circles sometimes divide people whom at other times they unite, but they do so in different ways. Concentric circles involve subgroups that often feud with one another but that sometimes combine in the larger group to which they belong on the next level to oppose another group on that level. Thus, cities in an area may be in conflict over water rights but unite in a court fight of their state against other states involving federal revenue allocations. Crosscutting circles divide the population along different lines on different issues. Union and management are on opposite sides at the bargaining table; both are often found on the same side in conflicts of their industry with other industries or the government; and in a controversy about abortion, religious affiliation may largely govern people's position, regardless of their occupation or industry. The basic distinction is that the narrowest group remains the same when concentric circles divide along different lines, whereas there is no permanent ingroup when crosscutting circles redivide. Not all crosscutting groups to which a person belongs have necessarily any other member in common, but when feuding clans join in their tribe's war against another, each person's clan remains with him on the same side. Concentric circles never divide the narrowest ingroup, but intersecting circles may. The permanent nature of the narrowest concentric circles probably is a major source of the strong ingroup pressures as well as the strong ingroup support in simple societies, which are predominantly characterized by concentric rather than crosscutting circles.

Concentric circles are indicative of social distance, just as the interval scales of graduated parameters are. Two mechanical engineers are closer in their work than two professionals in different occupations; siblings are more closely related than first cousins, who are closer than second cousins; just as two college graduates are less far apart in education than either is to someone who has not completed high school. There is an important difference, however, which corresponds to Parsons' (1951:61–63) distinction between particularistic and universalistic criteria of evaluation. Whether a person is a close or distant relative of ego cannot be ascertained by applying an external standard but only in reference to ego's own position in the kinship system, whereas whether someone's annual wage is $10,000 or $20,000 is measured by a universal standard that is independent of anybody else's economic position. The distinction drawn is not merely that between objective and subjective standards of judgment. Even for such an objective standard as physical distance, there is no way we can classify people by physical propinquity except in reference to a given person's location, whereas we can classify people by years of education without any particular reference point because the universal scale (years of schooling) suffices. Particularism also lacks the common value standards universalism provides. Which is the best religion depends on one's own religious commitment, but while some may believe that the poor are most blessed, poor and rich alike must acknowledge that the rich have more money.

Penetrating Differentiation

When more than two levels of subdivision are under investigation, the crucial question is how deeply differentiation—various forms of heterogeneity, of inequality, and of consolidated differences—penetrates into successive substructures. The substructures might be those of the educational systems of the 50 states—their school districts, the schools within districts, the grades in every school, and the classrooms for each grade, which are composed of different children. Thus, one can raise the question how much racial heterogeneity there is within school districts, within schools, and within classrooms, and then examine whether the differences observed influence interracial friendships. Alternatively, one could examine the geographical subunits on successive levels in the country, starting with regions and going to states, SMSAs (and possibly other county groups), cities or smaller incorporated places, and neighborhoods within them. How much does income inequality penetrate into towns and within them into neighborhoods? How much does ethnic heterogeneity penetrate? How much do consolidated differences in education, occupation, and income penetrate?

The systematic analysis of penetrating differentiation requires some preliminary considerations of basic quantitative properties of variations on several levels. First, as already noted, the average differentiation on any level is usually greater and cannot be smaller than the average differentiation on any lower level, that is, of the (weighted) mean differentiation within its subunits (whether on the next level or several levels below). For example, the racial heterogeneity in the state cannot be less than the average racial heterogeneity in all its communities (although it could be larger in some communities than in the state as a whole), and it could only be the same as the mean heterogeneity within communities if there is absolutely no difference in racial composition among communities. The reason is that the *total differentiation* in any unit is the sum of the mean differentiation within its subunits and a term representing differences among its subunits. Hence, the differentiation of any unit can be divided into two parts, that within and that among subunits. Thus, American income inequality is the result of income inequality within all its communities and income inequality among its communities.[4] This partition can be carried out on all levels, which provides an important clue for the analysis of penetration.

Total income inequality in the United States can be divided into several components, each of which represents economic inequality resulting from subdivision on a specific level. The income inequality on any one level refers to the variation among means on this level (whatever measure is used for income variation), ignoring for the moment income differences on lower as well as higher levels. Thus, American income inequality is produced by the following: the inequality among the mean incomes in the nine regions; the average income inequality among the states within every region, indicated by the deviations of state means from their region mean; the inequality within all communities in every state (also indicated by the differences among respective means); the inequality among neighborhoods within each community; and the residual inequality among the individuals or families within any neighborhood (the last, of course, refers to individual values and not means).

The procedure applies to any form of differentiation. To study industrial heterogeneity, for example, one would compute the heterogeneity among individuals (their industrial affiliations) within each of the subunits and a measure of the differences among the industrial compositions of the subunits.[5] For more than one intermediate level of subunits (between individuals and the whole population), the differences among all lowest-level subunits' industrial compositions can be further decomposed into the differences among the next-level units plus the differences among the subunits within each unit. This process can be repeated at each level of analysis. Analogously, to dissect the variation in SAT scores among seniors in American high schools, one could compute the variation in the mean scores for states, school districts within states, schools in each district, classrooms within a school, and among the individual scores within classrooms. The same principle applies to the analysis of consolidation: the results would indicate how much of the total covariation is accounted for within

---

[4]Though the formulae are not elementary, several persons have discussed how to decompose an overall measure of inequality into a weighted average of the inequality within each subunit plus a measure of between-subunit inequality. Theil (1967:123, also 1972:99–109) provides a concise but thorough discussion of the decomposition of measures of inequality, which is briefly summarized in Allison (1978:875–878).

[5]It can be algebraically shown that

$$H_{total} = \overline{H}. + [\Sigma_{ij} N_j (p_{ij} - \overline{p}_{i.})^2]/N,$$

where H_{total} is the total heterogeneity in the population; $\overline{H}.$ is a weighted average of the within-subunit heterogeneities [$\overline{H}. = (\Sigma_j N_j H_j)/N$]; N_j is the size of the jth subunit; N is the total size of the population; H_j is the heterogeneity in the jth subunit; p_{ij} is the proportion of those persons in subunit j who are in the ith (industrial) category; and $\overline{p}_{i.}$ is the proportion of the entire population in the ith category [$\overline{p}_{i.} = (\Sigma_j N_j p_{ij.})/N$].

the lowest level, and how much of it is accounted for by correlated between-subunit differences on every higher level.

The actual estimating procedure would be nested analysis of variance (ANOVA). However, the substantive interest in the study of penetrating differentiation is the opposite of that for which ANOVA is usually employed. Its usual purpose is to ascertain whether the proportion of the total variance accounted for by the variance among groups on a given level is sufficiently great to conclude that there are significant differences among groups on that level. But the substantive focus here is not the between-group variance on any level but the within-group variance on successive levels. It is important in this connection to keep in mind the distinction between the variance among units at a given level and the total amount of variance that penetrates to this level. Thus, the differences in SAT scores among school means in each district do not indicate the total variation among all students in a district; only the sum of all percentages (of variance) below and up to the school level indicate the total variation in scores within school districts. It is the total variation below a certain level that is of interest, specifically, how its proportion increases with successive levels.

Penetrating differentiation is indicated by the cumulative percentages, adding from the bottom up, yielded by the procedure described. If most of the division of labor in the entire country is accounted for by the division of labor within cities and towns, occupational heterogeneity penetrates deeply into substructures; if only the proportion of the total among cities within states (and on lower levels) is sufficient, penetration is less; and if only the occupational differences among the states in a region explain most of the country's division of labor, it penetrates hardly at all into substructures. One of two specific criteria of the extent of penetration can be used in actual research: either how many levels one has to move from the bottom up before 90%, or another high percentage, is reached; or how large the cumulative percentage on a given level is, for instance, how much of American religious heterogeneity can be explained by variations among states (including those within them). But the example only describes one case—this country. Comparative analysis of the consequences of penetrating differentiation must be based on numerous cases. If a given level is employed as the criterion, the ratio of the within-group to the total variance, which is one minus the correlation ratio (eta-square), indicates the degree of penetration. The measure is the complement of the one conventionally used in statistics because interest is not in how much variation differences among groups can account for but, on the contrary, how much variation remains within the different groups.[6]

[6]Those familiar with ANOVA, especially nested ANOVA, know that eta^2 is upwardly biased because some of the sample variation among group means results from sampling error. Therefore, ANOVA procedures for estimating *components of variance* (Snedecor and Cochran, 1967: Chapter 10) should be used to decompose total variance. (Several ANOVA computer routines automatically estimate these for the user.) For the decomposition of consolidation, components of covariance should be estimated in the same manner.

These procedures can be applied to consolidated differences as well as to differentiation in a single dimension, but the two are not independent. As a matter of fact, they are related both within and among levels. Two or more variables cannot be related unless they exhibit variation. If all people in a small town have the same education or the same occupation, one obviously cannot compute a correlation between years of schooling and occupational status. The same is true for the means on higher levels. If either the average education or the proportion of racial minorities is about the same in all communities in a state, education cannot be related to proportion of nonwhites among the communities in this state. Thus, differentiation of a dimension on a certain level is a prerequisite for this dimension to be correlated with others (which also must be differentiated) on that level. Regardless of how much racial heterogeneity there is within cities, if there is hardly any racial heterogeneity within neighborhoods, race cannot be consolidated with other social differences within neighborhoods (though it can, of course, within cities, that is, on a higher level).

Since consolidation on a given level implies differentiation of each of the consolidated factors on this level, it restricts the amount of differentiation of these factors within subunits on the next lower level. If average education and average socioeconomic index are highly correlated for neighborhoods, it implies much variation of each among neighborhoods and, consequently, relatively less educational and socioeconomic differences within neighborhoods. In other words, much consolidation on one level tends to diminish both this form of consolidation and the differentiation of the consolidated factors on lower levels. If much of a city's correlation between socioeconomic status and grade point average of pupils is accounted for by the correlation between the school means of the two, which also implies substantial variation in both respects among schools, it restricts the strength of the correlation between socioeconomic status and grade point average as well as the extent of variation in either within classrooms. In short, strongly consolidated social differences on a more encompassing level of social structure impede all three types of penetrating differentiation.

Implications of Penetrating Differentiation

Although heterogeneity promotes intergroup relations (T-2), the strength of its influence depends on the scope of the social structure under investigation. A society's ethnic heterogeneity does not exert much impact on interethnic relations if the various ethnic groups live in different regions or towns. Even a city's ethnic heterogeneity influences interethnic relations less when the ethnic groups are largely segregated in internally homogeneous neighborhoods than if ethnic heterogeneity prevails within neighborhoods. This conclusion is implied by the assumption that social associations depend on contact opportunities (A-2) because the smaller the spatial unit in which different groups live together, the greater are the contact opportunities between members of different groups. The significance of structural scope for social life is not confined to physical space. The assumption that social relations are more prevalent between persons in proximate than those in distant social positions (A-1) implies that ingroup tendencies are greater in narrower social circles than in the broader ones of which they are part. Surgeons have undoubtedly more in common than all professionals or even all physicians do. Generally, smaller groups have denser networks of social relations than larger ones, further strengthening ingroup bonds in subunits.[7] Since social relations are disproportionately prevalent in narrower than in broader social circles, the chances of association between two persons who differ on a crosscutting dimension are greater in a small group than in its encompassing larger collectivity, which implies more intergroup relations across intersecting dimensions in subunits. Accordingly, another theorem is deducible from A-2 and A-1.

The further heterogeneity penetrates into successive substructures, the more it promotes intergroup relations (T-21).[8] Members of different religious groups who work in the same office are more likely to associate with each other than those working only in the same large corporation, partly owing to the greater contact opportunities in the office and partly owing to the greater social proximity resulting from the common interests and ingroup bonds of fellow workers in an office. Essentially the same principles apply to inequality. Inequality promotes status-distant relations (T-3) because it increases the chances that any fortuitous meeting involves status-distant persons. But these chances of status-distant meetings are greater if the status-inequality penetrates into neighborhoods than if it is observable only among SMSAs because the former entails more intersection. In short, the more status differences penetrate into successive subgroups, the greater is the likelihood of status-distant associations. This conclusion, too, applies not only to spatial subunits but also to others. If rich and poor belong to the same congregation, their opportunities of meeting are greater than if they merely belong to the same religious denomination. Their social proximity is also greater, which further increases their likelihood of associating despite their income differences. If the prevalence of social relations depends on social

---

[7]*Density*, which is often considered an index of group cohesion, is the proportion of possible ingroup relations that actually exist. The formula is $2a/[n(n-1)]$, where a is the number of ingroup associations (multiplied by two to account for both participants) and n the number in the group. It is evident that density declines exponentially with an increase in group size, which reflects the common-sense impression that all people in a small group can and do have social relations but all people in a large city cannot possibly even know one another.

[8]This theorem essentially applies T-15—about the influence of within-substructure heterogeneity—to the decomposition of heterogeneity among more than two levels. Similarly, T-22 and T-23 apply T-16 and T-17, respectively, to multiple levels.

proximity (A-1) and on contact opportunities (A-2) and if people who differ in other ways are closer and have more contact opportunities when they share membership in narrower than in wider social circles, it follows that *the further inequality penetrates into successive substructures, the more it promotes status-distant relations* (T-22).

In both of these cases, the penetration of differentiation reinforces the influence of differentiation itself. The penetration of heterogeneity into narrower subdivisions increases the positive influence of heterogeneity on intergroup relations, and the penetration of inequality increases its positive influence on status-distant relations. One might therefore expect that penetrating consolidation similarly reinforces the influence of consolidation itself on social relations. Since consolidated social differences inhibit social relations (T-11), the apparent inference is that the penetration of consolidated differences into substructures inhibits intergroup relations still more. But this inference is wrong; the opposite is the case. This can be formulated as another theorem. *The further consolidated social differences penetrate into successive substructures, the more they promote intergroup and status-distant social relations* (T-23).

It is paradoxical that consolidation and differentiation have opposite effects on intergroup relations, whereas *penetrating consolidation* and *penetrating differentiation* have parallel effects on these relations. The clue for explaining the paradox is provided by remembering that T-23 does not compare more or less consolidated social structures (as T-11 does) but social structures with a given degree of consolidation that penetrates more or less deeply into their substructures.[9] Consolidation inhibits intergroup relations, and it inhibits them the most if the interrelated differences are also related to and, thus, reinforced by differences among regions or states. On the other hand, if these interrelated differences expressing consolidation penetrate into cities and neighborhoods, they will still inhibit intergroup relations, but they will do so less owing to the counteracting influences of physical propinquity and the contact opportunities it creates. If consolidated class differences do not penetrate into neighborhoods, their adverse effect on social relations between classes is most pronounced. Corresponding considerations apply to other than spatial subunits. If consolidated differences in race, parental occupation, and family income penetrate into the schools and classrooms of a school district, their negative influence on friendships, though probably still considerable, will tend to be less, owing to the counteracting effect of classmate proximity, than if the consolidated differences would occur largely among schools and not within them. (This is, of course, a

---

[9]A given degree of consolidation refers to the correlations of the variables under investigation (which must be controlled) and not to the relationships of these variables with the criterion for defining substructures (whether it is place of residence or another factor). Indeed, penetration promotes intergroup relations precisely because it entails weaker relationships of the investigated variables with the criterion of substructures.

main argument for desegregation.) The assumptions that social associations are promoted by contact opportunities (A-2) and by social proximity (A-1) imply the theorem that the penetration of consolidation fosters intergroup relations (T-23) and thus reduces the adverse effect consolidation itself has on these relations (T-11).

Penetrating differentiation also improves chances of mobility because it gives people access to and connections in other companies, other occupations, other social classes. The three last theorems, jointly with T-6, imply three corresponding theorems about social mobility. If penetrating heterogeneity promotes intergroup relations (T-21) and if intergroup relations foster mobility (T-6), it follows that *the penetration of heterogeneity into substructures promotes social mobility* (T-24). If penetrating inequality promotes status-distant relations (T-22) and if status-distant relations promote social mobility (corollary of T-6), it follows that *the penetration of inequality into substructures promotes social mobility* (T-25). If penetrating consolidation promotes intergroup relations (T-23) and if intergroup relations foster social mobility (T-6), *the penetration of consolidated differences into substructures promotes social mobility* (T-26). It is worthy of note that these three theorems are deduced in two steps from three assumptions, namely, that social proximity encourages social relations (A-1), that contact opportunities do (A-2), and that associates in other groups or classes facilitate mobility there (A-3).[10]

Consolidated inequalities are at the roots of class differences. One might have surmised that the effects on people's life chances and social circles of the class differences within the communities where they live and work are greater than the effects of the ecological correlations between mean class differences among communities. Actually, the opposite is the case, at least if the theoretical inferences drawn are correct. Class differences within communities and neighborhoods have less adverse effects on social mobility and social intercourse between classes than do the average class differences among communities. The reason is that class differences among communities are reinforced by the spatial segregation of classes, whereas the penetration of consolidated class differences into substructures—communities and neighborhoods—diminishes their inhibiting in-

---

[10]It should be pointed out that research to test the penetration theorems would require a very large data set. Let us take the 50 American states as units of analysis and analyze penetration into two levels only. Thus, we would want a sample of cities in every state, a sample of neighborhoods in every city, and a sample of individuals in every neighborhood. Even if we use only 25 cases for every subunit, which is very few, we would need 625 cities, 15,625 neighborhoods, and nearly 400,000 individuals, which is a very large sample indeed. Although the census public use sample is even larger, it does not contain the needed subdivisions, that is, it does not identify neighborhoods within specific SMSAs. The above calculations do not even take into consideration that there would be fewer than two young couples in the average neighborhood for computing marriage rates, nor that variation in size would produce many units with fewer than 25 subunits.

fluence on social relations and mobility, owing to the counteracting effects of physical and social proximity and the opportunities for contact between classes they provide. It is when concomitant inequalities in resources and status not only consolidate class positions but also lead to physical segregation and other lines of group distinctions (based on ethnic or family background, for example) that class boundaries are most likely to crystallize.

Penetrating differentiation is a centrifugal force that directs the social life and career interests of group members outwards and, therefore, helps cement the diverse segments of a large and complex society into a coherent structure. Such differentiation weakens ingroup bonds and allegiances, which undoubtedly undermines the profound support people in traditional societies received from their strong integration in their ingroups. But what is experienced as ingroup bonds and support by the insider is typically experienced as prejudice and discrimination by the outsider. Strong ingroup bonds—whether based on ethnic or class divisions or both—fragment a complex society with a diverse population. Pluralism in food, dress, music, and folk dances is one matter; maintaining social distance from outsiders and excluding them from jobs and neighborhoods is quite another. Much as one may favor the first notion of pluralism, one must be wary that it does not turn into the second. Penetrating differentiation minimizes the danger of such a development. It loosens ingroup ties and loyalties, counteracts fragmentation, and thereby contributes to the integration of the various segments of a complex society.

Conclusions

Complex structures are nested series of interdependent elements that repeatedly combine with other substructures on the same level into increasingly encompassing systems. Thus, societies have a social structure, and so do the communities composing them and the neighborhoods within the communities. But the structure of all its communities does not describe the structure of society because any level of structure has emergent properties not found in its separate elements. The national government would be such an emergent property of society, if structure were conceptualized on the basis of institutions. Even if structure is conceptualized ultimately in terms of the characteristics of its population, as it is here, it has emergent properties produced by the variations and concomitant variations in its population, which have been conceptualized as heterogeneity, inequality, and consolidation-intersection. Communities as well as the entire society can be characterized by various forms of these three structural features. Society's total heterogeneity, inequality, or consolidation can be decomposed into two parts, one that results from differences within and another that results from differences between communities.

The larger the proportion of society's differentiation that is the product of differentiation within rather than among communities, the more prevalent are intergroup relations. Whether race or class differences or any others are under consideration, the social differences inhibit intergroup relations less when the groups or classes live together in the same communities than when they live in different ones because the inhibiting effect of social distance is moderated by physical propinquity in the former case but reinforced by physical distance in the latter.

Substructures can be distinguished not only in space but also in various other dimensions. Unions have locals; organizations have departments; universities have specialized colleges and professional schools; and companies have branches. In all these cases, the total differentiation in the larger unit can be divided into the proportion resulting from within-unit and the proportion result-ing from between-unit differentiation. The theorems advanced are assumed to apply to all these cases. Moreover, more than two levels of subdivision can often be distinguished. Universities have colleges and schools that are composed of different departments; large organizations have many levels of subunits; occupa-tional groups consist of detailed occupations which can be subdivided into finer and finer specialities; and societies can be divided into regions, provinces or states, districts or counties, communities, community zones, neighborhoods, and blocks. Differentiation within and among subunits can be analyzed on every level, and one can inquire how far differentiation penetrates into successive substructures.

The further differentiation of any kind penetrates into substructures, the more it promotes social relations between persons in different social positions. Pen-etrating heterogeneity fosters intergroup relations; penetrating inequality fosters status-distant relations; and penetrating consolidation minimizes the adverse ef-fect consolidated social differences generally have on social relations. Even consolidated class positions do not constitute as great barriers to social inter-course and mobility if they penetrate into communities and neighborhoods (that is, if different classes live together in the same places and thus have much opportunity for social contact) than if they do not (which means that classes are segregated in different places and the social distance between them is reinforced by physical distance). As long as race and class differences persist, they are least divisive if they do not distinguish large communities and groupings but penetrate deeply into the substructures of society. For penetrating differentiation is a centrifugal force which helps integrate diverse groups and classes by pulling people out of their particular ingroups and encouraging them to search for friends and careers outside their old surroundings.

The social integration of a polyglot society like ours requires a loosening of ingroup bonds sufficient to permit substantial close relations between members of all different groups. Consolidated social differences inhibit such intergroup relations. The penetration of consolidated differences mitigates their detrimental effects on the integration of diverse groups and classes. Ultimately, however, the greatest contribution to the social solidarity of a diverse society is made not merely by the penetration of consolidation but by reductions in the consolidation of social differences, that is, by more intersection of the various forms of inequality.

CHAPTER 7

Conflict

Not all social relations are positive and involve integrative social bonds. Some are negative and find expression in discordant social interaction. There is animosity and conflict as well as love and friendship. The theory and research in this book have centered attention on cordial social relations that integrate individuals and unite groups in a larger community. The marital relations used to test the implications of the theory, though they are surely not free of conflict, illustrate such basically integrative social bonds. In this last chapter before the concluding summary, we turn briefly to an analysis of negative social interaction and conflict. What structural conditions lead to hostility and conflict? Are some of them the same as those that lead to cordial and intimate social associations? Even if this is the case, what are the distinctive structural features that engender divisiveness and even violent aggression?

Conflict between groups and individuals in society is ubiquitous. Antagonism can take many forms. Although many impair social integration and in extreme cases create cleavages that can tear society asunder, some forms of conflict make essential contributions to the institutional system of Western societies. Political conflict among parties with different programs is a requirement of democracy, and economic competition and conflict among firms is a prerequisite for a market economy. Democratic institutions can be thought of as mechanisms for diverting conflict from destructive channels and directing them into constructive channels, albeit not always with success. Just as conflict is not necessarily detrimental for social integration, strong social bonds that unite individuals with their groups are not always beneficial for it. In complex modern communities composed of diverse groups, the opposite is the case; strong ingroup bonds can be a divisive force that fragments the larger collectivity and weakens the integration of its various groups and classes.

Two major sources of conflict are distinguished in this chapter, one of which has its roots in excessive ingroup salience, the other in the conflict of interest over the distribution of resources. Then the question is raised as to what social conditions tend to redirect conflict from a realistic pursuit of interests to diffuse aggression, and some empirical analysis of such violent aggression is presented.

Two Major Sources of Conflict

Concern is confined to conflict within societies and communities. No attempt is made to analyze international conflict, whether in the form of war, conquest, economic exploitation of one country by another, or competition between them. Attention centers on the prevalence of overt conflict in a community or society, not on mere conflict of interest nor on feelings of hostility, but on explicit antagonistic action of some persons against others, acting individually or collectively. The significance of cultural dissension for conflict is noted, but the emphasis is on the structural conditions that lead to conflict.

Overt conflict between persons depends on a conflict of interests or values, which is the source of their animosity, and on contact opportunities, without which the animosity cannot become manifest in explicit antagonistic confrontations, be they mere verbal disputes or acts of physical violence. Thus, negative as well as positive associations depend on contact opportunities (A-2). The greater the number of people who live together in the same place, which implicitly refers to the size of a metropolis (though the underlying factor is density), the greater are their chances of contact, which makes abrasive as well as friendly associations more probable. Accordingly, A-2 implies another theorem: *The large size of a community increases the rate of overt conflict* (T-27).[1]

Opportunities for expressing antagonism are not utilized, however, unless there is some reason for the antagonism. Two major sources of conflict are excessive ingroup salience typically rooted in a group's distinctive value system and a conflict of interest generally resulting from an unequal distribution of resources. The distinction between the two is related to that between nominal and graduated parameters. Nominal dimensions divide a population into unordered groups with boundaries, such as religion or ethnic group. Graduated dimensions divide people on the basis of a status gradation that usually involves differences in resources,[2] such as income, wealth, or power. (The discussion of conflict is restricted to graduated parameters that do refer to the distribution of some re-

---

[1]Mayhew and Levinger (1976) develop a mathematical model which predicts the specific form of the relationship in this theorem (a logistic S-shaped curve), and they successfully test their model with data on crimes against persons.

[2]This is usually but not necessarily true. Not all variables involving interval scales reflect a monotonic increase in resources. Age illustrates one that does not; neither physical strength nor earnings nor prestige increases monotonically with age.

source.) Nominal parameters permit only qualitative distinctions because there is no scale or rank order, and the basic distinction usually made is that between one's own group and outsiders, whereas graduated parameters entail quantitative comparisons—amount of money, or scope of authority. This difference is related to Parsons' (1951:61–63) concepts of particularism and universalism. Particularism refers to social distinctions based on the particular relation between ego and alter, notably their common membership in some group, while universalism involves social distinctions that rest on an objective criterion independent of the specific relations, like education or skill in computer programming. The two criteria of evaluation lead to different social relations and conflicts.

The assumption made in the theory is that people associate disproportionately with others in the same or proximate social positions (A-1). This does not mean, of course, that everybody has the same ingroup preferences or that everybody has strong ingroup preferences in all respects. On the contrary, in a complex society with intersecting differences, people frequently must set aside their weaker ingroup preferences in order to satisfy their stronger ones. However, it does imply that everybody has substantial ingroup preferences in some respects. Whereas such ingroup preference may be confined to close friendships, it may extend to living in the same neighborhood and working in the same place, especially for social differences for which ingroup salience is pronounced. Great salience often involves some outgroup prejudice and discrimination. Preferences for some people result in the exclusion of others from one's clubs, unions, and jobs. Such exclusion from positions on which benefits depend is likely to provoke antagonism, which frequently leads to counter-antagonism. The result is that strong ingroup preferences tend to be accompanied by outgroup hostility, as Sumner (1940) has emphasized.

Ingroup tendencies are inevitable, and cohesive ingroups on many levels are essential for the members of large societies to become integrated and receive social support. Yet ingroup salience contains the seeds of outgroup rejection and group conflict. The chances that ingroup tendencies turn into outgroup hostility are particularly great if a group has a distinctive ideology—a value system that sets the group apart and that either defines it as superior, like racism, or that makes it an obligation to spread the gospel, like Calvinism or Communism. Religious and political fanaticism are dramatic illustrations of the nexus between ingroup devotion and outgroup hostility and of the significance of value commitment as a catalyst to produce the nexus. The ideology of the true believers reinforces and sanctifies their conviction that their own group is superior and that their mission is to oppose and even destroy the infidels. The fight between Hindus and Moslems that led to the division of India is an illustration, and so are the fights between Catholics and Protestants in Northern Ireland, between Trotskyites and Stalinists in the 1930s, and generally between extremist political and religious sects (Simmel, 1950:87–98; L. A. Coser, 1956:111–119). Ideologies are, of course, elements of culture. In our theoretical scheme, which focuses on social structure, the concept of salience reflects the significance of cultural factors and transmits their influence on social relations.

A second major source of conflict is the unequal distribution of resources in a population. Resources can be defined as means for reaching a variety of ends, and the most important resources are generalized means for obtaining virtually all material benefits. Money is the prototype; power is a second basic type; other resources, such as education and physical force, are more limited in the range of benefits obtainable with them. In any case, if resources are means for gaining many advantages, it is in the interest of everybody to maximize his resources, which implies that any distribution of resources, uneven or not, entails a conflict of interest. This is particularly the case for zero-sum situations (Thurow, 1980). But the individual's interest in maximizing resources, which engenders competitive conflict of every person's interest with everybody else's, must be distinguished from the implications for the individual's interest in the resource distribution in a community because this distribution makes most people's self-interest consistent with the common ideal of reducing inequality but some people's self-interest inconsistent ·vith it. Thus, inequality creates a potential split between the majority whose upward mobility (or economic advancement) would diminish inequality and the rest whose upward mobility would increase it: those below and those above the upper-lower boundary specified in Chapter 3. Often as not, however, many people below that boundary do not realize that they would benefit not only from success in competing with others but also from collective pursuit of reductions in inequality.

The uneven distribution of resources creates two classes with opposite interests, but it usually does not precipitate overt conflict (unless other conditions are also met). There are several reasons for the acquiescence of the disadvantaged. The uneven distribution of resources may provide the investments in wealth and power necessary for the coordination of the work of large numbers, and it may thereby improve the collective accomplishments and raise the benefits available to all—lower as well as higher recipients. This is the contribution successful leadership can make to the employees of a firm, the supporters of a political party, the members of a union, or the citizens of a country. An unequal distribution may also yield benefits to the commonwealth if it furnishes rewards for exercising skills and efforts to improve economic conditions. These are the contributions incentives make to directing energies into productive channels. In short, the less affluent may receive compensating advantages from an unequal distribution of resources and for this reason willingly accept such a distribution.

However, the failure of the disadvantaged to fight for a more equitable distribution of resources may not rest on such rational economic consideration but on fear of retaliation or lack of awareness of their collective interests, what Marx has termed *false consciousness*. The weak and poor have good grounds to be afraid that fighting the rich and powerful will provoke retaliation that would leave them much worse off. They may not be willing to fight for their common interests because their divergent immediate interests—who will be laid off? who will be promoted?—are more conspicuous and immediate. They may believe the conservative propaganda that the best way to help the poor is to increase the profits of the rich—the so-called trickle-down theory. They may put credence into the popular myth that superior resources and standards of living are the just rewards for superior merit and achievement and hence blame themselves for their failure to get ahead, particularly if they experience lack of success alone while witnessing more successful careers of others around them. In sum, although severe inequalities engender a basic conflict of interest that may manifest itself in much strain and tension in interpersonal relations, many counteracting social forces tend to suppress this conflict and make it improbable that it expresses itself in overt conflict, particularly when individuals experience their deprivation in isolation.

Consolidated Inequalities

The situation is entirely different when nearly all members of a group—an entire town or industry or race—suffer similar deprivations, that is, if inequalities are consolidated by group boundaries. As Marx observed long ago, inequalities that involve people who are isolated from one another—the farmers on their home-steads, for instance—are not likely to find expression in overt conflict. But if inequalities, especially correlated differences in resources that consolidate dif-ferences in positions, affect an entire group the same way—the workers in an industry's various factories or a racial minority—the boundaries circumscribing the groups transform individuals with similar socioeconomic status into a distinct social class (in Marx's terms, from a *Klasse an sich* to a *Klasse fuer sich*), which may begin to act collectively to improve the economic conditions of its members. People are much less likely to believe that universalistic standards of merit have determined the superior position of some and to blame themselves for their lack of success if it is apparent that the difference is related to membership in a group, particularly if it is an ascribed group—being Puerto Rican or Southern or Catho-lic or black. Ascriptive inequalities absolve individuals from guilt for failure.

It is when the two major sources of conflict—strong ingroup salience and much inequality—occur in combination that their conflict potential is most likely to be realized in overt conflict. Ideological disagreements that erupt into violent battles generally involve groups whose economic and political interests differ and are at stake. Religious clashes, ostensibly fought solely for the sake of the true faith, typically entail an underlying struggle over economic and political resources. This is the case in the fighting between the poorer and powerless

Catholics and the more affluent and powerful Protestants in Northern Ireland, just as it was the case in the recent rebellion in Iran, and the fighting, more than three centuries ago, in the Thirty Years War. Some may interpret this as indicating that the ideological conflict merely occurs in the superstructure and the economic conflict is the only fundamental one. But it is not necessary to dismiss the significance of ideological salience entirely. It suffices to note that ideological differences are not likely to give rise to violent battles unless they are reinforced by differences in economic interests. By the same token, looking at it from the alternative perspective, the conflict of interest created by inequality in resource distribution is unlikely to precipitate concerted fights by the underprivileged to effect a more equitable redistribution unless the economic differences are strongly related to group differences, which implies that the group boundaries transform isolated sets of individuals in similar economic situations into distinct social classes. From either perspective, the consolidation of salient group affiliations and inequalities in resources is what increases the likelihood of overt conflict between groups or classes with contrasting interests.

The interpretations advanced resemble some recent versions of the theory of political pluralism, except for reversing the focus of the argument. Political sociologists as well as political scientists have noted that stable democracy depends on two seemingly contradictory conditions: freedom of expression of opposing political views, regardless of how extreme, and an absence of a deep cleavage that divides society into hostile camps willing to fight each other by any means. Simmel's concept of crosscutting affiliations resolves the dilemma because it implies that different combinations of groups will be on the opposing sides of different issues. The choice of which side people support may be largely governed by their religion in one controversy, their income in another, and the industry in which they work in a third. Moreover, intersecting group memberships put people under cross pressures, internal ones because some of the groups to which they themselves belong—for instance, their union and their church— may take opposite sides in a controversy, and even more external cross pressures because their various friends are likely to belong to groups that take opposite stands. The hostility against the opposition cannot be extreme for people who have allegiances to both sides or friends on both sides. Hence, crosscutting group affiliations mitigate conflict and help sustain democratic processes (L. A. Coser, 1956:72–81; Coleman, 1957:21–23; Lipset, 1960:31–32; 88–92; Rae and Taylor, 1970:85–90, 105–11).

The implicit assumption in these discussions of pluralism seems to be that there is actually much intersection of social differences in industrialized Western societies that can explain why they are usually stable democracies. Whereas this assumption is undoubtedly correct for some dimensions of social differences, such as race and sex differences, it is undoubtedly not correct for other dimensions, such as the consolidation of race and administrative authority. In any case, how strongly various combinations of social affiliations are interrelated is an empirical question, and the claim that they are less strongly related in stable democracies than in other countries must be empirically tested. On an abstract theoretical level, these pluralistic analyses of democratic processes and our analysis of consolidated inequalities are in agreement. Both hypothesize that the extent to which group and status differences are related in a population intensifies the conflict between bitterly opposed adversaries. But in sharp contrast to their emphasis on the significance of intersection for diminishing conflict and keeping it within bounds, ours is on the significance of consolidation for crystallizing conflict and bringing it into the open.

The consolidation of economic inequalities by group boundaries, resulting from the correlation of graduated and nominal parameters, tends to make the underprivileged aware of their collective interest in redistribution and thus increases the likelihood that they will engage in concerted action to seek to reduce inequalities. The group boundaries are essential for creating the common identification that induces people to let the collective interests override their diverse individual interests and to take the risks that organizing collective action against those with large resources involves. Although extreme consolidation of social differences creates an unbridgeable cleavage between two hostile camps that tends to destroy democratic processes, a minimum of consolidation is essential for democracy because without it the disadvantaged are unlikely to be able to organize to represent their interests. Democracy is not synonymous with equality, but it does require that the common interests of all classes and groups, not only those of the educated and resourceful, are effectively represented in the political forum. This is not now the case in the Soviet Union, which has no party to oppose the interests of the ruling group. Nor is it now the case in the United States, which has no labor party representing the interests of workers. It is as yet an ideal to strive for. To be sure, rudimentary forms of collective action to improve the conditions of the underprivileged can be observed. Workers organize unions to bargain collectively for higher wages. People support minority parties to achieve radical economic reforms. Protesters assemble in large demonstrations against the growth of nuclear armaments. Women mount a campaign to have equal rights extended to the entire American population. The record of success is not impressive.

There is an inherent dilemma in endeavors to abolish the unequal distribution of basic resources. The very people whose lack of resources makes them most interested in redistribution lack the resources that would give them a good chance in a fight for a more equitable distribution, whereas those who have an interest in sustaining or increasing existing inequality have the resources to protect their interests.

Blocked Conflict

To recapitulate the main argument briefly: Resources that are generalized means for achieving a great variety of ends pose an inherent conflict of interest because it is in the interest of everybody to maximize them. The unequal distribution of resources superimposes upon this individualistic conflict of interest, in which everybody competes with everybody else, a new potential conflict between those whose interests would be advanced by a less unequal redistribution and those whose interests would suffer from such a redistribution. For this potential to become realized in actual political conflict over redistribution requires that the difference in resources be closely related to some group difference because this implies that group boundaries consolidate distinct classes or groups with common economic interests, which greatly increases the likelihood of collective action to further these interests. If inequalities are consolidated by ascriptive group differences from which individuals cannot escape, it makes their common interest more conspicuous, which should lead to joint action to effect a more equitable distribution. These conditions describe the case of ethnic minorities who have suffered many disadvantages for long periods. Some of them were successful in improving their conditions, but others were not. If a minority's endeavors to obtain a fair share of resources are consistently frustrated, it means that their attempts to give realistic expression to their conflict of interest are blocked.[3] The blocking of realistic conflict produces pent-up aggression, which manifests itself in diffuse hostility and violence. Vandalism, kicking dogs, and yelling at children illustrate such blind (not goal-oriented) aggression.

A conflict is realistic if it is designed as a means to achieve objective goals or interests, according to L. A. Coser (1968:233). But if the realistic expression of a conflict of interest is blocked or crushed by the superior strength of the opposition, it is likely to find expression in what Coser calls *nonrealistic conflict*, which involves indiscriminate hostility, with individuals more driven by diffuse aggression than governed by the rational pursuit of certain ends through appropriate means. The distinction may be symbolized by wildly thrashing about in angry rage rather than taking deliberate aim to hit an enemy target. Repeated frustration of people's hopes and aspirations and of collective attempts to improve opportunities leads to pent-up aggression which is given vent at the slightest irritation. Frequent violent crimes against persons[4] in a community are indicative of the prevalence of such diffuse aggression. Property crimes are not because they may be considered to serve rational self-interests and surely are so considered by those committing them.

[3]Even in a democracy a minority's interests may be blocked, which is why basic rights of citizenship are needed to protect minorities against domination by the majority.

[4]The terms *violent crimes* and *crimes against persons* are synonymous (comprising four types: murder, rape, robbery, and assault). Robbery is also a property crime, of course.

Racial differences in the United States are strongly consolidated with differences in various resources and aspects of socioeconomic status, which makes the black minority group a typical case of blocked realistic conflict. Blacks have less education than others, lower-status jobs, less prestige, lower earnings, less wealth, fewer positions of authority, and less power. In contrast to the socioeconomic status of other ethnic groups, moreover, which has risen on the average with the number of generations in this country (Warner and Srole, 1945:67–102), that of blacks has not, although there have been limited improvements in recent years. Accordingly, the foregoing considerations suggest a hypothesis about the implications of racial inequality for conflict. Although the hypothesis derives from the structural theory advanced, it is not formulated as a theorem because it is more inferential and cannot be rigorously deduced from the assumptions and other theorems. The hypothesis is that persisting inequalities between ascribed groups lead to nonrealistic conflict. Since racial inequalities are the best illustration of such persisting inequalities in this country and criminal violence manifests nonrealistic conflict, the specific implication of the hypothesis is that socioeconomic inequalities between races promote criminal violence.

It is important to distinguish what the hypothesis claims to explain from what it does not seek to explain, and also to specify what alternative explanations it implicitly denies. As a structural hypothesis, it addresses itself to the question of why rates of crimes against persons are more frequent in some places than in others, and it does not specifically address the question why some individuals rather than others commit them, though it does suggest that people whose opportunities are blocked are most likely to do so. Accordingly, the independent variables are not traits of individuals but attributes that characterize the structure of communities, such as community size, income inequality, and racial inequality in socioeconomic status. Besides, the hypothesized structural explanation implicitly rejects several alternative explanations of crime couched in terms of cultural influences.

Three major empirical findings are that crime rates, including rates of violent crime, are exceptionally high in poor urban slums, in the South, and in black ghettos. Various theories have been developed that explain these empirical regularities on the basis of cultural orientations that stress the value of violence. Thus, the earlier interpretation that the poverty in slums breeds social disorganization and delinquency has been transformed by W. B. Miller's (1958) theory that attributes crime not to poverty itself but to the culture of poverty with its emphasis on toughness, smartness, excitement, and fatalism, which encourage conduct that is likely to bring a person into conflict with the law. In a similar vein, Wolfgang and Feracuti (1967) explain the disproportionately high incidence of criminal violence in the South as a manifestation of the Southern tradition of violence, which has for historical reasons become part of the regional culture. The high crime rates among blacks have also been interpreted as an expression of a subculture that legitimates violence, because life is tough, survival and success often depend on fighting ability, and the laws and mores imposed by prejudiced outsiders command little respect.

Our hypothesis suggests a different explanation and thus implies rejection of these three alternatives. Economic inequality is assumed to account for high crime rates, not poverty as such or the culture of poverty. The greater inequality in the South than in other regions, and not any Southern culture of violence, is considered to be responsible for the regional differences in crimes against persons. The high crime rates of neighborhoods and cities with many blacks are also hypothesized to be the result of socioeconomic inequality between races, not of race itself. The claim that our explanation is correct and the alternative in all three cases is wrong is subjected to empirical tests.

Racial inequality in resources is, of course, not the only condition in social structures that may affect criminal violence. Three other possible influences are examined, partly because they are of intrinsic interest and partly to check whether the predicted influence of racial inequality persists under controls. First, the theorem (T-27) that the size of a place influences the probability of conflict should be tested with the SMSA rates of crimes against persons, replicating Mayhew and Levinger's (1976) research. Second, the influence of total economic inequality in a metropolis on violent crime should be examined, if only to compare its influence with that of socioeconomic inequality between races. Third, a general indicator of the extent of conflict and disruptions of close personal relations should be found to explore whether it influences rates of criminal violence and whether it mediates the structural influences on them.

Criminal Violence[5]

The dependent variables for the analysis of violent conflict are the 1970 rates (per 100,000 population) of the four major violent crimes—murder, forcible rape, robbery, and aggravated assault. The data are the crimes known to the police, taken from the *Uniform Crime Reports* (F.B.I., 1971). Crimes known to the police, although they are not data without shortcomings, are generally considered to be more reliable than other official statistics, such as arrest figures. Thus, Hindelang (1974:14), after discussing many criticisms of this source, concludes that "the weight of the evidence is that the UCR data provide robust estimates of the *relative* incidence of index offenses known." OLS regression analyses for

---

[5]The research reported in this section has been carried out by Judith R. Blau in collaboration with one of the authors. It has been published, in considerably different form, in Blau and Blau (1982).

TABLE 7.1
Regression of Violent Crime Rates on Family Income Inequality and Poverty

	Total[a]		Murder[a]		Rape[a]		Robbery[a]		Assault[a]	
	b	β	b	β	b	β	b	β	b	β
Family income inequality	5.22	.52	6.73	.56	2.45	.26	5.72	.49	4.81	.47
Poverty	-.01*	-.07	.01*	.09	.01*	.11	-.03	-.30	.01*	.12
R^2		.23		.40		.12		.12		.32

* Not significant at the .025 level (one-tailed).

[a] Log_{10} transformation.

the four types and for all of them combined are presented, and so is a path diagram for the combined total.[6]

Ever since the early ecological studies in Chicago (for example, Shaw and McKay, 1942), research has found that crime rates in poor urban slums are disproportionately high. The first issue raised is whether it is economic inequality rather than poverty that is responsible for high crime rates. To be sure, the two economic conditions are related (for the 125 SMSAs, $r = .70$), but the question is whether poverty exerts an influence of its own on violent crime or is only correlated with it because economic inequality influences it and much inequality entails much poverty. Five regression analyses of rates of violent crime on family income inequality and the Social Security Administrations's index of poverty,[7] presented in Table 7.1, give an unequivocal answer to this question. Income inequality has substantial positive relationships with all forms of criminal violence, whereas poverty does not once income inequality is controlled.[8] Poor countries do not have higher crime rates than rich ones—the high crime rates in this country being a dramatic illustration of this point—and the same is apparently true when metropolitan places are compared. Not poverty as such but poverty in the midst of plenty is what fosters violence.

[6]OLS procedures can be used because the UCR data do not raise problems of unreliability of estimates and variation in standards errors which require WLS procedures, whereas the intermarriage rates do raise these problems. The five rates of criminal violence have been logarithmically transformed, as has SMSA size.

[7]The poverty index of the Social Security Administration takes into account family size, sex of family head, number of children under 18, and farm-nonfarm residence.

[8]There is some multicollinearity in Table 7.1 ($r = .70$), but it is not excessive, and the replications for the four specific rates increase confidence in the conclusion that the two influences can be distinguished. The only significant coefficient for poverty is opposite in direction from the prediction of poverty theory.

The proportion of adults in an SMSA who are divorced or separated is considered an index of the extent of conflict and disruption in close personal relations.
Marital breakups rupture profound and lasting human relations, manifest serious
conflict, and usually occur after a prolonged period of estrangement and recur-
rent conflict. Such upheavals in intimate relations are indicative of instabilities
and disorientations in social life, what Durkheim (1951:246–258, 270–273)
termed *anomie,* of which he considered divorce to be a main indicator. In his
discussion, he describes anomie as a sign of the weakening of institutional norms
and the restraints they exert upon individual passions, freeing desires and appetites from the restrictions imposed by moral authority. These conditions are most
likely in areas of transition or rapid change, when traditional values clash with
emergent new ones and old established norms no longer provide firm guidance in
an altered situation. The higher divorce rate accompanying women's emancipa-
tion and growing participation in the labor force may be a contemporary illustration of Durkheim's argument.

Divorces (and separations) clearly involve disruptions of important personal
relations with significant others, which undoubtedly are upsetting and disorienting experiences. Since not every marital spat ends up in the divorce court,
frequent divorces probably reveal widespread discord and friction in intimate
relations, involving many more persons than those who have actually experienced divorce or separation. Durkheim's concept of anomie has increasingly
acquired the connotation of such prevalent disturbances and disorientations in
social life, as distinguished from its literal meaning of normlessness. Social
upheaval and rapid change upset established routines, and are therefore likely to
increase strife, disputes, and rifts in personal relations. In all these respects, our
interpretation agrees with and, indeed, derives from Durkheim's. But we see no
reason to make the further inference that the disruptive and disorienting social
experiences reflected in divorce rates are the results of normlessness and insufficient restraints of human passions and appetites.[9] Accordingly, the prevalence of
divorce (or separation) in a metropolis is viewed as indicative of much dissension
and disorientation in social life, without assuming that the cause is the failure of
social norms to restrain human desires.

This indicator of the pervasiveness of conflict in significant personal relations
is highly related to the likelihood of the extreme form of conflict manifest in

---

[9]Durkheim (1951:272) notes, but his theory conveniently ignores (except for a remark in a
footnote, p. 276), that this major measure of anomie—divorce rates—is positively related to suicide
rates, as his theory implies, only for half the population, whereas the two rates are negatively related
for the other half. He dismisses the negative findings about the rates for females with such quaint
remarks as the following (p. 272): "Woman's sexual needs have less of a mental character because,
generally speaking, her mental life is less developed. . . . Being a more instinctive creature than
man, woman has only to follow her instincts to find calmness and peace."

TABLE 7.2
Regression of Rates of Violent Crimes

	Total[a]		Murder[a]		Rape[a]		Robbery[a]		Assault[a]	
	b	β	b	β	b	β	b	β	b	β
Size[a]	.26	.33	.12	.13	.10*	.13	.41	.45	.16	.19
South	.03*	.05	.06*	.09	-.00*	-.01	-.06*	-.09	.11*	.18
Family income inequality	.40*	.04	2.33	.19	-.18*	-.12	-.96*	-.08	1.30*	.13
Percentage black	.67	.22	1.23	.33	.41*	.14	.69	.19	.49*	.15
Log ratio SES[b]	.62	.22	.71	.21	.28*	.11	.80	.25	.54	.19
Percentage divorced	8.45	.36	6.08	.22	11.57	.52	10.52	.39	6.95	.29
R^2	.64		.69		.44		.61		.57	

* Not significant at the .025 level (one-tailed).

[a] Log_{10} transformation.
[b] The logarithm$_{10}$ of the ratio of white to nonwhite mean (Duncan's) SEI.

violent crimes against persons, as Table 7.2 (last row) shows.[10] The frequency of divorce (and separation) in an SMSA exhibits substantial relationships with all forms of criminal violence. This finding must not be interpreted to indicate that divorced persons are more likely than others to commit violent crimes. As a matter of fact, it is quite possible that the ecological relationships observed are not the result of underlying individual correlations. Since about nine-tenths of the sampled population in the average SMSA is white, chances are that the proportion of divorced persons largely refers to the whites in an SMSA (despite the higher divorce rates of blacks). On the other hand, crimes of violence are disproportionately committed by blacks against blacks (Mulvihill et al., 1969:208–215; Curtis, 1974:24–27).[11] Thus, the findings suggest that a structure of inter-

[10]The population is divided into blacks and nonblacks—rather than into whites and nonwhites, as in previous analyses—because we are interested in the relationship of Southern location and racial composition, for which blacks are the pertinent subgroup. Honolulu is not an outlier on percentage blacks; hence, the analysis is based on all 125 SMSAs.

[11]Despite the antiblack bias in official crime statistics, the differences are so large that they cannot reasonably be attributed to this bias alone. Thus, there can be little doubt that blacks commit more violent crimes than whites, mostly against other blacks (with the possible exception of robberies, which often have white victims).

personal relations characterized by much conflict and disruption increases the likelihood of violent conflicts, although the measures of the two kinds of conflict may well be largely based on the conduct of different individuals.

The data in the fifth row of Table 7.2 support the hypothesis that the consolidation of race and socioeconomic status increases the likelihood of nonrealistic conflict in the form of criminal violence.[12] Socioeconomic inequality between whites and blacks increases three of four types of violent crime, the exception being rape, the type of crime most often not reported to the police. The influence on violent crimes of racial differences in socioeconomic positions is not the result of the higher incidence of violence in the South nor is it the result of the higher rates in places with large proportions of blacks, because both of these factors have been controlled. On the other hand, these two conditions exert an influence on the white–black difference in socioeconomic status and through it indirectly influence criminal violence, as the path diagram in Figure 7.1 reveals. Racial differences in socioeconomic status are larger in the South than in other regions and are larger in SMSAs with many than those with few blacks, which produces an indirect influence, transmitted by racial inequality, of Southern location and of racial composition on violent crimes.

Of the four conditions treated as exogeneous influences, two exert a direct influence on criminal violence and two do not. The size of a metropolis (first row, Table 7.2) makes criminal violence of all four types more likely (though the rape coefficient is not quite significant), corroborating the theorem that the large size of a place raises the probability of overt conflict (T-27) because opportunity for friction as well as opportunity for cordial contacts increases with the number of people living in the same place. SMSA size influences criminal violence not only directly but also indirectly, mediated by the proportion divorced (Figure 7.1). In other words, the greater opportunities for friction in larger SMSAs influence both types of conflict—those manifest in many marital breakups and those manifest in frequent violence—and by increasing the likelihood of conflict in intimate relations they also indirectly increase the likelihood of violent crime.

Inequality in family income exerts no influence on violent conflict (except murder), but it does increase marital conflict and through it, exerts some indirect influence on violent conflict (Figure 7.1). In short, economic inequality increases disruptive conflict in marriages and, perhaps, disturbances in human relations generally.

Criminal violence is more frequent in the South than in other parts of the

---

[12]J. Braithwaite (1979) finds racial inequality not related to violent crimes for American SMSAs. We originally suspected this to be the result of multicollinearity between his measures of poverty and racial inequality, but he reports (in a personal communication) that the correlation of his measures of the two is only .33. It is not clear whether the difference between his finding and ours is the result of the different (larger) sample of SMSAs he used, the quite different measure of inequality employed, or something else.

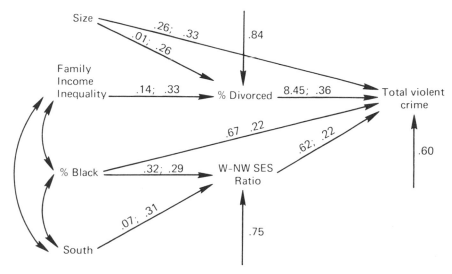

Figure 7.1   Path diagram for rates of all violent crimes. Note: The first coefficient is *b*; the second is β. For clarity, only paths that are significant at the .025 level (one-tailed) are presented, but calculations are based on all paths (see Table 7.2).

country. For the 125 largest SMSAs, the correlation between location in the South and the total rate of violent crimes is .41. As already noted, this relationship has been interpreted in terms of the subculture of violence that pervades human relations in the South. Southerners presumably have a lower threshold for aggression and a greater tolerance or even admiration for violence as a means to gain one's objectives. The frequency of violent crimes is considered to be an extreme manifestation of this cultural tradition. The regression analysis does not support this interpretation, however. When other conditions are controlled, SMSAs in the South do not have higher rates of any of the four types of violence than others. The reasons that Southern SMSAs have higher total rates of violent crimes than others is that they have larger proportions of blacks and that there is more discrimination against blacks there, as indicated by the white-black ratio in socioeconomic status (Figure 7.1). Once these conditions are controlled, location in the South no longer has any significant bearing on the rate of violent crimes. The correlation between the two must be accounted for in structural terms (racial composition and racial economic inequality) and not in cultural ones.

When the other variables in the regression analysis are controlled, racial composition continues to exert some influence on the rates of criminal violence, contrary to expectations. The percentage of black people in an SMSA increases the total rate of violent crimes—and two of the four component rates—but its influence is much less than the simple correlation (.57) seems to imply. The five other structural conditions in the equation account for three-fifths of the variation among SMSAs in their total rates of criminal violence, and adding the percentage of blacks increases the variation accounted for by merely 3%, one-tenth of the explanatory power one would have attributed to racial composition on the basis of the zero-order correlation alone. To be sure, the proportion of blacks also exerts some indirect influence on rates of violent crimes, which is primarily transmitted by racial differences in socioeconomic status (Figure 7.1). But this is precisely the point. Even assuming that the ecological relationships presented reflect higher rates of criminal violence of blacks than whites—and there are good grounds for assuming that (Wolfgang, 1964; Mulvihill et al., 1969)—the findings indicate that much of this difference is the result of racial inequality in socioeconomic status.

There is some multicollinearity in the regression analysis in Table 7.2, but it is not pronounced. The two highest simple correlations are those of the Southern SMSAs with percentage of blacks (.67) and family income inequality (.64). The multiple correlation of racial inequality with the four exogenous variables is .65, and that of percentage of divorced with its five antecedents is only .56. To check whether the inclusion of South distorts the finding, it was excluded and the five crime rates were each regressed on the other five independent variables in Table 7.2. For total violent crimes, the R^2 is reduced from .64 to .62, and none of the standardized regression coefficients change by more than .02. For the four regressions of specific rates, only two of the 20 coefficients change appreciably, both involving assault: the standardized coefficient for percentage of blacks increases some (from .15 to .23) and so does that for family income inequality (from .13 to .20). None of the four R^2s for specific crimes is reduced by more than .03.

Inequality apparently weakens the structure of social relations in a community because it engenders disruptive conflict in several respects. It increases the likelihood of conflict in lasting personal relations that may ultimately undo them, as indicated by its relationship with divorce, and it increases the likelihood of violent conflict. Inequalities between races as well as those within them lead to conflict. Since socioeconomic inequality between races is controlled in the regression analysis, family income inequality refers primarily to intraracial inequality. Accordingly, the path diagram (in Figure 7.1) is interpreted to indicate that economic inequality *within* races is what affects conflict in marriages and perhaps also in other close relations, which is plausible because marriages and other intimate relations occur largely between persons of the same race, and the effect of intraracial inequality on violent conflict is largely mediated by its general effect on conflict in personal relations (as indicated by frequent divorce).[13] Intimate relations between blacks and whites are rare. Pronounced socioeconomic inequalities between races have a direct positive effect on the

---

[13]The total effect of family income inequality on the combined rate of violent crime is .19, which is significant at the .01 level (one-tailed).

extent of criminal violence in a community, and they mediate the influence of Southern location and partly that of proportion of blacks on such violence.

Conclusions

People's associates depend in part on their own preferences and in part on the kinds of persons they have an opportunity to meet in the place where they live and work. The theory in this book analyzes the influences on the social relations in a metropolis of its population composition and opportunity structure, not those of the personal preferences of individuals. In turning to the study of conflict in this chapter, however, a shift in focus is necessary because the influences of contact opportunities and population distributions are the same on cordial and on discordant social relations, on marriage and on conflict. Why contact opportunities lead to conflict rather than friendly relations must be ascertained by investigating what conditions antagonize people and create animosity between them.

Two major sources of overt conflict are excessive ingroup salience and great inequality in the distribution of important resources. Ingroup preferences, by their very nature, entail outgroup exclusion and discrimination that are likely to be resented by outsiders and arouse their antagonism, and reciprocal processes tend to produce progressive animosity, particularly when group leaders exploit outgroup hostility to stifle internal opposition and strengthen their position as is often the case. Commitment to an ideology greatly strengthens ingroup salience and may amplify aversion into fanatic hatred of the outgroup. Ideological commitment is a cultural factor, and its influence on conflict is represented and transmitted in our structural scheme by salience.

The second major source of conflict, which is structural, is an unequal distribution of essential resources, notably those that are general means for obtaining most material ends, such as income, wealth, and power. It is in everybody's interest to maximize their resources, and resource distribution creates competitive conflicts of everybody against everyone else. But inequality superimposes upon this individualistic competition a conflict of interest between two potential classes because it splits the population into those whose interests are served by egalitarian ideals and those opposed to them. In short, inequality draws a line that distinguishes two classes with opposing interests (for any dimension of resources). Applying this line to important resources, such as wealth or power, may be a more useful criterion for separating the ruling class from the rest of the population than Marx's criterion of ownership of the means of production, which has been made ambiguous and obsolete by the corporate structure of contemporary society, but which many Marxists today feel obliged to defend at all costs. The term *potential class* has been used advisedly because the two groups are not aware of their opposing interests; they are not "class conscious." One reason is that the lower class also has divergent interests and the upper class uses strategies of *divide et impera* to exploit them. Another reason is that most middle-class persons do not realize that they are still below this line and would benefit from a more even distribution.[14] But great inequalities, even when they do not produce class conflict, increase friction and strife in social life, as indicated by their positive influence on marital breakups.

The combination of its two sources is what makes overt conflict most likely. Ideological conflicts are intensified when the two groups also have conflicting economic interests, and the unequal distribution of resources crystallizes into group or class conflict if differences in resources are closely related to differences in group affiliation. Economic interests reinforce ideological commitments, and group boundaries transform individual self-interests into collective interests. If the legitimate political expression of conflicting interests is suppressed, the pent-up aggression may find diffuse expression in angry outbursts of violence, as illustrated by the influence of racial inequality in socioeconomic status on criminal violence. But the pluralistic assumption in a democracy, which is not always met, is that legitimate channels for expressing conflict lessen them sufficiently to prevent the outbreak of violence. Crosscutting social affiliations that produce crisscrossing conflicts on different issues are a major structural mechanism serving this purpose. However, social structures do not assure functional integration, and there are also many consolidated social differences—race and economic position being only an extreme example—which have the opposite effect of intensifying conflict and even violence.

[14]The line that divides the part of the population who would benefit from a redistribution that diminishes inequality from those who would be hurt by such a redistribution depends on the existing degree of inequality, as we saw in Chapter 3.

CHAPTER 8

Implications and Conjectures

The objective of this book is to present a deductive macrosociological theory of social structure and empirical tests of the implications of its main theorems. What we consider distinctive about the analysis is the combination of a deductive theoretical system, a focus on the structure of social relations and positions, a macrosociological approach, and the empirical research testing many of the theoretical predictions.

There has been much emphasis in methodological discussions of sociological theorizing on the importance of developing axiomatic theories that entail deductive systems of testable propositions (Zetterberg, 1963; Merton, 1968:139–155) rather than merely conceptual clarifications and ad hoc interpretations. The focus here on deductive or axiomatic theorizing—the terms are used interchangably— is in full agreement with this admonition. However, there is a danger that we throw out the child with the bath and forget the crucial significance of conceptual insights for theoretical innovation and scientific advancement. The distinction between analytic and synthetic propositions is relevant here. *Analytical propositions* are essentially definitions of concepts and are, as such, not empirically testable. *Synthetic propositions* specify relationships between two (or more) independently defined concepts, which makes them testable in research, either directly or, if the concepts are too abstract, indirectly through their implications for relationships between operational variables. Hence, theorems in a scientific discipline must be synthetic propositions that are, directly or indirectly, testable. But this does not mean that the basic assumptions or axioms of a theory must also be. A theory's primitive synthetic propositions may be assumptions postulated as the given conditions that circumscribe its range of applicability, whereas its basic operating principles are grounded in its analytic propositions that define its object of inquiry.[1] This is the procedure followed in this book. The assumptions are not

[1]The use of analytical propositions here is related to Liska's (1969) *relational tautologies,* which he considers legitimate elements of deductive theories, in contrast to the redundant *contentual tautologies.*

dignified by the term *axiom* because they are not the basic explanatory principles but merely conditions assumed to be universal, whereas the operating force underlying the explanatory theorems is derived from the analytic propositions in terms of which structure is defined. Simmel's concept of crosscutting circles is a notable example, but this concept had to be clarified to use it in formulating a deductive system of testable theorems.

A structural theory centers attention on the significance of patterns of social positions and relations, whereas a cultural theory focuses on the importance of shared values and norms. Microstructural theories are concerned with the networks of social relations of individuals. However, the idiosyncratic interpersonal networks of many thousands of persons are not of primary significance for understanding the structure of entire societies or large communities. Here, a two-step procedure is used to describe social structure: first the population is classified by social attributes, including background, and then tests are made to determine whether the initial classification actually does distinguish positions that influence patterns of social relations. Thus, in macrosociological analysis people are classified by positions, but positions are defined on the basis of their influence on patterns of social relations.

Résumé of Theory

Social structure can be described as the population's distribution in a multidimensional space of social positions. The properties of the distribution of the people in a community or society are called structural parameters. A population's variation in ethnic composition, division of labor, age structure, income distribution, and power structure illustrate parameters. Parameters refer only to those differences among people in terms of which they themselves make social distinctions in their relations with one another and that therefore influence social relations, which is the criterion of social position. Thus, parameters of differentiation delineate the social structure. Three generic kinds have been distinguished, under which all specific forms of differentiation can be subsumed. Heterogeneity is the differentiation of people among nominal categories, such as racial heterogeneity or industrial heterogeneity. Inequality is the degree of differentiation in terms of status or resources, such as educational differentiation or income inequality. Whereas these two concepts refer to differences in a single dimension, the third refers to joint differentiation in several dimensions. Consolidation indicates how strongly one difference among people is related to several others, for example, how much occupational differences are related to differences in education, prestige, and income. The opposite of consolidation is intersection, which manifests how weakly several differences are related and thus how much their boundaries intersect, for instance, how much differences in ethnic background crosscut differences in occupation and in income.

These analytic propositions define social structure and elaborate various aspects of it. Since they are definitions and do not specify relationships between independently defined terms, they are arbitrary in the sense that they cannot be empirically tested. But this does not mean that one cannot deduce how variations in these conditions, jointly with certain other conditions assumed to exist, influence social relations. Indeed, this is precisely the objective of the theory. The aim is to explain how the structure of opportunities and constraints resulting from variations in population compositions and distributions affect people's relations, independently of their psychological preferences and cultural norms, indeed, frequently in ways that are the exact opposite of their own preferred choices.

Four assumptions are introduced, from which the 27 theorems stipulated are directly or indirectly derived. The first two are employed in the derivation of many theorems, and the other two are the basis of only a few. The four assumptions postulated as necessary conditions for deducing the structural explanations incorporated in the theorems are: The prevalence of associations between persons depends on their social proximity (A-1), which implies that ingroup relations are more prevalent than intergroup relations and that the prevalence of social relations declines with status distance. Social associations depend on opportunities for social contact (A-2). Associates in other groups or strata facilitate mobility there (A-3). In a large population, every salient dimension of social differences exerts some influence on social life independent of those of other dimensions on it (A-4).

The 27 theorems deduced from these assumptions and the analytical propositions explicating social structure can be divided into two categories. Most of the ones directly deduced from primitive structural terms and postulated assumptions deal with influences on intergroup relations, whereas most of those indirectly derived from other theorems pertain to influences on social mobility. Intergroup relations and social mobility are the two main aspects of social life the theory seeks to explain, although a few other factors are of concern as well, such as social change and conflict. Figure 8.1 presents a diagram summarizing the derivations of the 27 theorems.

Structural conditions often have paradoxical consequences for social life. The seven theorems deducible from the combination of the first two assumptions and primitive terms defining relevant aspects of social structure illustrate such paradoxical implications. Heterogeneity increases the probability of intergroup relations (T-2), and inequality increases the probability of status-distant relations (T-3). How can these follow from the assumption that people have the very opposite tendencies of associating with others in proximate positions (A-1)? The reason is that this sociopsychological tendency is counteracted by the structural conditions in the community. If there is much heterogeneity or inequality in a

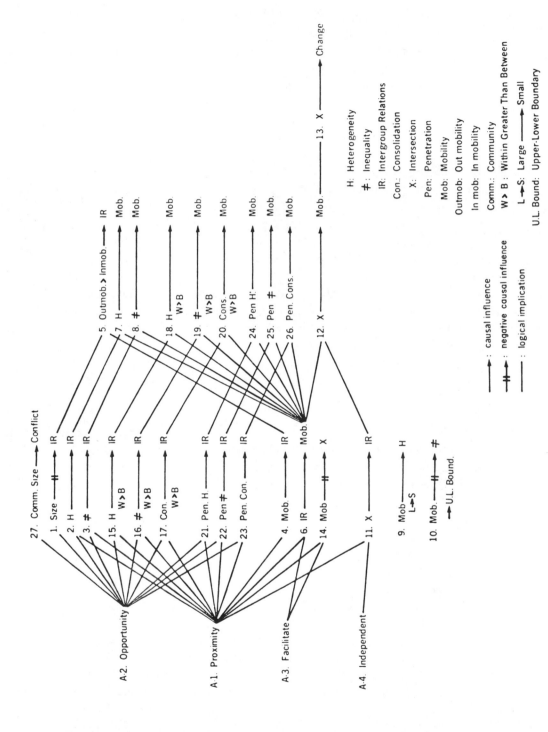

Figure 8.1 Logical structure of the theory.

community, there is less opportunity for meeting people in proximate positions and a greater chance of fortuitous contacts between socially distant persons (A-2), and these structural conditions exert constraints that make intergroup relations more likely, notwithstanding preferences for ingroup relations.

Any form of differentiation in a large population can be decomposed into the differentiation within and that among its subunits. For example, a city's racial heterogeneity can be decomposed into the racial heterogeneity within and that among its neighborhoods. A society's income inequality can be decomposed into the inequality within and that among communities. Consolidated differences also are the sum of concomitant variations within and those among subunits. A-1 and A-2 also imply that heterogeneity within substructures promotes intergroup relations (T-15); inequality within substructures promotes status-distant relations (T-16); and consolidated differences within substructures promote both (T-17). This is because the inhibiting effect of social differences on social relations (A-1) is counteracted by the contact opportunities (A-2) within subunits but is reinforced by the lack of such opportunities if most of the differences exist among subunits. Ethnic heterogeneity promotes interethnic relations much less in cities that are composed of ethnically segregated neighborhoods (between-subunit variation) than in those with ethnically heterogeneous neighborhoods (within-subunit variations). Status-distant associations are more likely if rich and poor live in the same towns than if they live in different ones. More than two levels of substructure can be considered, and the same considerations apply on all levels; that is, differences within subunits compared to those among subunits enhance the chances of intergroup relations. Accordingly, A-1 and A-2 also imply that intergroup or status-distant relations tend to increase the further heterogeneity penetrates into substructures (T-21); the further inequality penetrates into substructures (T-22); and the further consolidated differences penetrate into substructures (T-23). Whatever the existing differences in national descent, the smaller the subunits within which national differences can be observed—towns, neighborhoods, blocks within neighborhoods—the greater is the probability of intergroup relations across national lines.

Contact opportunities (A-2) are responsible for the influence of size on both friendly and antagonistic social interaction. The relative size of a group in a community governs its members' opportunities for ingroup contact, with large size making such opportunities abundant and small size making them rare. Hence, A-2 implies that group size and intergroup relations are inversely related (T-1). Since such an inverse relationship is true by definition for two groups—the smaller of the two must have more outgroup relations than the larger—T-1 can also be derived from this tautology for two groups as a theorem for many, qualified by ceteris paribus. Community size makes abrasive as well as cordial contacts more likely because both depend on contact opportunities (A-2), which implies that interpersonal conflict increases with increasing city size (T-27).

The multiple intersection of social differences promotes intergroup relations (T-11). This is the central principle of the theory, based on Simmel's insightful concept of crosscutting circles. It could serve as an alternative source for deriving the theorems about the significance of internal differentiation (T-15, T-16, T-17) and of penetrating differentiation (T-21, T-22, T-23). It follows from A-1 and A-4; if people in proximate positions associate disproportionately (A-1) and if every dimension of social differences exerts some independent influence (A-4), crosscutting social circles constrain people to have many intergroup associates because they imply that ingroup associates in one dimension are often intergroup associates in other dimensions. The more social circles intersect, the more difficult it becomes to choose a partner who is in your own group in all or most dimensions. On the other hand, if differences along various lines are strongly related and consolidate group boundaries, most people's associates will be largely confined to their ingroups, even in dimensions in regard to which they have little or no ingroup preference, as long as these dimensions are related to others for which they do have ingroup preferences. Structural conditions determine whether there will be extensive intergroup relations despite strong ingroup preferences or few intergroup relations even in areas where ingroup preferences are weak.

The ingroup assumption (A-1) jointly with the assumption that associates in other groups or strata facilitate mobility (A-3) implies that intergroup and status-distant relations improve the chances of social mobility (T-6). Another implication of the combination of these two assumptions is that there is a structural strain limiting crosscutting social circles and enhancing the consolidation of various dimensions of social differences. If people who occupy similar positions associate in disproportionate numbers (A-1) and if having associates in different positions facilitates mobility there (A-3), the persons with the best chance of mobility to a new position in one dimension are those who have many ingroup associates in another dimension in that position. The lower-class children who have gone to college have the best chance to be upwardly mobile into a higher occupational stratum. People usually move into a new neighborhood where they have disproportionate associates who share their ethnic background or social class or religion or age. In all these illustrations, mobility makes social circles less intersecting and more consolidated (T-14). In sociopsychological terms, it may be viewed as an improvement in balance resulting from a reduction in status inconsistency. But from the structural perspective it involves greater consolidation of resources and social positions at the expense of lesser countervailing forces and flexibility.

Mobility influences social associations and the population distributions in a community. Mobile persons can be considered to occupy two positions in the same dimension—an origin and a destination position. If proximate positions promote social associations (A-1), people who have moved from one position to another are likely to have associates in both, which implies that social mobility promotes intergroup relations (T-4). This tendency for mobility to increase intergroup relations may be reinforced because mobile persons are apt to bring their friends from their old groups and those from their new groups together, so that these nonmobile friends of the mobile also often become intergroup associates as the result of frequent mobility. T-4 and T-6 together indicate that mobility and intergroup relations exert mutual influences on each other. Mobility, moreover, alters the population distribution, unless the number of persons moving in opposite directions is the same. Excess mobility from larger to smaller groups increases heterogeneity (T-9). Although this theorem is implied by the definitions of terms and thus strictly speaking tautological, not all tautologies are useless in theorizing (Liska, 1969), and this one has corollaries that are not without interest. If the same proportion of members of two groups move to the other group, it increases heterogeneity because if the proportion that leaves a large for a small group is the same as the proportion that leaves the small for the large group, the number moving from the large to the small group is greater than the number moving in the opposite direction, making the distribution more even, which is the criterion of heterogeneity. The corresponding theorem for a graduated parameter is that mobility, upward or downward, toward the upper-lower boundary in a status hierarchy reduces inequality (T-10). The upper-lower boundary is the dividing line in a population's status pyramid where the proportion below minus the proportion above is the same as the Gini index. Since the Gini index is the operational definition of inequality, this theorem is also entailed by the definitions of terms and, hence, tautological. Yet it, too, has unexpected corollaries. For instance, it implies that upward mobility from the 70th to the 75th percentile reduces inequality if the Gini index is greater than .50, which is surprising, particularly in view of the fact that the index for inequality in personal income in the average SMSA was just .50 in 1970.

All these theorems are directly derived from primitive terms and assumptions. In contrast, the following theorems are deduced from the theorems already formulated, which means that they are two steps removed from the structural foundations of the theory. A caveat about chains of deductions in social theorizing is in order. The theorems are not deterministic—if x, then y—but all require qualification by ceteris paribus because they refer to one but not the only influence on the dependent variable, although the presumption is that the theorems stipulate dominant influences and that their empirical implications are observable, normally without any controls or, if necessary, when just a few counteracting influences are controlled. Nevertheless, long chains of deductions that link probabilistic propositions may yield wrong conclusions (Costner and Leik, 1964; Blalock, 1969:16–17), because the many other influences at each step are likely to reduce the one traced to the vanishing point. To minimize this danger, only two-step deductions—with a single intermediate link—are used with the exception of one three-step chain (see Figure 8.1). Most of the theorems deduced from other theorems refer to influences on social mobility. One of the two that does not asserts that net outmobility from a group increases its outgroup relations more than net immobility (T-5). Since intergroup relations are fostered by both mobility (T-4) and small size (T-1), the two influences reinforce each other in the case of net outmobility but counter each other in the case of net inmobility.

Structural conditions that promote intergroup relations thereby indirectly improve the chances of social mobility (on non-ascribed characteristics) because extensive intergroup relations raise rates of social mobility (T-6). Intergroup relations provide people with associates in other groups (or strata), and such associates facilitate mobility (A-3). Hence, T-6 jointly with any theorem that specifies influences on intergroup relations implies corresponding influences on social mobility. (Of course, theorems about mobility cannot be applied to ascribed traits.) Thus, jointly with the theorems that heterogeneity promotes intergroup relations (T-2) and that inequality does also (T-3), T-6 implies that heterogeneity increases mobility among groups (T-7) and that inequality increases status-distant moves (T-8). Jointly with the theorems that intergroup relations are more likely the more a social structure's heterogeneity exists within its subunits (T-15), the more its inequality exists within its subunits (T-16), and the more its consolidated differences exist within its subunits (T-17), T-6 implies that social mobility is more prevalent in those societies whose heterogeneities primarily result from the great heterogeneities within communities and neighborhoods (T-18), whose inequalities are primarily manifest in the inequalities within subunits (T-19) and whose consolidated differences, too, largely express such internal differences (T-20). Parallel considerations apply to the three theorems that intergroup relations are furthered by the penetration of heterogeneity into society's substructures (T-21), the penetration of inequality into substructures (T-22), and the penetration of consolidated differences into them (T-23). Jointly with T-6, these three theorems imply, respectively, that chances of social mobility are improved by penetrating heterogeneity (T-24), penetrating inequality (T-25), and penetrating consolidation (T-26).

The attempt to summarize briefly the complex derivations of six intricate theorems makes the last paragraph so concise and abstract that it is hardly understandable. Perhaps a few illustrations can help convey its meaning. A pronounced division of labor in a city increases the likelihood of occupational mobility, because people are likely to have more associates in other occupations (T-7). Much income inequality implies a greater average difference in income, so that any mobility—for example, from clerk to supervisor—tends to involve a greater income difference (T-8). If different classes, which are expressions of the consolidation of various resources, live in different suburbs and work in different companies, the likelihood of having some contacts with persons in a higher class who can improve one's chances of mobility are less than if various classes live and work nearby in the same towns and firms (T-20). If entire regions have largely different industries, the likelihood of moving from one industry to work in another is much less than if industrial diversity penetrates into increasingly narrower subunits—states, counties, towns (T-24).

Since multiple intersection promotes intergroup relations (T-11) and since intergroup relations improve the chances of social mobility (T-6), it follows that multiple intersection increases the chances of social mobility (T-12). Many crosscutting social circles help integrate the diverse segments of complex societies or communities both by fostering social relations between their members and by facilitating social movement from one segment to another. Social mobility entails structural change, not only if the mobility is predominantly in one direction and, thus, alters the population distribution—for example, from mostly rural to mostly urban—but also if mobility in opposite directions effects little change in the population distribution (so-called exchange mobility). The latter as well as the former almost always alters how much various characteristics of people—their background and occupation and income, for example—are related, and such an increase in intersection or consolidation constitutes a most important form of structural change. Hence, an implication of T-12 is that multiple intersection furthers structural change (T-13). Whereas exogenous conditions, such as technological developments, are the ultimate causes of social change, multiple intersection makes the social structure more flexible and responsive to such exogeneous pressures for change.

The nexus between crosscutting circles and social change poses a paradox. Multiple intersection facilitates social mobility, adjustment to new external conditions, and thus structural change (T-13). However, the social mobility that is most probable involves movements of persons to new positions in one dimension where they have ingroup associates in other dimensions, and such mobility diminishes intersection (T-14). If these theorems are formulated correctly, they suggest that the results of structural change tend to undermine the very condition (multiple intersection) that facilitates it. Perhaps these countervailing tendencies reflect the dialectics of historical developments. They may well also be indicative of the capacity of vested interests to slow down structural change.

Theory Testing

Systematic theorizing involves harnessing the imagination by anchoring it at both ends in disciplined analysis. The fruitfulness of a theory depends on the profound original insights embodied in its central concepts, such as natural selection in biological evolution or marginal utility in economics. But rigorous theory requires going beyond the insight and grounding it, on the one hand, in a system of logically related propositions and, on the other, in empirical research designed to test the implications of these propositions. In the process, it is usually necessary to dissect the insight and distinguish the various operational criteria implicit in it. Starting with Simmel's perceptive concept of crosscutting social circles, we have endeavored to distinguish its various elements, formulate a theory embodying it, and test its main theorems. The preceding section reviewed the deductive theory. Now we summarize the tests of the basic theorems.

The theory is couched in abstract terms. It can only be tested by examining the empirical implications of these abstractions. One cannot carry out research on social structure as such but only on the social structure of a community or society or some other population. Similarly, one cannot study heterogeneity or inequality in the abstract, only specific forms of heterogeneity and specific forms of inequality, such as ethnic heterogeneity or income inequality. To study what influence structural conditions exert on social life, one must compare numerous social structures with varying conditions to ascertain how these variations are related to differences in patterns of social relations. The social structures used to test the theory were those of the 125 largest metropolitan areas in the United States in 1970, all metropolitan places with a population of more than 250,000.

People's cultural values and psychological preferences influence, of course, their social relations. But these are not the influences on which the structural theory presented focuses. Instead, it centers attention on the ways people's relations are influenced by the social structure of their environment, notably the population compositions and distributions in their communities. Population compositions obviously affect the chances of casual contacts. Hence, using casual meetings would not constitute a stringent test of the theory. Lasting and intimate relations like marriage, however, are strongly influenced by psychological dispositions and cultural norms. The impact of an SMSA's population structure on the marriage rates of young couples, which is the dependent variable examined, furnishes a very strict test of theorems that assert that the opportunity structure exerts substantial influences on marriages independent of those of personal preferences, indeed, often in the opposite direction.

Empirical tests of the major theorems were performed. It was not possible to conduct any research on propositions that include either mobility or several levels of social structure because the data set (the public use sample of the U.S. Census) does not supply the needed information. But some investigation of the relationship between intermarriage and mobility, based on another data source, has been carried out. Before testing the theorems, the assumption that ingroup relations are more prevalent than intergroup relations (A-1) was tested because many theorems are true but vacuous unless this assumption is correct. For this purpose, the influences of population distributions in eight dimensions (for instance, the racial or occupational distribution) on marriage rates were analyzed within each SMSA, which produced, as there were a few missing cases, 966 chi-square tests. Although inmarriage tendencies vary greatly—most spouses have the same race but very few have the same occupation—the proportion of ingroup marriages far exceeds chance expectations for all attributes under investigation, in accordance with the assumption.

The theorem that the relative size of groups is inversely related to its outmarriage rate (T-1) cannot be tested by comparing group size and outmarriage rate for a large number of groups within SMSAs because the subsample of young couples on which marriage rates are based is not large enough to permit subdividing it within each of 125 SMSAs into a large number of different groups. Instead, for each of 10 attributes separately, it is ascertained whether its proportionate size in an SMSA and its outmarriage rate in that SMSA are inversely related. For example, are the variations in the proportion of whites of native stock among the 125 metropolitan places inversely related to the proportion of them who marry either people of foreign stock or blacks? The answer is yes ($r = -.78$). The same analysis was carried out for nine other groups; all tests—which admittedly are not entirely independent—exhibit the predicted negative correlation, supporting the theorem.

The core of the theory comprises the three theorems stipulating the influences of heterogeneity, inequality, and consolidated differences on intermarriage. The heterogeneity theorem posits that a population's heterogeneity in any respect determines its opportunity structure and, therefore, affects the rate of intergroup relations (T-2), including not merely superficial contacts but even such profound relations as marriage. The theorem was tested by analyzing nine group differences. Since some of the variables are substantially related, the nine furnish six essentially independent tests of the implications of the theorem. The six refer to the relationship between heterogeneity and intermarriage with respect to race (two measures), ethnic background (three measures), birth region, major industry, major occupation, and detailed occupation.[2] Even simple (WLS) correlations of the 125 SMSAs reveal the predicted positive correlations between heterogeneity and intermarriage in four of the six independent tests (and in those based on related measures), and refined analysis reveals them also for the other two. The two exceptions are detailed occupation and race. A ceiling-effect distorts the measure of (detailed) occupational heterogeneity; the mean for the 125 SMSAs is .988, only .012 from the maximum possible value. To correct for this, logit transformations are performed, and when these are used, the predicted positive correlation is observed. The consolidation of race with socioeconomic differences discourages intermarriage, as stipulated by the 11th theorem, and it consequently suppresses the positive effect of heterogeneity on it. When racial differences in socioeconomic status are controlled, racial heterogeneity is revealed to be positively related to racial intermarriage. Thus, for a variety of attributes that differ extremely in their salience for marriage, heterogeneity increases the likelihood of intermarriage. It does so for race, although racial

[2]Major-occupation and detailed-occupation heterogeneity are virtually unrelated ($r = -.03$).

intermarriage is very rare, and it does so for detailed occupation, although most couples who both work have different occupations. These empirical results corroborate T-2.[3]

The inequality theorem, which has been completely revised from its initial formulation, claims that inequality *increases* the average status distance of social relations (T-3). It is tested with four measures of status differences: in education, socioeconomic status, income, and earnings (the main difference between the last two, which are highly correlated, is that income includes and earnings exclude public assistance). Since income and earnings may well have changed between the time the couple decided to get married and a few years later when the census was taken, the difference scores in either are not good indications of the possible significance economic differences have on marital decisions. Nevertheless, the theoretically predicted structural effects are apparent. For three of the four—education, socioeconomic index, and earnings—inequality in an SMSA and the status difference between spouses exhibit a positive simple (WLS) correlation, and for the fourth—income—a positive relationship between the two becomes apparent in the regression analysis that controls for the consolidation of income with other social differences. In short, the empirical findings support the revised formulation of the theorem.[4]

The theorem about crosscutting social circles, which has also been somewhat revised on the basis of empirical tests, stipulates that multiple intersection of social differences in various dimensions promotes intergroup relations (T-11). Indexes of multiple intersection are constructed by starting with a given variable in an SMSA (such as industry or income); computing the mean of all its available correlations with any other variable within the SMSA; eliminating any item if its deletion improves alpha by .05; and using the complement of the result as the index of the degree to which the given variable intersects with various others in the SMSA. Ten such intersection measures are devised that permit eight independent tests of the theorem about crosscutting circles. Inasmuch as heterogeneity and inequality are known to influence intermarriage, the tests are performed by regressing intermarriage on both intersection and differentiation (either heterogeneity or inequality), using the same attribute—for example, birth region—for all three variables. Nine of the 10 regression coefficients reveal the theoretically predicted positive coefficient, and the 10th (education) does, too, if one addi-

---

[3]For five of the six independent tests, 1960 measures of heterogeneity could be obtained from published sources, which were used to test the causal assumptions made in the cross-sectional analysis of 1970 data. The 1960 measures of heterogeneity exhibit very similar correlations with 1970 marriage as the 1970 heterogeneity measures do, supporting the causal inferences.

[4]Using 1960 measures of inequality to check the causal assumptions, the results are: for education, the correlation is similar and positive (.59); for SEI, it is positive but not significant (.13); for income, no 1960 measure is available; for earnings, the regression coefficient is positive and significant if one other variable (earnings intersection) is controlled (beta = .28).

tional variable is controlled. These empirical tests corroborate the intersection theorem.[5]

To explore whether there is a basic dimension of structural consolidation that distinguishes SMSAs, a factor analysis is performed on all available measures of bivariate association between variables. The analysis yields one dominant factor; the items with the highest loading indicate how strongly race is related to various achieved positions; and the SMSA's racial composition explains nearly nine-tenths of the variance in this factor. Thus, the racial composition of a metropolis largely accounts for variations in the degree to which the metropolitan structure consolidates social positions and fortifies group boundaries. (There is also much consolidation of socioeconomic attributes, but it varies little among SMSAs.) A more consolidated structure (as indicated by the factor score) inhibits not only racial intermarriage but also intermarriage between ethnic groups and intermarriage between social classes, whether class is measured by income, earnings, or socioeconomic status. All these influences are independent of those of heterogeneity or inequality on intermarriage.

The empirical evidence confirms the implications of the theory's major theorems for various forms of intermarriage and thereby indirectly supports the underlying assumption of the structural approach. The structural opportunities and constraints in communities produced by their population compositions govern the patterns of social relations that develop, often notwithstanding opposite tendencies produced by cultural values and psychological preferences. However, this is not meant to suggest that all theorems are corroborated as originally formulated. Many could not be tested, as already mentioned. Some were reformulated either already while designing the empirical research to test them or in response to negative evidence, and one theorem, together with its corollaries, had to be discarded altogether. It is instructive to examine these three cases.

The original formulation of the inequality theorem states that "a decline in inequality reduces the impact of status on social associations" (Blau, 1977:44, italics removed). Although the wording is ambiguous, which undoubtedly reflects uncertainty about the proposition, the intent apparently is that inequality makes status proximity more important for social intercourse and, consequently, reduces the status distance in established social relations. The reasoning derives from individual preferences and tendencies, which are reflected in the assumption that social associations disproportionately often involve persons in proxi-

[5]Four 1960 indexes of multiple intersection could be derived from published sources. All four are based on relatively few items, but two are fairly reliable (race and earnings), whereas the other two, based on only two items each, are not (occupation and income). Regression analyses were carried out with all four, nevertheless. The two reliable ones reveal the predicted positive coefficients with intermarriage; the other two do not.

mate social status (A-1). But to infer from this assumption that less inequality, which implies less average status distance in the population, will increase the status distance between associates ignores the limiting constraints the social structure of the community imposes on the choices of individuals. Although people tend to associate with others in proximate status, great status differences (much inequality) in a population reduce the opportunities to meet people in proximate status and constrains individuals to find more distant associates, despite their preferences for less distant ones. Schwartz pointed this out[6] while we were designing the research, and the empirical results show that inequality increases status distance in social relations, even in such intimate ones as marriage.

Although the original discussion of the influence of crosscutting social circles emphasizes the importance of *multiple* intersection of social differences for intergroup relations (Blau, 1977:83–88), the theorems formulated left out the qualifying adjective and merely stipulated that intersecting differences promote intergroup relations. This hypothesis implies that bivariate measures of association should be negatively related to rates of intermarriage. The stronger the relationship between any two attributes in an SMSA is, the rarer should be rates of intermarriage with respect to either. This prediction is tested with more than 50 correlations between a bivariate measure of association and the intermarriage rates referring to the two variables in the measure. Some supported the predictions; others did not: there is no consistent pattern. These findings negate the theorem as formulated. The theorem is thus reformulated to stipulate that only multiple intersection promotes intergroup relations. The implications of this revised theorem for intermarriage are supported by the data summarized above.

One of the theorems originally formulated turned out to be wrong. The theorem states that a small group in a given dimension is more likely than a large group in the same dimension to establish intergroup relations in another dimension (Blau, 1977:94). The argument seems plausible enough. For instance, blacks are undoubtedly more likely than whites to have social associates across class lines. Although this is true enough, the reason is not that there are fewer blacks than whites but that there are fewer middle-class persons among blacks than whites because the two parameters are *not* intersecting. But does not the argument apply to actually intersecting parameters, like religion and left-handedness? A left-handed Jew who wants to associate with another left-handed person would seem to have a better chance of finding one among Christians, owing to their larger number, than among Jews, constraining him to associate across religious lines. But this argument is fallacious because the determining factor is not the absolute number but the proportion. If the same percentage of Jews and of Christians are left-handed—which is the criterion of intersection—the chances to

---

[6]As did Steven Rytina (see Rytina *et al.*, 1982) and one of the anonymous reviewers of our NSF proposal.

find a left-handed buddy in either group are exactly the same. In conformity with this reasoning, the data fail to support the empirical implication of the above proposition, that is, they do not reveal that group size in one dimension is inversely related to intermarriage in intersecting dimensions.

In concluding this short synopsis of the extensive tests of the theory, a final word should be said about the qualification of the theorems by ceteris paribus. Whereas all theorems require such a qualification, because they do not claim to specify the only influences on the dependent variables, it should be reiterated that the ceteris paribus is not meant to imply that the influences noted are minor ones that are easily overwhelmed by the effects of other conditions. On the contrary, the influences specified are assumed to be dominant ones that are usually apparent in simple correlations, unless they are suppressed by other influences stipulated by the theory, as exemplified by the influence of racial heterogeneity on racial intermarriage that is revealed only when racial socioeconomic inequality is controlled.

Theoretical Extensions

Exploratory research often stimulates theoretical ideas, but the ad hoc interpretations of empirical results do not constitute systematic theory. To be sure, the initial insights are frequently derived from research findings and attempt to explain them, but to transform these ideas into a rigorous theory requires disciplining the insights by incorporating them into a deductive hierarchy of propositions and then testing new empirical implications of the propositions. This approach, which is not the conventional one in sociology, has been adopted here. The central theorems of a previously formulated deductive theory[7] are recapitulated in more succinct and, we hope, clearer form, and their implications are tested in research on the influence of metropolitan structure on marriage. In addition, the application of the theoretical scheme is extended to the analysis of new problems, although we were not able to incorporate most of the elaborations of the study into the deductive theoretical system. By using the theoretical scheme beyond the confines of the already existing deductive system, the groundwork is laid for future expansions of the theory.

The deductive theory focuses on the consequences of various aspects of a social structure for patterns of social relations, and an obvious question this raises is how the theoretical scheme can be applied to analyze the conditions and processes that help shape the social structure. Given the importance of consoli-

[7]The fact that the theorems have been previously published is of considerable methodological significance because it demonstrates that the explanations were not derived from the empirical results (although, as we have noted, a few theorems were revised on the basis of these results).

dated social differences for enhancing the likelihood of ingroup relations, it is of interest to ask what conditions influence variations in consolidation among metropolitan structures. We have seen that the most important difference in this respect among SMSAs is the degree to which people's race is consolidated with their other social positions, particularly their education, occupation, and income. It is therefore not surprising that the major influence on SMSA variations in structural consolidation is the metropolis' racial composition. The larger the proportion of blacks in an SMSA, the stronger is the consolidation of race with people's other social positions, even when the effect of Southern location is controlled. The reason may well be, as Blalock (1967) and others have suggested, that discrimination against minorities tends to increase with their expanding size.

Since the population structure strongly influences patterns of marriage and friendship as well as those of conflict, it is of interest to dissect in greater detail the underlying social processes that give rise to the distinctive characteristics of metropolitan structures. For this purpose, we have combined two sociological traditions, the structural approach adopted in this monograph and the status-attainment model of stratification studies. The focus of status-attainment research is on the characteristics of individuals that influence their chances to achieve superior occupational status and income. The model treats ascribed background characteristics (such as race and age) and social origin (such as parental occupational status) as exogeneous variables; the typical endogenous variables are education, occupational status, and income, in that causal sequence. We unfortunately have no indication of social origins, so we cannot analyze social mobility, but our data make it possible to investigate other aspects of status attainment. Although the measures used in the two research traditions are not identical, the measures of both approaches refer to univariate variability and multivariate concomitant variation, which may be considered to reflect roughly equivalent concepts—differentiation and consolidation. The status-attainment model makes it possible to dissect the structural conditions in the metropolis to discover the social processes that have produced them.

The population distributions in our data file were used to construct a correlation matrix for every SMSA, which is analyzed, together with the means and standard deviations, to produce a path model for every SMSA. The three exogeneous variables are sex, race, and age; education, occupational status (SEI), and earnings are the intervening or dependent variables. The average coefficients for the 125 SMSAs in 1970 indicate that blacks had cumulative disadvantages; they had less education than whites; controlling education, they had lower occupational positions; and controlling occupation, their earnings were less. Education influenced both occupational status and, even when occupational position is controlled, earnings, which indicates that better educated workers earn more in the same occupations than less educated ones. The earnings of women were much lower than those of men, independent of their education and occupational status, probably in part because more women than men have part-time or temporary jobs, but undoubtedly in part owing to occupational segregation and wage discrimination by sex. However, these average coefficients conceal the substantial variations among parameters.

Path models are usually constructed for entire countries, and the implicit assumption is that the path coefficients are the same for different populations—for instance, for different parts of the country or different communities. To be sure, the population composition in different places is expected to differ and to produce differences in other distributions—in occupation and in income—but the path coefficients reflecting the influences of antecedents on attainments are expected to be largely the same throughout, lest the model fails to explain differences in occupational and other attainments (Duncan, 1975:57). But our analysis reveals that there are large and systematic differences in path coefficients among SMSAs, which implies that there are substantial differences in consolidation among SMSAs. An exploratory analysis of what SMSA characteristics might be related to differences among SMSAs in the effect of one variable on another reveals that black–white differences (and therefore consolidation) are much greater in Southern SMSAs, compared to SMSAs in other parts of the country. (Some of this regional variation may in turn be due to the higher proportion of blacks—greater racial heterogeneity—in Southern SMSAs, which is entirely consistent with our analysis of the antecedents of multiple racial consolidation in Chapter 4.) We also found that more populated SMSAs tend to have greater sex differences in earnings. As a final example, economic growth (in per capita GNP) appears to reduce race differences in earnings. Thus, the status-attainment process—the process by which differences in one dimension are converted into differences in another, thereby consolidating the two dimensions and generating differentiation in the latter—varies substantially among SMSAs, in ways that are systematically related to other characteristics of the SMSA. These results suggest the need to study variation in social process, in addition to variation in individuals' traits, abilities, and rewards.

According to the theory, the same structural conditions that promote social relations among groups and strata also promote social mobility among them because intergroup relations and mobility mutually influence each other (T-4, T-6). It is not possible to test the mobility theorems, however, because the Census source did not contain the needed information on social origins. But data from another source can be used to analyze the underlying principle that the structure of social positions exerts similar influences on the patterns of social relations and the patterns of social mobility among the positions. The data are for a sample of men in the entire country, not for separate samples in the various SMSAs, and they refer to occupational mobility and intermarriage (defined in terms of the two spouses' parental occupations). The analysis is based on two 12

× 12 matrixes, in which occupations are arranged in order of status. Occupational intermarriage and mobility reveal very similar patterns; the rarer intermarriage is between two occupational groups, the rarer also is mobility. Principal component analyses disclose two dimensions that account for nine-tenths of the observed variation in either matrix of log odds ratios (indicating inmarriage or immobility for pairs of occupations). The major dimension that accounts for both occupational mobility and intermarriage is proximity in socioeconomic status, and a second dimension, the meaning of which is not entirely clear, seems to be freedom from bureaucratic supervision.

An attempt is made to broaden the theory to encompass discordant as well as cordial social relations. But the discussion of conflict is admittedly more speculative and does not entail a theoretical system with a logical structure. Two main sources of conflict are suggested: highly salient group boundaries that make outsiders aliens if not enemies and pronounced inequalities in resources that intensify the conflict of interest over their distribution. The salience of group distinctions is indicative of the significance of cultural values on social life. Cultural norms are the foundations of the highest moral principles of people, but they can turn into fanaticism that inspires the worst atrocities. The profound moral standards of the Bible led to such excesses as the Inquisition and the Salem witch hunts. All ingroup salience contains the germs of outgroup prejudice, but it is the ideological conviction of the superiority of one's own group—the white race or the Aryans—that tends to crystallize outgroup rejection into hostility. This book, because it focuses on structural influences on social life, does not deal much with these cultural influences except as they combine with structural ones, such as inequality.

If resources are defined as generalized means that everybody is interested in maximizing, great inequality of resources makes a conflict of interest over their distribution virtually inevitable. Even if some differences in resources act as incentives for exerting efforts and contribute to coordination and thereby improve the *absolute* amount of resources of the lower strata, great inequality entails, by definition, more *relative* deprivation, which probably has greater significance for conflict than absolute deprivation.[8] Inequalities in resources tend to produce festering discontent, irritability, and friction in one's relations with others, which make conflict and disruption of close relations more likely, as exemplified by the influence of inequality on marital breakup.

What makes overt conflict particularly probable is the combination of these two conditions—salient group boundaries and much inequality of resources. The combination means that salient group differences are reinforced by a conflict of interest over the possible redistribution of generally significant resources, and it

[8]This is illustrated in Table 7.1, which indicates that income inequality (relative deprivation), not poverty (absolute deprivation) affects aggression in the form of criminal violence.

means that inequalities are not experienced by individuals in isolation but by groups many of whose members are in direct contact. Individuals who experience deprivation in isolation, while seeing others around them who are more successful, often blame themselves for their failure, but this is unlikely if most members of a group or all of them—an entire firm, a large part of an industry, most members of an ethnic group—experience the same economic hardships, especially if the group is an ascribed one. If all Japanese–Americans on the West Coast are thrown out of their jobs and homes, how can an individual Nisei feel responsible for his or her misfortune rather than direct the aggression against the outgroup that committed or, at least, tolerated the injustice? If disadvantaged groups can mobilize sufficient strength, they may organize concerted action to fight for a larger share of the resources, as illustrated by collective bargaining and strikes of unions or by elections of labor parties. But the very lack of resources of the most underprivileged groups tends to make them too weak for a successful fight to improve their conditions substantially. In such a situation the prevailing frustration tends to turn into diffuse aggression, with conflict no longer being channeled into realistic battles to improve economic interests but finding outlets in blind rage and violence. Socioeconomic inequalities between blacks and whites are a prime case of inequalities consolidated by ascribed group boundaries, and racial differences in socioeconomic status have the expected influence on criminal violence.

Concluding Conjectures

Contemporary sociology is characterized by a great variety of approaches to the study of social life and the construction of theories about it. This diversity of sociological orientations and theoretical paradigms is often criticized as indicative of the immaturity of the discipline, a growing crisis in its development, and a sign that it has not been possible, and may never be possible, to develop a coherent body of systematic knowledge about society and social life. Whereas most sociologists would agree that sociology is not yet a mature science, by no means do all view the plurality of sociological viewpoints and theoretical schemes as a regrettable or unusual state of affairs that impedes the advancement of systematic knowledge. Thus, Merton (1975:47–48) stresses that "while the unified consolidation of paradigms remains a useful but distant ideal of Pareto T-type, a plurality of paradigms has its own uses in an evolving discipline." He goes on to single out for attention two important advantages of multiple theoretical orientations: they lead to the study of a wider range of different problems, and they foster competition for cognitive attention and for new recruits, and such competition stimulates research endeavors to bolster theoretical claims. If a single theory dominates a field, it threatens to stifle scientific progress. Conflict among opposing theoretical orientations helps to sift theories and advance systematic knowledge, just as conflict among opposing political parties is essential for giving voters a meaningful choice and, thus, for democracy.[9]

In concluding this book, the approach presented is briefly contrasted with a few others in sociology. Much sociological analysis is concerned with the influences of social conditions on the attitudes and behavior of individuals. Why do people in industrialized countries have lower birth rates than those in less developed nations? Why do people in rural areas have more children than those in cities? Why do disproportionate numbers in slums vote Democratic? Although the questions are worded in terms of influences of social conditions rather than personality traits, which presumably makes them sociological rather than psychological issues, it is evident that they actually refer to the properties of individuals and can easily be translated into such terms. The last question, for example, really asks why poor people are more likely than affluent ones to vote Democratic. Sampling surveys, which have been the main tool of systematic social research for several decades, encourage the study of relationships of factors by which individuals can be characterized, and the problems are usually formulated in terms of the relationships between such factors, leaving implicit the significance of social conditions. How does a person's religion influence her political attitudes and voting? Does work satisfaction influence productivity? How do social origins influence education, occupation, and income; how does education in turn influence occupation and income; and how much of its influence is mediating that of social origins and how much of it is independent of origins? Since such questions ask how or why factors that characterize individuals are related, they require answers that refer to the psychological processes that connect various states of individuals, which may be acquired attributes (education), socially inherited positions (class origin), attitudes (political preference), or behavior patterns (party vote). The analysis of this type of data that describe individuals lends itself to Homans' (1961) theoretical approach of methodological individualism, often referred to as psychological reductionism, according to which all sociological explanations must themselves ultimately be explained in terms of underlying psychological principles.

When sociology originated in the last century, the questions it raised did not refer to the relationships of characteristics of individuals but to the relationships of characteristics of societies. How does society's economy influence its political system? What was the significance of the Reformation for the development of capitalism? Do economic developments affect religious dogma? How does the

---

[9]Our inability to develop a deductive theory of conflict must not be taken to mean that we consider conflict unimportant for social life. The reason that we present some empirical analysis of violent crimes is not that we think it is a typical expression of conflict but that data on it are available, which are indicative of unrealistic manifestations of conflict when realistic expressions of conflicting interest are suppressed and frustrated.

division of labor influence social solidarity? These broad questions cannot be answered on the basis of psychological principles. The changes in social solidarity Durkheim seeks to explain had nothing to do with changes in psychological attributes but were, according to him, the result of changes in society's occupational structure. These big issues do not lend themselves to systematic research. Sampling surveys provided a research tool for sociology, but they simultaneously redirected the focus of its concerns from macrosociological to essentially sociopsychological questions.

Not all recent sociologists turned away from the study of macrosociological problems. Parsons, who is probably the most influential social theorist of this century, was one who did not. In his first book, Parsons (1937:768) defines sociology as the science that attempts to explain social action in terms of *common-value integration,* and although his theories undergo considerable changes in the many books he wrote during the subsequent forty years, his emphasis on the dominant significance of the integration of cultural values and norms persists throughout. The gist of his functional theory (Parsons and Smelser, 1956) is that all social systems must meet four basic requirements; they do so by developing specialized subsystems, that also must meet the four functional requirements and develop more specialized sub-subsystems for this purpose. In this way, modern societies have become increasingly differentiated. All institutional systems and subsystems are ultimately defined and governed by their distinctive cultural values.

Of course, not all macrosociological theories center attention on order, functional integration, and the ultimate significance of common values for all institutions. The prototype of the opposite perspective is Marx's theory, according to which shared values and norms are merely ideologies that help the ruling class to sustain the status quo and preserve their vested interests. They are part of the superstructure, as are society's political, religious, and family institutions. The infrastructure that is the foundation of all these characteristics is the economy, characterized by the dialectical interplay between productive forces and relations of production, which find expression in the class structure and class conflict and in historical developments that ultimately lead, when internal contradictions become too great and class consciousness of the exploited develops, to revolutions. Marx's theory continues to have a dominant influence on social science in Europe, but it was virtually ignored in this country until quite recently. Now there are a few theories building on that of Marx. A well-known example is the world-system theory (Wallerstein, 1974).

The recent development of network analysis focuses on the microsociological study of interpersonal relations, in sharp contrast with Marx's focus on the class structure of entire societies, but on a more abstract level, it shares with his theory a common concern with a relational structure rather than shared values, norms, or attitudes. It derives from Moreno's (1934) sociometry and analyzes the struc-

ture of relations between individuals in small groups. Thus, Harary and colleagues (1965) explain the constellations of direct links in terms of psychological
balance theory. Mitchell (1969) presents a conceptual analysis of network structures, distinguishing, for example, whether social relations are confined to one
sphere, like work, or are multiplex, involving several joint activities and reciprocal attitudes. A recent development in network studies is blockmodeling, which
centers attention on indirect rather than direct links and classifies individuals,
regardless of whether they choose each other, together if they largely make the
same choices of third persons, which defines them as belonging to the same
block or having the same position (White *et al.*, 1976; Burt, 1976). A difficulty
with this type of analysis, which it shares with factor analysis, is that the
discovery of pattern—blocks in this case, factors in the other—is often the end
product of the study, without relating this pattern to other variables and trying to
explain it.

The approach in this book contrasts with the foregoing orientations in the
following ways: instead of analyzing the interrelated characteristics of individuals, it analyzes those of entire societies or communities; it is not concerned
with the influences of cultural values and norms but with those of population
distributions, in terms of which social structure is defined; there is no primary
theoretical emphasis on the economic structure but the question of which structure is most significant is left for research to answer (which means that the theory
has less empirical content[10] than Marx's); and the objective is not the microsociological analysis of the structure of relations and positions in small groups
but the macrosociological study of the structure of positions and relations in large
populations.

The core of sociology is the study and explanation of the structure of social
relations in a collectivity, whether a small group or an entire society. But the
kind of social relations of interest are different in these cases. In the study of
small groups, we are interested in the networks of interpersonal relations between individuals, and the roles and positions of individuals are defined by their
involvement in these networks. In the study of large populations, however, the
millions of personal relations are not of interest. To be sure, we may want to
know what factors determine whether a person is an isolate or how many friends
he has, but this would not be a study of the social structure. Since it is impossible
to get a meaningful description of the relations between all individuals in a large
population, macrostructural inquiry, as here conceived, first distinguishes social
positions and then analyzes the patterns of relations among positions, that is,
between people occupying different positions—Protestants and Catholics, for
instance, or members of different ethnic groups. But the definition of social

---

[10]Empirical content as discussed by Popper (1959:112–135).

positions takes their significance for social relations into account. Specifically, the criterion of position is that it influences the distinctions people make in their social life. This sounds tautological because social positions are first defined on the basis of their influence on social relations, and the structure of social positions is then used to explain the pattern of social relations. Actually, however, there is no tautology involved because the two influences of positions on relations—those defining positions and those explaining relations—are quite different ones. The difference is embodied in the first two assumptions and is of central importance for the nature of the theory advanced.

According to the first assumption, social relations are more prevalent between proximate than distant social positions. One could consider this assumption a defining criterion of position, which means that only those attributes are social positions which satisfy the assumption that associations between proximate positions exceed chance expectations. This means, of course, that the assumption is tautological,[11] true by definition, cannot be tested, and does not explain social relations. But this is not the explanation of people's relations the theory advances in any case. The theory's objective is represented by the second assumption, that social association depends on contact opportunities. This assumption does not rest on the conception of social position in terms of its influence on social relations, but it is the basic operating principle of the theory.

The population distributions in a community or society create opportunity structures and structural constraints that influence people's social relations independent of, and frequently in opposition to, the infuences of their ingroup preferences. As long as sociology tries to explain the behavior of individuals in terms of their own attributes and experiences, it is no more than wholesale psychology, as it has been sarcastically called, and its principles are ultimately rooted in psychological theory, as Homans insists. The distinctive objective of sociology is quite different. It is to explain patterns of social relations, not the individual motives and behavior underlying them, in terms of the population structure that sets limits to the influences of cultural values and psychological preferences. The endeavor here has been to present a macrostructural theory that furnishes such strictly sociological explanations.

Although the theory had been previously formulated, its core is recapitulated in more concise and, we think, more lucid language. This serves as a basis for drawing the empirical implications of the major theorems for the influences of metropolitan structures on intermarriage. The central aim of the book has been to present research findings to test the major theorems, based on data about the 125 largest metropolitan places in the United States, where more than three-fifths of

---

[11]In Liska's (1969) terms it is a *contentual tautology*, which merely relabels variables and does not further systematic analysis.

the American population live. The tests essentially corroborated the theorems, with a few minor revisions. Conducting research on the implications of theorems that had been previously formulated, although it unfortunately involves some duplication, has the great advantage that the analysis of theoretical explanations and research results does not involve, as it so often does, ad hoc interpretations of findings but genuine tests of a priori specified theorems.

Macrosociological theory in the United States has been dominated by an emphasis on the fundamental significance of cultural values and norms as the basic principles that determine the character of social systems and are the source of their social integration and order. The great influence of Parsons' theories is in good part responsible for this prevailing orientation. The structural theory advanced and tested may be considered as an attempt to compensate for this one-sided emphasis by calling attention to the significance of structural influences on social life. Both cultural and structural conditions undoubtedly influence it, and they mutually influence each other. Prevailing values and norms influence social relations, but structural conditions also influence them and may in the long run modify the common values and norms. For example, heterogeneity promotes intergroup relations despite ingroup preferences, as we have seen, and one may suspect that it ultimately mitigates the ingroup peferences themselves.

As a final illustration of structural influences on culture, we examine a few conjectures about the significance of structural conditions for art. One main thesis in the literature is that inequality fosters the development of superior art for several reasons. Wealthy individuals have traditionally been patrons of the arts, and they also constitute a leisure class that has the time and interests to develop refined tastes in art. The argument has also been advanced that a highly stratified society stimulates artistic creativity, though some claim that the reason is that the psychological security of clear-cut class lines stimulates artistic endeavors (Fischer, 1961), whereas others suggest that it is the alienation of artists in societies with much inequality that spurs their creativity (Wolfe, 1969). Most of the research on the subject, what little there is, has been done in simple societies where stratification constitutes the main form of differentiation. It is therefore not surprising that interpretations of art in terms of inequality are complemented by interpretations in terms of diversity or complexity. Several art historians have suggested that social and economic complexity stimulates greater artistic diversity in both style and subject matter (Pevsner, 1940; Henning, 1960; Haskell, 1963). Special importance has been attributed to the greater diversity of patronage resulting from the decline of support of art by aristocratic patrons and their replacement by sales in markets to diverse customers (White and White, 1965). Even such a purely cultural expression as artistic activity is apparently affected by structural conditions, although the precise nature of the influence is often not specified.

Coda

There is an inherent dilemma in pluralism and in heterogeneity. Since heterogeneity promotes intergroup relations, including intermarriage, the inference is
that it wipes out heterogeneity in the long run and produces homogeneous populations. But this cannot be true because we know that communities and societies
today are more heterogeneous than they used to be centuries ago. One reason for
this is that heterogeneity is self-reinforcing, not only because a heterogeneous
metropolis attracts diverse migrants from various places but also because the
lines of differentiation become more and more finely drawn—the division of
labor leads to increasing specialization; a variety of religious denominations
encourages the splitting off of sects who interpret the Bible differently; and a
multiparty political system facilitates the emergence of splinter parties. There is a
second reason. Crosscutting social circles sustain multiform heterogeneity because even if heterogeneity in one dimension or another should decline—and
ingroup tendencies are usually strong enough to prevent this—other forms of
heterogeneity tend to continue to expand. Although the extent of intersection is
limited by social mobility that increases consolidation, as has been suggested,
these limits are not sufficient to preclude the trend toward increasing multiform
heterogeneity. Ultimately, therefore, we come back to the crucial significance of
crosscutting social circles for understanding the structure of society.

List of Assumptions and Theorems

Assumptions

A-1   Social associations are more prevalent between persons in proximate than those in distant social positions. (Page 27)

A-2   Rates of social association depend on opportunities for social contact. (29)

A-3   Associates in other groups or strata facilitate mobility to them. (57)

A-4   The influence of every dimension of social differentiation is partly independent of that of any other dimension in a large population. (90)

Theorems

T-1   As group size increases, the probable rate of outgroup relations decreases. (31)

T-2   Heterogeneity promotes intergroup relations. (41)

T-3   The greater the inequality, the greater is the probability of status-distant social relations. (42)

T-4   Mobility promotes intergroup relations. (54)

T-5   Net outmobility from a group promotes outgroup relations more than net inmobility to it does. (56)

T-6   Intergroup relations increase the probability of social mobility. (57)

T-7   Heterogeneity is positively related to social mobility. (58)

T-8   Inequality is positively related to mobility across greater social distances. (58)

T-9   Net mobility from larger to smaller groups increases heterogeneity. (61)

T-10   Mobility toward the upper-lower boundary in a status hierarchy diminishes inequality. (66)

T-11   The multiple intersection of independent dimensions of social differentiation promotes intergroup relations. (90)

T-12   Multiple intersection tends to increase social mobility. (98)

T-13   Intersecting lines of differentiation further structural change. (100)

T-14   Social mobility increases the consolidation of various lines of differentiation. (100)

T-15   The more society's heterogeneity results from the heterogeneity within rather than that among its substructures, the more it promotes intergroup relations. (156)

T-16   The more society's inequality results from the inequality within rather than among its substructures, the more it promotes status-distant relations. (156)

T-17   The more society's consolidated differences result from concomitant variations within rather than among substructures, the less do the consolidated differences impede social relations. (158)

T-18   The more society's heterogeneity is the product of within-community heterogeneity, the better are the chances of social mobility. (160)

T-19   The more society's inequality is the product of within-community inequality, the better are the chances of social mobility. (160)

T-20   The more society's consolidated differences are the product of concomitant variations within rather than among communities, the better are the chances of social mobility. (160)

T-21   The further heterogeneity penetrates into successive substructures, the more it promotes intergroup relations. (167)

T-22   The further inequality penetrates into successive substructures, the more it promotes status-distant relations. (168)

T-23   The further consolidated social differences penetrate into successive substructures, the more they promote intergroup and status-distant social relations. (168)

T-24   The penetration of heterogeneity into substructures promotes social mobility. (169)

T-25   The penetration of inequality into substructures promotes social mobility. (169)

T-26   The penetration of consolidated differences into substructures promotes social mobility. (169)

T-27   The large size of a community increases the rate of overt conflict. (174)

APPENDIX A

Description of Variables

DEPENDENT VARIABLES: MARRIAGE RATES

All marriage rates for categorical (nominal) characteristics are computed from a crosstabulation (joint distribution) of wife's by husband's group membership with respect to the specified characteristic. The general form of such a crosstabulation is

	Husband's group						
	1	**2**	...	j	...	n	**total**
1	f_{11}	f_{12}	...	f_{1j}	...	f_{1n}	f_{1+}
2	f_{21}	f_{22}	...	f_{2j}	...	f_{2n}	f_{2+}
.	.	.	...	.	...	.	.
.	.	.	...	.	...	.	.
Wife's group i	f_{i1}	f_{i2}	...	f_{ij}	...	f_{in}	f_{i+}
.	.	.	...	.	...	.	.
.	.	.	...	.	...	.	.
n	f_{n1}	f_{n2}	...	f_{nj}	...	f_{nn}	f_{n+}
total	f_{+1}	f_{+2}	...	f_{+j}	...	f_{+n}	f_{++}

where n equals the total number of categories, or groups, for the characteristic, and f_{++} is the total number of young (subsample) couples with nonmissing data for both spouses.

Outmarriage Rates (Unconstrained)

This variable is defined for a group within an SMSA and equals the proportion of persons (men and women) in a specific group who are married to someone outside their group. Using the marriage crosstabulation, the outmarriage rate for group k is

$$OM_k = \frac{\sum_{i \neq k} f_{ik} + \sum_{j \neq k} f_{kj}}{f_{k+} + f_{+k}} = 1 - \frac{2 f_{kk}}{f_{k+} + f_{+k}}$$

	N	$\bar{X}$	S.D.
Ethnic group			
Nonwhite	115	.100	.221
Calculated from the crosstabulation of couples in the subsample according to their race			
White of foreign stock	119	.779	.237
White of native stock	125	.072	.060
Calculated from the crosstabulation of spouses' ethnicity			
Birth region			
Born in same region (as now living)	125	.155	.136
Born in different region	125	.694	.220
Calculated from crosstabulating spouses' regions of birth, using the nine census categories			
Industry			
Manufacturing	125	.651	.195
Other	125	.249	.118
Calculated by collapsing the crosstabulation of major industries of spouses			

	N	$\overline{X}$	S.D.

Occupation

	N	$\overline{X}$	S.D.
Professional and technical workers	121	.756	.225
Sales and clerical workers	125	.718	.138
Operatives and transportation workers	125	.736	.187

Calculated from the crosstabulation of
major occupational categories for spouses

Intermarriage Rates (Unconstrained)

The intermarriage rate is computed for the entire crosstabulation (in contrast to outmarriage, which can be computed for each group) and equals the proportion of couples in which the spouses belong to different groups. The intermarriage rate is

$$IM = \frac{\sum_i \sum_{j \neq i} f_{ij}}{f_{++}} = 1 - \frac{\sum_i f_{ii}}{f_{++}} \quad .$$

	N	$\overline{X}$	S.D.
Race (detailed)	125	.010	.029

Proportion of all couples intermarried with
different detailed races given the following
categories: 0-White, 1-Negro, 2-American
Indian, 3-Japanese, 4-Chinese, 5-Filipino,
6-Hawaiian, 7-Korean, 8-other

Race (dichotomy)	125	.009	.017

Proportion of all couples intermarried based
on a white-nonwhite dichotomy

Nativity	125	.114	.086

Proportion of all couples intermarried by
nativity, based on the following categories:
native stock (both parents born in the
U.S.A.—one foreign-born parent defines the
person's origin based on the parent's
country of birth), Puerto Rican, Northwest
European, Central European, Eastern
European, Southern European, Russian, Asian,
Canadian, Mexican, Central or South American,
other foreign stock

	N	$\overline{X}$	S.D.
Ethnicity	125	.117	.085

Proportion of all couple intermarried
ethnically, based on 15 categories:
three races (Black, American Indian,
Oriental), which override nativity, and
the 12 categories of nativity

	N	$\overline{X}$	S.D.
Mother tongue	125	.166	.167

Proportion of all couples intermarried by
mother tongue (language during childhood),
based on a dichotomy of English versus
all others

	N	$\overline{X}$	S.D.
Birth region	125	.254	.165

Proportion of couples intermarried by region
of birth, recoded to give nine geographic
divisions or regions as defined by the U.S.
Bureau of the Census: 1-New England, 2-Middle
Atlantic, 3-South Atlantic, 4-North East
Central, 5-North West Central, 6-South East
Central, 7-South West Central, 8-Mountain,
9-Pacific

	N	$\overline{X}$	S.D.
Industry	125	.809	.078

Proportion of couples in the civilian labor
force intermarried by major industrial group,
based on the following categories: 1-Agricul-
ture, 2-Mining, 3-Construction, 4-Durable
manufacturing, 6-Transportation, 7-Communica-
tions, 8-Utilities, 9-Wholesale trade,
10-Retail trade, 11-Finance, insurance, real
estate, 12-Business services, 13-Personal
services, 14-Entertainment services, 15-Pro-
fessional services, 16-Public administration

	N	$\overline{X}$	S.D.
Occupation (major)	125	.836	.061

Proportion of couples in the civilian labor
force intermarried by major occupational
group, based on the following categories:
1-Professionals, 2-Salaried managers, 3-Self-
employed managers, 4-Sales workers, 5-Clerical
workers, 6-Craftspeople, 7-Operatives, 8-Trans-
portion workers, 9-Laborers, 10-Farmers,
11-Farm workers, 12-Service workers, 13-Pri-
vate household workers

	N	$\overline{X}$	S.D.
Occupation (detailed)	125	.974	.033

Proportion of all couples in the civilian
labor force intermarried by 444 detailed
occupational categories defined by the U.S.
Bureau of the Census

Outmarriage Rates (Constrained)

The constrained outmarriage ignores those outmarriages that necessarily occur because of the difference in the number of husbands and wives in the specified category. It is

$$COM_k = 1 - \frac{f_{kk}}{\min(f_{k+}, f_{+k})}$$

	N	$\bar{X}$	S.D.
Ethnic group			
Foreign stock	99	.671	.301
Native stock	125	.053	.055
Birth region			
Born in same region	125	.114	.099
Born in different region	125	.596	.277
Industry			
Manufacturing	116	.470	.244
Other	125	.155	.110
Occupation			
Professional and technical workers	103	.611	.302
Sales and clerical workers	118	.327	.239
Operatives and transportation workers	107	.523	.262

Intermarriage Rates (Constrained Nominal)

The constrained intermarriage measure ignores that proportion of intermarried couples in the crosstabulation that necessarily occurs because of differences in the marginal distributions of wives and husbands. It is

$$CIM = 1 - \frac{\Sigma f_{ii}}{\Sigma \min(f_{i+}, f_{+i})}$$

	N	$\bar{X}$	S.D.
Nativity	125	.071	.072
Ethnicity	125	.073	.071
Mother tongue	125	.093	.078
Birth region	125	.184	.150
Occupation (major)	125	.604	.165
Occupation (detailed)	125	.948	.066
Industry	125	.657	.145

Intermarriage Rates (Unconstrained Graduated)

The intermarriage rates for graduated characteristics are based on the average relative difference between spouses' statuses. The unconstrained measure is

$$IM = \frac{\frac{1}{N} \sum_i |X_{mi} - X_{fi}|}{.5(\bar{X}_m + \bar{X}_f)}$$

where m is for males (husbands) and f is for females (wives) in the subsample. This is calculated only for couples where there is information on the characteristic for both spouses.

	N	$\bar{X}$	S.D.
Education	125	.128	.025

Unconstrained intermarriage based on the
number of years of education completed:
the variable is coded from 0 = never
attended to 16 = 4 years of college or more

	N	$\bar{X}$	S.D.
Earnings	125	.904	.173

Unconstrained intermarriage based on earnings

	N	$\bar{X}$	S.D.
Total personal income	125	.909	.119

Unconstrained intermarriage based on total
personal income

	N	$\bar{X}$	S.D.
SEI	125	.505	.080

Unconstrained intermarriage based on Duncan's
socioeconomic index

Intermarriage Rates (Constrained Graduated)

The constrained intermarriage rate for a graduated characteristic adjusts for any systematic tendency for wives to have more or less status than their husbands. It equals

$$CIM = \frac{\frac{1}{N}\sum_i |(X_{mi} - X_{fi}) - (\bar{X}_m - \bar{X}_f)|}{.5(\bar{X}_m + \bar{X}_f)} = \frac{\frac{1}{N}\sum_i |(X_{mi} - \bar{X}_m) - (X_{fi} - \bar{X}_f)|}{.5(\bar{X}_m + \bar{X}_f)}$$

	N	$\bar{X}$	S.D.
Education	125	.123	.025
Earnings	125	.607	.161
Total personal income	125	.613	.116
SEI	125	.493	.078

DEPENDENT VARIABLES: CRIME RATES

	N	$\bar{X}$	S.D.
Total violent crime rate	125	2.45	.280

Log (base 10) of total crime rate per 100,000 persons for 1970, data from the Uniform Crime Reports

Murder rate	124	.805	.336

Number of murders per 100,000 for 1970 ($\log_{10}$ transformation)

Rape rate	125	1.23	.269

Number of rapes per 100,000 for 1970 ($\log_{10}$ transformation)

Robbery rate	125	2.06	.327

Number of robberies per 100,000 for 1970 ($\log_{10}$ transformation)

Assault rate	125	2.13	.289

Number of aggravated assaults per 100,000 for 1970 ($\log_{10}$ transformation)

PRIMARY INDEPENDENT VARIABLES: MEASURES OF SOCIAL STRUCTURE

Size Measures

The size measures are the percentage of an SMSA's relevant population that belongs to a group, based on the total sample.

	N	$\bar{X}$	S.D.

Ethnic group

Nonwhite	125	.120	.098

Number of nonwhites/total number of whites and nonwhites in the SMSA

Native stock	125	.728	.112

Number of native ethnics/total number of all ethnics in the SMSA

Foreign stock	125	.160	.109

(Number of Puerto Ricans + North West Europeans + Central Europeans + Eastern Europeans + Southern Europeans + Asians + Russians + Canadians + Mexicans + Central and South Americans + other ethnicities)/ total number of all ethnics in the SMSA

Birth region

Born in same region	125	.759	.153

Number of respondents born in region in which they are now living/total number with a reported birth region

Born in different region	125	.241	.153

Number of respondents not born in region in which they are now living/total number with a reported birth region

Industry

Manufacturing	125	.260	.105

(Number of durable manufacturing + number nondurable manufacturing)/total number in all the major industrial groups in the SMSA

Other	125	.740	.105

[Total number in all the major industrial groups - (number in durable + nondurable manufacturing)]/total number in all the major industrial groups in the SMSA

Occupation

Professional and technical workers	125	.149	.028

Number of professional and technical workers/total number in all the major occupational groups in the SMSA

Sales and clerical workers	125	.262	.033

(Number of sales workers + number of clerical workers)/total number in all the major occupational groups in the SMSA

Operatives and transportation workers	125	.172	.051

(Number of operatives + number of trans- portation workers)/total number in all the major occupational groups in the SMSA

Heterogeneity Measures

The heterogeneity measures are the Gibbs–Martin index of the division of labor, which equals $1 - \Sigma p_i^2$ where p_i is the fraction of the population in the ith group.

	N	$\overline{X}$	S.D.
1970 Measures			
Detailed race Gibbs-Martin	125	.195	.131
White-nonwhite Gibbs-Martin	125	.192	.123
Nativity Gibbs-Martin	125	.273	.166
Ethnicity Gibbs-Martin	125	.426	.134
Mother tongue Gibbs-Martin	125	.308	.108
Birth region Gibbs-Martin	125	.381	.190
Occupation (major) Gibbs-Martin	125	.872	.010
Occupation (detailed) Gibbs-Martin	125	.988	.001
Industry Gibbs-Martin	125	.873	.024

1960 Measures

White-nonwhite Gibbs-Martin	121	.183	.131
Nativity Gibbs-Martin	100	.321	.181
Occupation (major) Gibbs-Martin	121	.850	.016
Occupation (detailed) Gibbs-Martin	121	.998	.002
Industry Gibbs-Martin	121	.883	.029

Inequality Measures

The inequality measures are the Gini Index of Concentration (takes into account weights for the number of people in the SMSA with a given status level),

$$\text{Gini} = \frac{1 - \sum_i X_i f_i [f_i + 2(N - cf_i)]}{N^2 \bar{X}}$$

where X_i equals the status of the ith category, f_i is the number of persons with this status, cf_i is the number of people with this status <u>or less</u>, and N is the total number of persons.

	N	$\bar{X}$	S.D.

1970 Measures

Education Gini	125	.165	.020
Earnings Gini	125	.463	.023
Total personal income Gini	125	.495	.019
SEI Gini	125	.325	.018
Family income Gini	125	.343	.028

1960 Measures

Education Gini	100	.202	.028
Earnings Gini	100	.389	.028
SEI Gini	121	.358	.020

Intersection Measures

The intersection measures are equal to 1 − the average of the bivariate associations of the specified variable with several others (see Appendix C) within an SMSA.

	N	$\bar{X}$	S.D.
1970 Measures			
Nominal			
Race intersection (dichotomy)	125	.167	.093
Nativity intersection	125	.133	.038
Ethnic intersection	125	.207	.060
Birth region intersection	125	.131	.025
Occupation intersection	125	.324	.018
Industry intersection	125	.276	.027
Graduated			
Education intersection	125	.361	.037
Earnings intersection	125	.223	.026
Total personal income intersection	125	.221	.024
SEI intersection	125	.304	.042
1960 Measures			
Race intersection (dichotomy)	125	.498	.299
Occupation intersection	125	.541	.231
Industry intersection	125	.408	.303
Earnings intersection	125	.532	.262

OTHER INDEPENDENT (CONTROL) VARIABLES

	N	$\bar{X}$	S.D.
Occupation-earnings eta	125	.419	.032
The 1970 eta between major occupation and earnings of persons in the experienced civilian labor force			
Consolidation factor	125	15.77	6.77
Factor scores based on factor analysis of the covariance matrix of 46 measures of bivariate consolidation			

Race (dichotomy) mean   125   .120   .098

   Mean of the nonwhite-white dichotomy

South   125   .336   .474

   A geographic region, used as a dummy variable
   distinguishing SMSAs located in the South
   (South Atlantic, East Southern Central, West
   Southern Central) from those in other regions

Percentage foreign stock   125   .160   .109

   Number of non-American ethnics/total number
   of ethnics in SMSA

Poverty   125   8.97   3.60

   Proportion of all families below the low
   income level: low income levels are based
   on a poverty index developed by the Social
   Security Administration in 1964; the index is
   adjusted for family size, sex of family head,
   number of children under 18, and farm/nonfarm
   residence

Log white-nonwhite SEI   125   .169   .102

   Ratio of white to nonwhite SEI (Duncan score)
   in logarithmic transformation

Size (population)   125   9941   14,551

Log size   125   3.81   .356

   The size of the population, which is highly
   skewed, is used in logarithmic transformation
   (base 10)

Percentage divorced   125   .055   .012

   The percentage divorced is (number divorced in
   the SMSA + number separated in the SMSA)/total
   number of marriages in the SMSA

Age of SMSA   125   58.40   38.74

   Number of years since central city attained
   a population of 50,000

Economic growth   125   76.72   13.02

   Percentage increase from 1960 to 1970 in
   per capita GNP

APPENDIX B

Correlations among Independent Variables

Analysis for Table 2.5: detailed race Gibbs–Martin with log white-nonwhite SEI ratio = .48

Analysis for Table 4.1: 1970 heterogeneity and inequality with corresponding multiple intersection measure

Differentiation	Multiple intersection
Heterogeneity	
Race (dichotomy)	-.79
Mother tongue	-.74
Ethnicity	-.39
Birth region	-.16
Industry	.15
Occupation	-.10
Inequality	
Education	-.55
Earnings	-.22
Total personal income	-.25
SEI	.10

Analysis for Table **4.2**:

	1970 Occupation- earnings eta	Education Gini index
Education Gini index	-.06	
Education intersection	-.23	-.55

Analysis for Table 4.3: 1960 heterogeneity and inequality with corresponding multiple intersection measure

Differentiation	Multiple intersection
Heterogeneity	
Race (dichotomy)	-.87
Industry	-.12
Occupation	.05
Inequality	
Earnings	-.66

Analysis for Table **4.5**:

	Race (dichotomy) mean	South
South	.66	
Foreign stock mean	-.39	-.51

Analysis for Table 4.6:

	Consolidation factor
Racial heterogeneity (dichotomy)	.73
Ethnic heterogeneity	-.06
Total personal income inequality	.31
Earnings inequality	.23
SEI inequality	.08

Analysis for Table 5.6:

	South	Population	Log population	Percentage poor	Economic growth
Population	-.15				
Log population	-.14	.83			
Percentage poor	.70	-.15	-.26		
Economic growth	.41	-.004'	.003	.30	
SMSA age	-.15	.56	.70	-.24	.009

Analysis for Table 7.1: family income inequality with poverty index = .70

Analysis for Table 7.2:

	Log size	South	Family income Gini	Race (dichotomy) mean	Log w-nw SEI ratio
South	-.14				
Family income Gini	.06	.64			
Race (dichotomy) mean	.12	.67	.52		
Log w-nw SEI ratio	-.09	.61	.49	.56	
Percentage divorced	.30	.29	.44	.38	.26

APPENDIX C

Components of Multiple Intersection Indexes

INDEX	Components (bivariate measures)	Deleted	a
1970 Measures			
RACE	R-IND,[*] R-OCC, R-EDUC, R-INC, R-SEI	R-NAT, R-BREG	.96
NATIONAL ORIGIN	N-RACE, N-BREG, N-IND, N-OCC, N-EDUC, N-INC, N-SEI		.75
ETHNIC ORIGIN	E-EDUC, E-EARN, E-INC, E-SEI	NAT-RACE	.85
BIRTH REGION	B-NAT, B-IND, B-OCC, B-EDUC, B-INC, B-SEI	B-RACE	.72
INDUSTRY	I-NAT, I-BREG, I-OCC, I-EDUC, I-INC, I-SEI	I-RACE	.80
OCCUPATIN	O-NAT, O-BREG, O-IND, O-EDUC, O-INC	O-RACE	.70
EDUCATION	E-RACE, E-ETHN, E-BREG, E-IND, E-OCC, E-INC, E-SEI	E-NAT	.71
INCOME	I-RACE, I-NAT, I-ETHN, I-BREG, I-IND, I-OCC, I-EDUC, I-SEI		.68
EARNINGS	E-RACE, E-NAT, E-ETHN, E-BREG, E-OCC, E-EDUC, E-SEI	E-IND	.68
SEI	S-RACE, S-NAT, S-ETHN, S-BREG, S-IND, S-EDUC, S-INC		.72
1960 Measures			
RACE	R-IND, R-OCC, R-EDUC, R-EARN		.94
INDUSTRY	I-RACE, I-EARN	I-OCC	.45
OCCUPATION	O-EARN, O-RACE	O-IND	.34
EARNINGS	E-RACE, E-OCC, E-IND		.67

[*] R-IND is the bivariate association of race (the index variable) with industry.

References

Abrams, Ray H.
  1943   "Residential propinquity as a factor in marriage selection." American Sociological Review 8:288-294.
Abramson, Harold J.
  1973   Ethnic Diversity in Catholic America. New York: Wiley.
Alba, Richard D.
  1976   "Social assimilation among American Catholic national-origin groups." American Sociological Review 41:1030-1046.
Allison, Paul D.
  1978   "Measures of inequality." American Sociological Review 43:865-879.
Athanasiou, Robert and Gary A. Yoshika
  1973   "The spatial character of friendship formation." Environment and Behavior 5:43-65.
Atkinson, Anthony B.
  1970   "On the measurement of inequality." Journal of Economic Theory 2:244-263.
Blalock, Hubert M.
  1969   Theory Construction. Englewood Cliffs: Prentice Hall.
  1967   Toward a Theory of Minority-Group Relations. New York: Wiley.
  1956   "Economic discrimination and Negro increase." American Sociological Review 21:584-588.
Blau, Judith R. and Peter M. Blau
  1982   "The cost of inequality." American Sociological Review 47:114-129.
Blau, Peter M.
  1977   Inequality and Heterogeneity. New York: Free Press.
Blau, Peter M., Carolyn Beeker and Kevin M. Fitzpatrick
  Forthcoming   "Intersecting social affiliations and intermarriage." Social Forces 62.
Blau, Peter M., Terry C. Blum and Joseph E. Schwartz
  1982   "Heterogeneity and intermarriage." American Sociological Review 47:45-62.
Blau, Peter M. and Otis Dudley Duncan
  1967   The American Occupational Structure. New York: Wiley.
Blau, Peter M. and Richard A. Schoenherr
  1971   The Structure of Organizations. New York: Basic Books.
Bollen, Kenneth A. and Sally Ward
  1979   "Ratio variables in aggregate analysis." Sociological Methods and Research 7:431-450.

Bose, Christine
    1973   Jobs and Gender. Baltimore: Johns Hopkins University Center for Metropolitan Plan-
              ning and Research.
Bossard, James
    1932   "Residential propinquity as a factor in marriage selection." American Journal of
              Sociology 38:219–224.
Bowles, Samuel and Herbert Gintis
    1976   Schooling in Capitalist America. New York: Basic Books.
Braithwaite, John
    1979   Inequality, Crime, and Public Policy. London: Routledge and Kegan Paul.
Braithwaite, Richard B.
    1953   Scientific Explanation. Cambridge: University Press.
Breiger, Ronald L.
    1974   "The duality of persons and groups." Social Forces 53:181–189.
Brown, David L. and Glenn V. Fuguitt
    1972   "Percent nonwhite and racial disparity in nonmetropolitan cities in the South." Social
              Science Quarterly 53:573–582.
Bumpass, Larry
    1970   "The trend of interfaith marriage in the United States." Social Biology 17:253–259.
Burt, Ronald S.
    1976   "Positions in networks." Social Forces 55:93–122.
Cain, Glen and Harold Watts
    1970   "Problems in making inferences from the Coleman Report." American Sociological
              Review 35:228–241.
Campbell, Norman
    1952   What is Science? New York: Dover.
Caplow, Theodore and Robert Forman
    1950   "Neighborhood interaction in a homogeneous community." American Sociological
              Review 15:357–366.
Carter, Hugh and Paul C. Glick
    1970   Marriage and Divorce. Cambridge: Harvard University Press.
Centers, Richard
    1949   "Marital selection and occupational strata." American Journal of Sociology
              54:508–519.
Coleman, James S.
    1957   Community Conflict. Glencoe: Free Press.
Coser, Lewis A.
    1968   "Conflict: Social aspects." Vol. 3, pp. 232–236 in David L. Sills (ed.), International
              Encyclopedia of the Social Sciences. New York: Macmillan.
    1956   The Functions of Social Conflict. New York: Free Press.
Coser, Rose L.
    1975   "The complexity of roles as a seedbed of individual autonomy." Pp. 237–264 in
              Lewis A. Coser (ed.), The Idea of Social Structure. New York: Harcourt Brace
              Jovanovich.
Costner, Herbert L. and Robert K. Leik
    1964   "Deductions from axiomatic theory." American Sociological Review 29:819–835.
Cranor, Linda A., Robert A. Karasek and Christopher J. Carlin
    1981   "Job Characteristics and Office Work: Findings and Health Implications." Cincinnat-
              ti: Paper presented at NIOSH conference on Occupational Health Issues Affecting
              Clerical/Secretarial Personnel.

Cronbach, Lee J.
  1951   "Coefficient Alpha and the internal structure of tests." Psychometrika 16:297–334.
Curtis, Lynn A.
  1974   Criminal Violence. Lexington, Massachusetts: Heath.
Darwin, Charles
  1958 [1859]   On the Origin of Species. New York: New American Library.
Davis, James A.
  1966   "The campus as a frog pond." American Journal of Sociology 72:17–31.
Duncan, Otis Dudley
  1975   Introduction to Structural Equation Models. New York: Academic Press.
  1961   "A socioeconomic index for all occupations." Pp. 109–138 in Albert J. Reiss (ed.),
          Occupations and Social Status. New York: Free Press.
Duncan, Otis Dudley, David L. Featherman and Beverly Duncan
  1972   Socioeconomic Background and Achievement. New York: Seminar.
Durkheim, Emile
  1951 [1897]   Suicide. New York: Free Press.
England, Paula
  1979   "Women and occupational prestige: A case of vacuous sex equality." Signs
          5:252–265.
Featherman, David L. and Robert M. Hauser
  1978   Opportunity and Change. New York: Academic Press.
Federal Bureau of Investigation
  1971   Crime in the United States: Uniform Crime Reports—1970. Washington, D.C.:
          USGPO.
Festinger, Leon, Stanley Schachter and Kurt Back
  1950   Social Pressures in Informal Groups. New York: Harper.
Fischer, J. L.
  1961   "Art styles as cultural cognitive maps." American Anthropologist 63:79–93.
Freeman, John H. and John E. Kronenfeld
  1973   "Problems of definitional dependency." Social Forces 52:108–121.
Frisbie, W. Parker and Lisa Neidert
  1977   "Inequality and the relative size of minority populations." American Journal of
          Sociology 82:1007–1030.
Fuguitt, Glenn V. and Stanley Lieberson
  1974   "Correlations of ratios or difference scores having common terms." Pp. 128–144 in
          Herbert Costner (ed.), Sociological Methodology 1973–1974. San Francisco: Jossey-
          Bass.
Gans, Herbert J.
  1970   "Planning and social life." Pp. 501–509 in Harold M. Proshansky, William H.
          Ittelson and Leanne G. Rivlin (eds.), Environmental Psychology: People and Their
          Physical Settings. New York: Holt, Rinehart, and Winston.
Gibbs, Jack P. and Walter T. Martin
  1962   "Urbanization, technology, and the division of labor." American Sociological Re-
          view 26:667–677.
Goldberger, Arthur S., and Otis Dudley Duncan
  1973   Structural Equation Models in the Social Sciences. New York: Seminar.
Gordon, Milton M.
  1964   Assimilation in American Life. New York: Oxford University Press.
Gouldner, Alvin W.
  1970   The Coming Crisis of Western Sociology. New York: Basic Books.

Grant, W. Vance and Leo J. Eiden
    1982   Digest of Educational Statistics. Washington, D.C.: USGPO (National Center for Education Statistics).

Harary, Frank, R. Z. Norman and Dorwin Cartwright
    1965   Structural Models. New York: Wiley.

Haskell, Francis
    1963   Patrons and Painters. New York: Knopf.

Hauser, Robert M., Peter J. Dickinson, Harry P. Travis and John N. Koffel
    1975   "Structural changes in occupational mobility among men in the United States." American Sociological Review 40:585–598.

Heer, David M.
    1974   "The prevalence of black–white marriage in the United States, 1960 and 1970." Journal of Marriage and the Family 36:246–258.

Henning, E. E.
    1960   "Patronage and styles in art." Journal of Aesthetics and Art Criticism 18:464–471.

Hindelang, Michael J.
    1974   "The Uniform Crime Reports revisited." Journal of Criminal Justice 2:1–17.

Hollingshead, August B.
    1950   "Cultural factors in the selection of marriage mates." American Sociological Review 15:619–627.
    1949   Elmtown's Youth. New York: Wiley.

Homans, George C.
    1961   Social Behavior: Its Elementary Forms. New York: Harcourt, Brace and World.

Hope, Keith
    1971   "Path analysis: Supplementary procedures." Sociology 5:225–241.

Jencks, Christopher S.
    1979   Who Gets Ahead? New York: Basic Books.

Karasek, Robert A., Joseph E. Schwartz and Carl Pieper
    1982   "A Job Characteristic Scoring System for Occupational Analysis." New York: Columbia University Center for the Social Sciences, Pre-Print #89.

Kasarda, John D. and Patrick D. Nolan
    1979   "Ratio measurement and theoretical inference in social research." Social Forces 58:212–227.

Kendall, Morris G. and Alan Stuart
    1969   The Advanced Theory of Statistics, Vol. 1, Third Edition. London: Charles Griffin.

Kennedy, Ruby J.
    1944   "Single or triple melting pot?" American Journal of Sociology 39:331–339.

Laumann, Edward O.
    1973   Bonds of Pluralism. New York: Wiley.

Lieberson, Stanley
    1969   "Measuring population diversity." American Sociological Review 34:850–862.

Lipset, Seymour M.
    1960   Political Man. Garden City: Doubleday.

Liska, Allen E.
    1969   "Uses and misuses of tautologies in social psychology." Sociometry 32:444–457.

Macmillan, Alexander and Richard L. Daft
    1980   "Relationships among ratio variables with common components." Social Forces 58:1109–1128.
    1979   "Administrative intensity and ratio variables." Social Forces 58:228–248.

Mayhew, Bruce H. and Roger L. Levinger
    1976   "Size and density of interaction in human aggregates." American Journal of Sociology 82:86–110.
Merton, Robert K.
    1975   "Structural analysis in sociology." Pp. 21–52 in Peter M. Blau (ed.), Approaches to the Study of Social Structure. New York: Free Press.
    1972   "Insiders and outsiders." American Journal of Sociology 78:9–47.
    1968 [1949]   Social Theory and Social Structure. New York: Free Press.
    1948   "The social psychology of housing." Pp. 163–217 in Wayne Dennis (ed.), Current Trends in Social Psychology. Pittsburgh: University of Pittsburgh Press.
Messner, Steven and Ephraim Yuchtman-Yaar
    1979   "The Socioeconomic Hierarchy of Occupations: Is it Invariant for Men and Women?" New York: Columbia University Program in Sex Roles and Social Change, Pre-Print #40.
Miller, Herman P.
    1966   Income Distribution in the United States. Washington, D.C.: USGPO.
Miller, Walter B.
    1958   "Lower class culture as a generating milieu of gang delinquency." Journal of Social Issues 14:5–19.
Mitchell, J. Clyde
    1969   "The concept and use of social networks." Pp. 1–50 in J. Clyde Mitchell (ed.), Social Networks in Urban Situations. Manchester: Manchester University Press.
Moreno, J. L.
    1934   Who Shall Survive? Beacon: Beacon House.
Mulvihill, Donald J., Melvin M. Tumin and Lynn A. Curtis
    1969   Crimes of Violence. Washington, D.C.: USGPO.
Murdock, George P.
    1949   Social Structure. New York: Macmillan.
Parsons, Talcott
    1951   The Social System. New York: Free Press.
    1937   The Structure of Social Action. New York: McGraw-Hill.
Parsons, Talcott and Neil J. Smelser
    1956   Economy and Society. Glencoe: Free Press.
Peach, Ceri
    1974   "Homogamy, propinquity, and segregation." American Sociological Review 39:636–641.
Pearson, Karl
    1897   "On a form of spurious correlation which may arise when indices are used in the measurement of organs." Proceedings of the Royal Society of London 60:489–497.
Pevsner, Nicholas
    1940   Academies of Art. Cambridge: Cambridge University Press.
Popper, Karl R.
    1959 [1934]   The Logic of Scientific Discovery. New York: Basic Books.
Rae, Douglas W. and Michael Taylor
    1970   The Analysis of Political Cleavages. New Haven: Yale University Press.
Ramsoy, Natalie R.
    1966   "Assortative mating and the structure of cities." American Sociological Review 31:773–786.

Reagan, Barbara B.
    1979   "De Facto job segregation." Pp. 90–102 in Ann Foote Cahn (ed.), Women in the
             U.S. Labor Force. New York: Praeger.
Robinson, Robert V. and Jonathan Kelley
    1979   "Class as conceived by Marx and Dahrendorf." American Sociological Review
             44:38–57.
Rockwell, Richard C.
    1976   "Historical trends and variations in homogamy." Journal of Marriage and the Family
             38:83–95.
Rytina, Steven, Terry C. Blum, Joseph E. Schwartz and Peter M. Blau
    1982   "Inequality and Intermarriage." (Unpublished Manuscript).
Schuessler, Karl
    1974   "Analysis of ratio variables." American Sociological Review 80:379–396.
Schwartz, Joseph E.
    1977   "An examination of CONCOR and related methods for blocking sociometric data."
             Pp. 255–282 in David R. Heise (ed.), Sociological Methodology 1977. San Francis-
             co: Jossey-Bass.
Schwartz, Joseph E. and Christopher Winship
    1979   "The welfare approach to measuring inequality." Pp. 1–36 in Karl F. Schuessler
             (ed.), Sociological Methodology 1980. San Francisco: Jossey-Bass.
Shaw, Clifford R. and Henry D. McKay
    1942   Juvenile Delinquency and Urban Areas. Chicago: University of Chicago Press.
Simmel, Georg
    1955 [1923]   Conflict and the Web of Group Affiliations. Glencoe: Free Press.
    1950 [1908]   The Sociology of Georg Simmel. Glencoe: Free Press.
Simon, Herbert A.
    1962   "The architecture of complexity." Proceedings of the American Philosophical Soci-
             ety 106:467–482.
Simpson, E. H.
    1949   "Measurement of diversity." Nature 163:688.
Snedecor, George W. and William G. Cochran
    1967   Statistical Methods. Ames, Iowa: Iowa State University Press.
Sumner, William G.
    1940 [1906]   Folkways. Boston: Athenaeum.
Taussig, Michael K. and Sheldon Danziger
    1976   "Conference on the Trends on Income Inequality in the U.S." Madison: Institute for
             Research on Poverty, University of Wisconsin (mimeo).
Theil, Henri
    1972   Statistical Decomposition Analysis. Amsterdam: North-Holland.
    1967   Economics and Information Theory. Chicago: Rand McNally.
Thurow, Lester C.
    1980   The Zero-Sum Society. New York: Basic Books.
Tukey, John W.
    1954   "Causation, regression, and path analysis." Pp. 35–66 in O. Kempthorne, T. A.
             Bancroft, J. W. Gowen and J. L. Lush (eds.), Statistics and Mathematics in Biology.
             Ames, Iowa: Iowa State University Press.
Turner, Ralph
    1951   "The relative position of Negro males in the labor force of large American cities."
             American Sociological Review 16:524–529.

Tyree, Andrea and J. Treas
    1974   "The occupational and marital mobility of women." American Sociological Review 39:293–302.
U.S. Bureau of the Census
    1980   "Money Income of Households, Families, and Persons in the United States: 1980." Current Population Reports, Series P-60, No. 132. Washington, D.C.: USGPO.
    1972   Public Use Sample of Basic Records from the 1970 Census. Washington, D.C.: USGPO.
    1963   U.S. Census of the Population, 1960, Detailed Characteristics. Final Report (PCC1)-10. Washington, D.C.: USGPO.
U.S. Employment Service
    1977   Dictionary of Occupational Titles, Fourth Edition. Washington, D.C.: USGPO (U.S. Department of Labor, Employment and Training Administration).
Wallerstein, Immanuel
    1974   The Modern World-System I. New York: Academic Press.
Warner, W. Lloyd and Paul S. Lunt
    1941   The Social Life of a Modern Community. New Haven: Yale University Press.
Warner, W. Lloyd and Leo Srole
    1945   The Social System of American Ethnic Groups. New Haven: Yale University Press.
White, Harrison C., Scott A. Boorman and Ronald L. Breiger
    1976   "Social structure from multiple networks." American Journal of Sociology 81:730–780.
White, Harrison C. and Cynthia A. White
    1965   Canvasses and Careers. New York: Wiley.
Williams, Robin M.
    1964   Strangers Next Door. Englewood Cliffs: Prentice-Hall.
Wilson, William J.
    1978   The Declining Significance of Race. Chicago: University of Chicago Press.
Winship, Christopher
    1976   "Psychological Well-Being, Income, and Income Inequality." Cambridge: Harvard University (mimeo).
Wolfe, Alvin W.
    1969   "Social structural bases of art." Current Anthropology 10:3–44.
Wolfgang, Marvin E.
    1964   Crime and Race. New York: Institute for Human Relations Press.
Wolfgang, Marvin E. and Franco Feracuti
    1967   The Subculture of Violence. London: Tavistock.
Wright, Erik Olin and Luca Perrone
    1977   "Marxist class categories and income inequality." American Sociological Review 42:32–55.
Yinger, J. Milton
    1968   "A research note on interfaith marriage statistics." Journal for the Scientific Study of Religion 7:97–103.
Yule, G. U.
    1910   "On the interpretation of correlations between indices or ratios." Journal of the Royal Statistical Society 73:644–647.
Zetterberg, Hans L.
    1963   On Theory and Verification in Sociology. Totowa, New Jersey: Bedminster Press.

Author Index

Numbers refer to citations in the text. For complete references, see reference section beginning on page 237.

Subject Index

A

Achieved characteristic, 17, 28, 36, 55, 60, 85, 94, 96, 102, 104, 105, 114–117, 119–120, 122, 123, 125, 136–137, 141–142, 149, 206

Acquaintance, *see* Casual acquaintance

Age, 11, 12n, 122, 123, 127–150, 174n, 206
of metropolitan area, 145–146, 148

Aggregation, 16, 40, 122

Alpha, 143–144; *see also* Cronbach's alpha

Analysis of variance, 22, 152
nested, 165

Anomie, 25, 184

ANOVA, *see* Analysis of variance

Art, 214

Ascribed characteristic, 17, 28, 36, 44, 55, 57, 60, 85, 94, 102, 104, 115–117, 119–120, 122, 123, 137, 148, 149, 177, 180, 181, 198, 206, 208

Assault, aggravated, 182–188

Assimilation, 57, 88

Assumption, 1, 5–6, 14, 22, 26–30, 32, 33, 57, 80, 90, 122, 191, 193, 197, 213, 215; *see also* Axiom; Domain assumption; Primitive, assumption

Axiom, 6, 27, 191–192: *see also* Assumption

B

b, see Regression, coefficient, unstandardized

Barrier, 28; *see also* Class, boundary; Salience
to occupational intermarriage, 70, 73, 79
social, 11, 28, 42, 49, 55, 56, 79, 83, 171
to social mobility, 54, 57, 70, 73, 79, 171

Beta, *see* Regression, coefficient, standardized

Birthplace, *see* Region, of birth

Bivariate correlation, *see* Correlation, coefficient

Blacks, 14, 39, 45, 145, 181–182, 185–188, 206–207, *see also* Nonwhite; Race

Blockmodel, 26, 212

Bureaucratic, 78, 81, 208

C

Case study, 115, 149

Casual acquaintance, 13, 15–16, 27, 29, 41, 43, 57

Catholics, 3, 32, 59, 177–178

Causal
model, *see* Path, analysis
order, 20, 45–49, 50, 98, 100, 110, 119–120, 122, 200, 202n, 206

Ceiling effect, 46

Census, U.S.
1960, 21
1970, 16, 122, 200, 207

Ceteris paribus, 21, 58n, 80, 98, 195, 197, 205

Chance expectation, 10, 11, 14–15, 17–18, 28n, 29, 33–34, 36, 41, 45, 94n, 200–201, 213

Change, 184, 193
structural, 53, 58–66, 80, 99–102, 110, 120–121, 199, 216

Chi-square, 33–35, 200

Class, 28, 30, 56
boundary, 28, 56, 57, 160–161, 169–170, 171, 177–178, 189–190
conflict, 2, 161, 176–177, 178, 190, 211

249

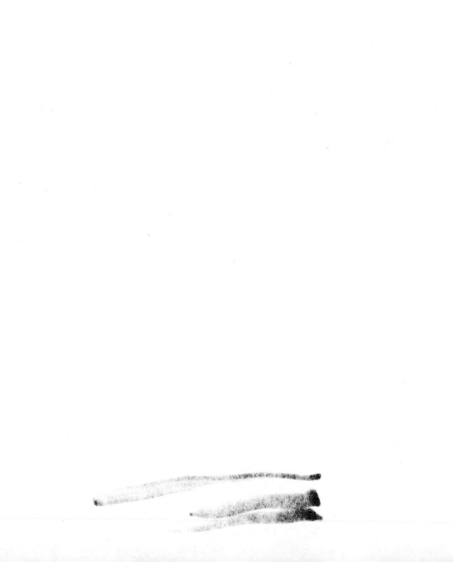

ADZ 0449

DATE DUE